D0984793

A New Species
of Man

Bucknell University Press Award

A New Species of Man (Gale C. Schricker)

A New Species of Man

The Poetic Persona of W. B. Yeats

Gale C. Schricker

Lewisburg
Bucknell University Press
London and Toronto: Associated University Presses

Associated University Presses, Inc.
4 Cornwall Drive
East Brunswick, N.J. 08816

Associated University Presses Ltd
27 Chancery Lane
London WC2A 1NF, England

Associated University Presses
Toronto M5E 1A7, Canada

Library of Congress Cataloging in Publication Data

Schricker, Gale C.
  A new species of man.

  Bibliography: p.
  Includes index.
  1. Yeats, W. B. (William Butler), 1865–
1939—Criticism and interpretation.   2. Self
in literature   3. Point of view (Literature)
I. Title.
PR5907.S32   821'.8   81-65860
ISBN 0-8387-5033-8   AACR2

PRINTED IN THE UNITED STATES OF AMERICA

FOR TOM

Contents

Preface

FOR the reader who wishes to consult individual chapters of this book for particular readings of the prose, fictional and nonfictional, and the poetry of Yeats, the Introduction that follows provides an outline and summary of the four chapters, their individual concerns, and their interrelations. The primary intent of this study, however, is to achieve an intensive and *inclusive* understanding of how Yeats's concept of "unity of being" becomes manifest over time in his prose and poetry through the development of the device I call the "poetic persona."

To fulfill this intention, I draw heavily on Yeats's writings as a whole, including several little-studied pieces, to elucidate the persona in theory and then focus on the function of the poetic persona in the most important creative writings: *Mythologies, The Autobiography, A Vision,* and especially *The Collected Poems.* (The Introduction explains the theoretical reason for my omission of Yeats's plays from consideration.) I also survey the important critical literature on Yeats's theory of persona, or mask, in order to demonstrate the need for an inclusive view of the development of the persona in Yeats's works as a whole in any critical discussion of "unity of being." In brief, since *A New Species of Man* pursues a holistic analysis of Yeats's works, it should itself ideally be read as a continuous, integrated work.

The title of this book is taken from a passage in Yeats's autobiography that I feel best expresses Yeats's own hopes for and achievements in the theory and practice of the poetic persona. In this passage from "Hodos Chameliontos," Yeats discusses two of his poetic "heroes," Dante and Villon:

The two halves of their nature are so completely joined that they seem to labour for their objects, and yet to desire whatever happens, being at the same instant predestinate and free, creation's very self. We gaze at such men in awe, because we gaze not at a work of art, but at *the re-creation of the man through that art, the birth of a new species of man.* (Italics added)

"Two halves" of human nature, "labour" and "desire," "predestinate and free"—these are all characteristics of the dual nature of the poetic persona, which I discuss and attempt to clarify in the following study. It is the union of this duality that comprises, in my view, Yeats's achievement of "unity of being."

Acknowledgments

SINCE *A New Species of Man* originally took form as a doctoral dissertation at Bryn Mawr College, I wish to acknowledge and thank the many teachers, colleagues, and friends there and in the surrounding academic communities who helped me in countless ways to pursue this study. Very special thanks go to Professor Sandra Berwind for her discerning and supportive guidance and for her unlimited generosity with her own thoughts and materials on Yeats. Many of the ideas developed in this book originated in my discussions with her.

I would also like to acknowledge the stimulating discussions and lectures by many excellent Yeats scholars at the 1979 Yeats International Summer School, in Sligo, Ireland, as well as the timely assistance of the Mrs. Giles Whiting Foundation, which funded the final year of composition of this book.

Finally, for the irreplaceable encouragement and confidence he has always given me in my work, I thank my husband, Tom, my most appreciative audience and critic.

I wish to thank the following for permission to quote from published works:

Macmillan Publishing Co., Inc., M. B. Yeats, Anne Yeats, and Macmillan London Limited for permission to quote from *The Autobiography* by William Butler Yeats, copyright 1916, 1935 by Macmillan Publishing Co., Inc., renewed 1944, 1963 by Bertha Georgie Yeats; *A Vision* by William Butler Yeats, copyright 1937 by W. B. Yeats, renewed 1965 by Bertha Georgie Yeats and Anne Butler Yeats; *Essays and Introductions* by William Butler Yeats, copyright 1961 by Mrs. W. B. Yeats; *Mythologies* by William Butler Yeats, copyright 1959 by Mrs. W. B. Yeats; *The Collected Poems* by William Butler Yeats, copyright 1940 by Georgie Yeats, renewed 1968 by Bertha Georgie Yeats, Michael Butler Yeats, and

Introduction

EARLY in 1910 W. B. Yeats presented a series of three lectures in London that he organized around a "plea for uniting literature once more to personality, the personality of the writer in lyric poetry or with imaginative personalities in drama."[1] In the second lecture, "Friends of My Youth," Yeats distinguished two aspects of self-identity that he called "character" and "personality" and defined as the habitual, everyday sense of self and a heightened, unique sense of self: "Character is made up of habits retained, all kinds of things. We have character under control in the normal moments of life. . . . Personality is greater and finer than character. . . . When a man cultivates a style in literature he is shaping his personality."[2] The lyric poet, who so often takes his own experiences for his subject matter and raises them to universal significance in the medium of poetry, was thus for Yeats the prime example of the process in literature of transcending character to personality. Yeats argued that the lyric poet's life constitutes, in fact, an experiment in the effort to achieve a unity of the two aspects of self:

> It is part of the principles of the whole art of our generation that we have no sympathy with that idea of Tennyson that the life of the poet does not belong to the people. The poet is what he is. If a good poet, because he lives sincerely, he makes an experiment in life, good or bad, but a sincere experiment. He may not live his life out of acquiescence, out of routine.[3]

In order to provide subject matter for his poetry, the lyric poet tries to live a life more of personality than of character, and so his life becomes an experiment in individual potential, a process which is recorded in his verse.

The result of this Paterian experiment was all too often disastrous for the "friends" of Yeats's youth who lived it, and Yeats

13

considered some of these tragic lives in his second lecture—the lives of his fellow Rhymers, members of what he elsewhere has called the "tragic generation."[4] The notes Yeats made for this lecture, even more than the lecture itself, show Yeats examining these poets and how their lives succeeded and failed. Because they reflect the movement of Yeats's thoughts on the topic in great detail, these notes in effect constitute an informal philosophy of poetry and reveal much about Yeats's goals and intentions in writing lyric poetry, even more intimately and clearly than do his later formal expressions of poetic theory in "Per Amica Silentia Lunae" and *A Vision.* Lionel Johnson's experiment is Yeats's primary focus:

> He was I think a great religious poet and he made his poetry out of the struggle with his own soul which the sword of Fate had as it were divided in two. All the great things of Life seem to me to have come from battle, and the battle of poetry is the battle of a man with himself. I do not think any nature comes to the self-knowledge that is genius without the original evil which gives the antagonist in that battle whose spoil and monument is knowledge.[5]

Yeats here generalizes character and personality into evil and good aspects of self; character, which Yeats later terms "self," works against genius, whereas personality, later to be termed "anti-self," is the self-knowledge that is genius. The fact that something which is "anti-self" can bring about self-knowledge is characteristic of the "battle of poetry . . . the battle of a man with himself." In this essay, Yeats begins by referring to this element of genius in an individual as "personality," and then substitutes "pose" and "mask." With each term Yeats is struggling to express that this aspect of self is simultaneously the true sense of individual self and, paradoxically, realizable only in artificial (in the sense of aesthetic) forms. Finally, as he does later in *A Vision,* Yeats settles on the term *mask* but insists on its connotations of enhancing individual identity rather than obstructing or altering it:

> Is not a mask laboured at all life long? But the soul which is bodiless and impalpable will find eyes to look through and lips to speak with. . . . Is it not that this mask is half unconsciously created, that there is so often something theatrical in the men of the vastest energy, that Napoleon will invade the east not for State craft only, but that he may copy the career of Alexander? . . . One thing alone would make it conscious, an element that has belonged to all great kings as well as to poets. The moment a man begins to speak to a large multitude of

people, and not to two or three people who will know him intimately, and to speak not of facts and figures, but of Life, and the wisdom of Life and the sorrow of Life, he becomes an actor, simplifying and enlarging that he may reach their eyes and ears. He may do it well or ill, but *his sincerity consists of making this enlarged and simplified being a fitting form for the utterance of his soul and not for his ambition that is vanity.*[6]

Many critics have misinterpreted Yeats's theory of mask and assumed that Yeats uses the mask to cover personal defects or to add variety to his writings; they speak at times of acting and of insincerity:

> In reading the poetry of William Butler Yeats's last decade, one need not and, indeed, one should not believe everything one sees and hears. . . . Even as we recognize and pay tribute to his gifts as a lyric poet, we should not overlook his talents as an actor, an actor who richly cultivated his poetic attitudes, who wore many masks and spoke in many voices. . . . Remembering his autobiographies . . . one might go further than mere praise and say that if Yeats had not been one of the greatest poets of the time through which he lived, he would have been its greatest charlatan.[7]

This is cutting criticism for a poet who lectures on sincerity and on "uniting literature once more to personality." Yet almost all of Yeats's critics have subscribed to this or a somewhat milder version of the charge of charlatanism, since few critics see any continuity or integrity in Yeats's lyric voice through the poetic canon. Richard Ellmann, as indicated by the title of his biography, *Yeats: The Man and the Masks*, sees the poet as a basically timid man who assumed the masks of various identities both to "connect himself with humanity" and to defend himself from others.[8] Ellmann does not convict Yeats of charlatanism but certainly of inconsistency or uncertainty. In his study of Yeats's poetry Ellmann extends this analysis of the man to the poet, finding that Yeats assumes three main masks, or "dramatic roles," in his verse: seer, victim, and assessor.[9] Thomas Parkinson similarly sees "five modes" of speaking in the "one poet": individual, social character, prophet, dramatist, and editor.[10] Both Ellmann and Parkinson break down the poet into these masks or roles in an effort to illuminate how one poet can speak sincerely through so many characters or perspectives.

Part of the problem in judging Yeats's sincerity, or the integrity

or continuity of his poetic voice, is in distinguishing poetic characters from the voice of Yeats himself. In 1910 Yeats identified two
approaches to the goal of "uniting literature once more to personality" as the theme of his lectures: assimilating the "personality of
the writer in lyric poetry" and integrating "imaginative personalities in drama." A survey of his *Collected Poems* shows that
Yeats actually does both in his verse; he creates "imaginative personalities," objective poetic characters in dramatic poetic settings,
and he expresses his own personality, as the poetic "I," in his more
meditative lyric poetry. Yet Yeats considered himself to be primarily a lyric poet—one who seeks to unite his own personality to his
verse. When he is being evaluated for sincerity or integrity, Yeats
must therefore be judged as a lyric poet and not as a creator of
dramatic characters. Indeed, when critical attention focuses on
Yeats's poetic "I," only one rather than three or five different roles
or masks is found—the poetic movement of one identity rising
beyond character to personality.

Two of Ellmann's roles isolate these two aspects of self and their
interrelation, those of victim and assessor. Ellmann's "victim," like
Yeats's "character," is the passive, habit-bound aspect of self: "As
the frustrated, unsuccessful lover of the early verse, as the hounded
public figure of the middle period, as the time-struck, age-worn
old man of the later work, he has always something of the
scapegoat about him." Ellmann's "assessor," like Yeats's "personality," is transcendent and unique:

> The assessment is conducted passionately, and disregards conventional
> morality to arrive at only those decisions which the imagination can
> accept because they are positive, imprudent, and dignified, never mean
> or narrow. . . . Because the assessment is made in particular and per-
> sonal terms, arising directly from some incident or development of the
> poet's life, the poems rarely seem didactic.[11]

Both Ellmann's division of the poet into victim and assessor and
Yeats's opposition of character and personality follow a time-
honored dialectical view of human identity. The human individual
has been analyzed variously through history as matter and spirit,
id and superego, empirical "I" and transcendental "I," the last the
formulation of Giovanni Gentile, an Italian idealist philosopher
whom Yeats greatly admired.[12] Each of these schemata of thesis
and antithesis, however, posits a synthesis: humanity, the ego, and
"mind as pure act." It is a similar synthesis of character and personality, man and mask, that is lacking in all critical readings of
Yeats's poetry to date.

Again, the implications of artificiality in the term *mask* seem to be at fault. Harold Bloom assumes that the doctrine of mask obliges the poet to "renounce mere *primary* experience,"[13] that of character, victim, or experiencing aspect of self. This is, of course, untrue; Yeats's poetic "I" is securely grounded in autobiographical experience. Yeats's mask rather is designed to cull the lasting value from that empirical experience as a "fitting form for the utterance of his soul"; mask is only one part of a dynamic relationship. The danger of giving more credence to either the personality / assessor / transcendent "I" part of the relationship or the character / victim / empirical "I" aspect can be commonly found in critical analyses of Yeats; a relatively recent example is Helen Regueiro's reading of "Sailing to Byzantium" (CP, 191–92).[14] Regueiro posits a separation of experience-bound poet and transcendent poetic protagonist and finds that they pursue different and irreconcilable courses in the poem:

> Poet and protagonist are presumably one in the first stanza, and by the end of the poem the poet discovers what the protagonist, trapped in eternity, cannot know. The "success" of the poem depends to some extent on our reading into it an ironic dimension by which Yeats remains detached from the "solution" which he posits. . . . The poet's is a constant sailing to Byzantium and a constant separation from the protagonist who arrives. . . . Redemption in Yeats's poem, if indeed it can be called that, lies not in the eternity of Byzantium, but in the constant "sailing to" by which the poet escapes the ficticity and silence of the protagonist in the last stanza.[15]

Although this is not an unusual reading of Yeats's poem, what textual evidence Regueiro finds either for the separation of poet and protagonist or for the protagonist's independent arrival in the "artifice of eternity" is unclear. In stanza 2, the "I" claims he has "sailed the seas and come / To the holy city of Byzantium"; but by stanza 4, the "I" paradoxically has still not transcended nature. The "I" merely contemplates the future possibility: "Once out of nature I shall never take / My bodily form from any natural thing." The persona, that is, has both arrived at a transcendent realm and not left nature. The significance of the "sailing to" in the title is thus not an affirmation of continual experiential process, as Regueiro argues, but a description of an imaginative act of transcendence. The imagination of the poet can travel out of this world and into an "artifice of eternity" but is ultimately dependent on the body, its source of empirical experience; it is never entirely "out of nature." It is not a question of two identities, of protagonist and poet, then, but one of transcendent and empirical aspects of the one self in a dynamic poetic interplay that explores and reveals the potentials and limitations of the compound self—once the persona is accepted as one continuous identity rather than a succession of masks.

Since *mask* is such a misleading term and represents only one part of the relationship in any case, and since a term of synthesis is required to express in critical analysis that dynamic relationship of character and personality or empirical and transcendent identities which Yeats achieves in verse, a term such as *persona* is a needed addition to the Yeatsian critical vocabulary. The etymology of this term includes meanings of both *mask* and *person*,[16] which cover both the transcendent and the empirical aspects of self. *Persona* also carries theatrical connotations, which suggest Yeats's poetic process of uniting the two aspects of self in terms of "simplifying and enlarging" the empirical self to universal significance before an audience. This theatrical element in the poet is further explained by Yeats in the same (1910) set of lecture notes:

> Perhaps even when that enlarged and simplified being is built up in all intensity, we come at last always to a form of wisdom and follow it, at last it may be beyond literature, beyond Life itself till it is with us when of old the stone was rolled back and linen cloths folded up.[17]

Yeats is describing the process of raising individual characteristics into archetypal symbols, and *persona,* with its simultaneous suggestions of person and poetry or art, suggests a like process.

Even accepting *persona* as a helpful term, however, its constituent aspects of empirical and transcendent identities need further definition. The empirical identity rather clearly denotes the historical man, the social man, the sense of self as an object in the world. The transcendent identity is harder to define, vaguely connoting as it does an escape from the empirical. Giovanni Gentile describes it as the sense of self as subject rather than object, the activity of thought or experience itself.[18] Yeats suggests, in the previously quoted passage, that the transcendent identity is a "form of wisdom" to be followed or emulated. Both Gentile and Yeats thus interpret the transcendent aspect of self as essentially a dynamic idea or structure of values and the empirical self as, conversely, a passive process, the self as body or object passively undergoing the experiences of everyday life. The interdependence and imprecise boundaries of these two aspects of self make for a true process of self-discovery within the persona of Yeats's lyric canon, as the empirical, experiencing self seeks and confronts a transcendent structure of values. Together, if united, these two aspects of self would achieve that concept of "unity of being" Yeats says Dante uses in comparing beauty to a "perfectly proportioned human body,"[19] itself a fitting symbol of the union of process and product, growth and form.

The empirical aspect of Yeats's poetic persona derives from the autobiographical input of the poet himself. Yeats's poetic "I" thus does not appear in his plays, in which each character has an objective identity of its own. Likewise, the transcendent aspect of the persona, as an embodied structure of values, does not appear in the "I" of the critical prose, since that "I" is openly analyzing rather than seeking to embody a truth itself. Yeats's poetic persona is thus to be found in the creative prose, primarily *Mythologies, The Autobiography,* and *A Vision,* and predominantly in *The Collected Poems.* In these volumes the empirical identity encounters several different manifestations of transcendence: the supernatural/spiritual world in the fictional prose, a quasi-philosophical abstract structure in *The Autobiography* and *A Vision,* and an archetypal life structure in *The Collected Poems* itself. Hugh Kenner has noted the influence of a transcendent poetic structure on the Yeatsian persona within a volume of poetry: "[Yeats] was an architect, not a decorator; he didn't accumulate poems, he wrote books. . . . It is a radical mistake to think of Yeats as a casual or fragmentary poet whose writings float on a current discoverable only in his biographable life."[20] Yeats, too, ponders the effect of art forms on a poet in his notes on the personal failures of the "tragic generation":

I have continually asked myself, why that generation followed more than any other I know of in the way of the mighty poets in their miserable end. . . . In [some] moods I find the cause in work itself. They were lyric poets, that only. Life existed for them in a few intense moments that when they were gone left darkness behind them. They had no causes, no general interests to fill up the common day, and then, look back through all the lyric poets of the world, how few of them have been happy or fortunate. . . . Dante, Homer, Shakespeare come only every now and then after hundreds of lines of circumstance, of mild or broken radiance, to the supreme moment of passion, but the lyric poet who sings his own passions must be always in the blue heart of the flame. . . . He will not write many poems no matter how passionate his life—and if his life were not passionate and troubled how should he write at all?[21]

Yeats implicitly recognizes in this passage that if lyric poets are destroyed by the act of living intensely enough to provide empirical subject matter for their own poetry, they require a mitigating structure—religious, epic, or social, such as Dante, Homer, and Shakespeare had—to provide a transcendent context for their intense lyric experiences. This larger than individual context is the source of the transcendent aspect of self, a source Yeats ultimately discovers for himself in his poetry.

The informal poetics that the notes for "Friends of My Youth" constitute is superseded in Yeats's later works by a formal essay Yeats wrote for a projected (but unpublished) collected edition of his works, the essay entitled "A General Introduction for My Work."[22] Since this essay reflects Yeats's mature views on poetry in an organized fashion, it is used in this study as both a structural and a thematic guide to a critical analysis of Yeats's persona and its quest for unity of being. The titles of the four sections of Yeats's essay and their topics are adopted as the main titles of the four primary chapters of this study and as their main topics. The first chapter, "The First Principle," discusses more fully the dual aspects of identity in the persona and considers the concept of persona as Yeats has inherited and developed it. "Subject-Matter," the second chapter, explores the relation of the empirical "I" to structures of transcendence in society and in literature, by tracing the continuity and development of the persona in the fictional prose collected in *Mythologies*. Chapter 3, "Style and Attitude," analyzes in greater detail the process of interaction of empirical and transcendent identities in the persona, by analyzing Yeats's developing theories and applications of self and anti-self in *The Autobiography* and *A Vision*. The final chapter, "Whither?," looks at Yeats's views on the fate of poets and societies that pursue empirical consciousness without the redeeming powers of a transcendent perspective and demonstrates how Yeats's persona escapes that fate and achieves unity of being by the synthesis of empirical development and the archetypal quest-romance structure of *The Collected Poems*. The integrity of concerns that this holistic approach to the poetic persona in Yeats's writings reveals finally ratifies the poetic persona as Yeats's achievement of unity of being.

A New Species
of Man

I have sought through all my life to find the secret of life. I was not happy in my youth, for I knew that it would pass; and I was not happy in my manhood, for I knew that age was coming; and so I gave myself, in youth and manhood and age, to the search for the Great Secret. I longed for a life whose abundance would fill centuries, I scorned the life of fourscore winters. I would be—no, I *will* be!—like the ancient gods of the land.

W. B. Yeats,
"The Heart of the Spring,"
Mythologies

1
"The First Principle":
The Poetic Persona in Theory

THE "first principle" of Yeats's poetics, as he outlines it in "A General Introduction for My Work," is the dual nature of the poet's identity. On the one hand, a "poet writes always of his personal life, in his finest work out of its tragedy, whatever it be, remorse, lost love, or mere loneliness." On the other hand, this personal identity is transformed, in the process of poetic creation, into a more universal concept of self: "Even when the poet seems most himself . . . he has been reborn as an idea, something intended, complete. . . . He is more type than man, more passion than type."[1] A poet begins writing with the given, personal self—"in the foul rag-and-bone shop of the heart," as Yeats says in a late poem—but he finishes with a re-created self—"complete" and grown "in pure mind" (CP, 336). Yeats puts it more personally in another poem:

> The friends that have it I do wrong
> When ever I remake a song,
> Should know what issue is at stake:
> It is myself that I remake.[2]

Writing poetry is for Yeats a matter of "making" himself; it is the process of refining or raising his personal identity into a whole and universal structure. Yeats refers to this composite identity in "A General Introduction for My Work" as the "Self," which reflects his concurrent readings of the Upanishads[3]; in his earlier writings, this "Self" is variously conceived and discussed primarily in terms of its constituent elements of primary self and antithetical mask or

23

anti-self. The critical term of synthesis of these elements in such a re-created poetic self is, however, the *persona*.

Yeats's contradictory uses of the term *persona* in his prose and poetry bear out its dual implications for him. One of Yeats's autobiographies is titled "Dramatis Personae, 1896–1902," which refers to Yeats's examination in that volume of the people who helped found the Irish dramatic movement—a use of the term *persona* in the sense of a fictional character, borrowed from the theater. In an early article on Browning, Yeats makes this meaning more explicit: "It is hard to know when he is speaking or when it is only one of his *dramatis personae*"; *persona* here distinguishes a created character from the creating artist himself. In the later essay "J. M. Synge and the Ireland of His Time," however, the term is associated with the artist's self: "Misfortune shook [Synge's] physical nature while it left his intellect and his moral nature untroubled. The external self, the mask, the *persona*, was a shadow; character was all." Yeats's association of *persona* with *mask* here reflects the derivation of *persona* from the Latin word for a dramatic mask; it is Yeats's own conception of the term, however, that permits him to refer to the physical body of a man as a *persona*. A clue to Yeats's meaning in using *persona* in this context may be found in *A Vision* and in the essay "Swedenborg, Mediums, and the Desolate Places," in which Yeats discusses the *persona* in antithetical relationship to the waking mind: "Swedenborg has written that we are each in the midst of a group of associated spirits who sleep when we sleep and become the *dramatis personae* of our dreams, and are always the other will that wrestles with our thought, shaping it to our despite."[4] *Dramatis personae* here has two connotations: the ordinary theatrical sense of the "characters of our dreams," and a more esoteric reference to spirits that act as the directors of human thoughts. The combination of these two connotations, characters and directors, seems also to be the meaning of Yeats's only use of *persona* in poetry:

> Eternity is passion, girl or boy
> Cry at the onset of their sexual joy
> "For ever and for ever"; then awake
> Ignorant what Dramatis Personae spake.
>
> (CP, 286)

Persona as character and director, body and spirit—Yeats's uses of the term indicate that it encompasses for him the dual aspects of the poet's identity, or indeed those of any human being: body and mind, object and subject. In this complex use of the word, Yeats goes beyond modern colloquial definitions of *persona* that limit its meaning either to the theatrical sense of "character of a fictional presentation" or to the Jungian sense of "aspect of personality as shown to or perceived by others."[5] Each of these definitions takes an external perspective on personality, human or fictional, and leaves the inner thoughts or spirits to another set of terms. This linguistic limitation of *persona* to the sense of a facade or fictional character, however, has precedent in ancient Greece and perhaps even derives from the "possibilities and hazards of the deliberate creation of a persona by the orator or poet" in the famous example of Socrates' expulsion of the poets in Plato's *Republic*.[6] Socrates objects to the act of poetic imitation that is inherent in a conception of *persona* as facade or fictional character. He fears that assuming a persona by donning a mask (as the Greeks did) both distracts the poet from pursuing his own proper role in life ("the same person will hardly be able to play a serious part in life, and at the same time to be an imitator and imitate many other parts as well") and instructs the poet and audience in dangerously volatile emotional roles rather than in controlling reason ("the wise and calm temperament, being always nearly equable, is not easy to imitate or to appreciate when imitated, especially at a public festival when a promiscuous crowd is assembled in a theatre"). Socrates thus perceives only the visible, external effects of assuming a persona on the actions of poet and audience and concludes that the associated roles cause "strife and inconsistency" in the imitator's life, rendering him "not at unity with himself."[7]

Yeats's constructive rather than reductive concept of persona is more closely related to the use and significance of the mask in classical Greek drama, mask in this context being "not what it is in our ordinary usage, a device for disguising or hiding the face";

> on the contrary, the mask of drama, or of primitive dance, is clearly intended to reveal more than it hides, to affirm more than it obscures. In these forms the face is not important, but the stylized mask symbolizes, stands for, something—an attitude, a view of life, one aspect of the universe—which is of too great significance for the expressiveness of any human face to be able to convey.[8]

Far from the modern definition of *persona* as one "aspect of per-

sonality," the ancient Greek concept of *persona* refers more generally to "one aspect of the universe" that fills the person who assumes a mask. The Greek Stoics, especially, emphasized an
"ethical sense" in the universal role associated with a dramatic
mask in their concept of *prosopon,* the apparent root of the Latin
persona. The interplay of mask and role in the doctrine of *prosopon,* as Adolf Trendelenburg reconstructs it, anticipates Yeats's
conception of persona as the union of body and spirit, or self and
art:

> The well-written part *[prosopon]* . . . particularizes the universal in
> accordance with the nature peculiar to each individual and grounds it in
> a rational mean. . . . The universal law of nature works in agreement
> with the individual will. For everything is as it should be and the course
> of life is beautiful when the will of the universal disposer and the
> *daemon* of the individual are in harmony. . . . Accordingly, the wise
> man, who ought to resemble a good histrionic artist, must not only
> write the part himself but must also interpret it.[9]

Although in *A Vision* Yeats specifically condemns the Stoics as the
"first beneficiaries of Plato's hatred of imitation" and the "first
benefactors of our modern individuality, sincerity of the trivial
face, the mask torn away," being apparently unfamiliar with the
concept of *prosopon,* in "Per Amica Silentia Lunae," he reaches a
conclusion similar to the Stoic conception of *prosopon,* in arguing
that the act of assuming a mask invokes the individual's daimon,
which facilitates his entry to "anima mundi," a rough equivalent of
the Stoics' "will of the universal."[10] Robert Langbaum concludes
from this use of the mask that "Yeats discovered a new sense of
identity by rediscovering the ancient process of identity-making
through imitation. . . . We pass from the individual to the archetypal order of identity at that psychological depth where we desire to
repeat mythological patterns."[11]
    Modern literary criticism has begun, perhaps partly in response
to the influence of Yeats among other modern poets, to include the
subjective narrator or controlling consciousness of a poem or novel
in the concept of persona. A recent dictionary of critical terms
includes among its definitions of *persona* the "sum of all the author's conscious choices in a realized and more complete self as
'artist,'" as distinguished from the "man who sits down to
write."[12] Wayne Booth, in *The Rhetoric of Fiction,* refers to this
"more complete self" as the "implied author," who, "as he writes,
. . . creates not simply an ideal, impersonal 'man in general' but an
implied version of 'himself' that is different from the implied au-

thors we meet in other men's works." Booth adds, "To some novelists it has seemed, indeed, that they were discovering or creating themselves as they wrote"; but he hesitates to call this re-created self simply "persona," "mask," or "narrator," because of their colloquially narrow reference to the "speaker in the work who is after all only one of the elements created by the implied author and who may be separated from him by large ironies."[13] The modern critical debate over the identity of Chaucer's per-sona—whether it is the voice of the historical Chaucer himself (the "man who sits down to write") or a created, fictional self[14]—exemplifies current critical confusion over the reference of the word *persona*. Chaucer's "Geffrey" could be (and has been) vari-ously interpreted as an ironic portrait of a limited mentality, an accurate historical self-portrait by the author, and Chaucer's artis-tic and constructive re-creation of his personal identity in more broadly universal terms. With such a diversity of reference, it is little wonder modern critics hesitate to employ the term *persona*, except within fairly narrow limits.

Leo Spitzer helps to clarify the literary concept of persona in revealing that the medieval poet sought to transcend his personal identity, or "empirical 'I,'" and speak in his art as the voice of truth, or the vehicle of a more universal "poetic 'I.'" Even Dante in the *Divine Comedy*, according to Spitzer, projects a universal identity dressed in personal details: "Dante is not interested, po-etically, in himself *qua* himself . . . but *qua* an example of the generally human capacity for cognizing the supramundane—which can be cognized only by what is most personal in man."[15] Yeats himself debates whether Dante "utterly found himself" in his po-etic persona or found a "spectral image/ . . . fashioned from his opposite" (CP, 158) but concludes, with Spitzer, that the empirical being that informs the poetic "I" "is so clear and simple that it has the quality of art",[16] that poet and poetic character meet in the artistic persona. Yeats finds a similar unity of art and life in Chau-cer's persona:

> I took great pleasure in certain allusions to the singer's life one finds in old romances and ballads, and thought his presence there all the more poignant because we discover it half lost, like portly Chaucer, behind his own maunciple and pardoner upon the Canterbury roads.[17]

What attacts Yeats to Dante and Chaucer is their assimilation of self and poetry as "an idea, something intended, complete." Yeats thus sympathizes with the medieval concept of persona, as with the Stoic, and fails to appreciate the modern critical distinction between a poet and his "poetic 'I.'" The crucial characteristic of the persona for Yeats is that it develops from the "empirical 'I'" and remains anchored in that personal aspect of self and thus maintains a consistency of identity. In other terms, Yeats in his poetry gazes steadily through one permanent but flexible mask rather than continuously assuming different identities behind different masks. In this concept of persona as continuous and personally derived, Yeats differs from other modern poets and theorists who conceive of a poetic persona as an objective, dramatically presented character within a particular poem and bearing little if any relation to the poet himself, and yet Yeats remains the truer to the ancient concept, as redefined here by Walter Ong:

> The symbol of the exteriority of a literary creation is the mask, for in such a creation the author does not communicate directly but through a kind of covering or disguise, fictitious persons or characters, who are more or less in evidence and who speak in his works. As T. S. Eliot remarks, poetry "is not the expression of personality, but an escape from personality." . . . And yet, is it not highly indicative that the word for mask, persona ("that through which the sound comes"), has given both to the ancients and to us the word for person? It is as though this ability to take on the role of another shows the actor's own humanity, shows that the other is already within him, and is, indeed, the shadow of his most real self. . . . Thus acting a role, realizing in a specially intense way one's identity (in a sense) with a someone who (in another sense) one is not, remains one of the most human things a man can do.[18]

Much as Yeats's thoughts on the dual identity of the poet and its resolution in the poetic persona resemble the Stoic doctrine of *prosopon*, there is no evidence of any conscious borrowing by Yeats from or knowledge of *prosopon*. Rather, it seems that Yeats arrived at his ideas through firsthand experience in the rituals of mystical societies, through contact with the aesthetic theories of such acquaintances as Edward Dowden and Oscar Wilde, and through study of the philosophies of certain proponents of the idealist implications of the persona, primarily William Blake, Bishop Berkeley, and Giovanni Gentile. Virginia Moore has described certain masking rituals of the Order of the Golden Dawn (a mystical society to which Yeats belonged in early adulthood), which emphasize the spiritual force that accompanies a symbolic mask much in the manner of the Stoics:

> [Yeats] did not hear about, but *saw*, masks of lion, eagle, and ox; masks of Osiris and Isis. Moreover, the god-form of each Officer *as faculty* was an "astral shape suitable to the force he represented." . . . Consider the function of masks in soul-development, said his Order course. . . . Look backward; acknowledge thy debt to evolution for having perfected that instrument thy body; then realize that, because outer never exactly coincides with inner, every human being wears a mask. Thus Yeats learned to see himself as "self-conscious—as one who receives impressions—one who criticises and watches, one whose will is interfered with—one who is misunderstood—one to whom others are 'persons' or masks. . . ." Then, "standing outside himself," he "became one who endeavours to sense how his mask appears to others."[19]

Here is perhaps one source of Yeats's compound understanding of persona, as encompassing body and spirit, mask and role, as well as of his conception of it as developing continuously in identity.

A more traditional influence on Yeat's theory of persona was his acquaintance with Edward Dowden, a friend of his father's, professor at Trinity College, and literary critic. In the course of his critical career, and specifically in a study of George Eliot, Dowden developed a theory of the poetic persona, which he called the "second self." In terms of Eliot, this persona was identified as "if not the real George Eliot," the self that "writes her books, and lives and speaks through them":

> Such a second self of an author is perhaps more substantial than any mere human personality encumbered with the accidents of flesh and blood and daily living. It stands at some distance from the primary self, and differs considerably from its fellow. It presents its person to us with fewer reserves; it is independent of local and temporary motives of speech or of silence; it knows no man after the flesh; it is more than an individual; it utters secrets, but secrets which all men of all ages are to catch; while, behind it, lurks well pleased the veritable historical self secure from impertinent observation and criticism.[20]

Yeats did not always approve of Dowden's critical opinions and took special issue with Dowden's admiration of George Eliot, feeling that she "seemed to have a distrust or a distaste for all in life that gives one a springing foot."[21] Yeats was, however, familiar with Dowden's writings on Eliot[22] and so was exposed to the concept of a transcendent artistic self which is created in the course of writing and which communicates with a universal realm. Yeats perhaps reserved judgment on Dowden's Victorian satisfaction in the fact that this "second self" allowed the "historical self" to lurk "secure from impertinent observation and criticism," as Yeats later would declare that a poet's life is "an experiment in living and those that come after have a right to know it."[23]

As Dowden influenced Yeats in terms of critical theory, Oscar Wilde taught Yeats by example that an artist need not create a book and characters in order to transcend the empirical self but only re-create himself, day to day in conversation, by assuming a dramatic mask. In *The Autobiography*, Yeats reveals that Wilde read to him from proofs of his *The Decay of Lying* on Christmas day 1888[24]; as Yeats listened he was impressed with Wilde's daring claims for an artistically assumed personality:

> In point of fact what is interesting about people in good society . . . is the mask that each one of them wears, not the reality that lies behind the mask. It is a humiliating confession, but we are all of us made out of the same stuff. . . . Where we differ from each other is purely in accidentals: in dress, manner, tone of voice, religious opinions, personal appearance, tricks of habit, and the like. . . .
>
> Life imitates art far more than Art imitates life. . . . A great artist invents a type, and Life tries to copy it, to reproduce it in popular form. . . .
>
> The self-conscious aim of Life is to find expression, and . . . Art offers it certain beautiful forms through which it may realize that energy.[25]

Yeats thus absorbed from Wilde the idea that artistic form improves and even idealizes nature, that the mask betters the face and the lie tells more than the truth. But Yeats took more than Wilde's aesthetic theories from that Christmas meeting; he left with the germ of his own theory of self and anti-self as well. Wilde's aesthetic concept of the mask did not account for his motivations in actualizing the concept, as Yeats inferred them. Yeats consequently theorized that donning a mask must constitute an act of personal self-completion, and Wilde became the object of Yeat's own growing critical theories:

> Of late years I have often explained Wilde to myself by his family history. His father was a friend or acquaintance of my father's

father. . . . The Wilde family was clearly of the sort that fed the imagination of [Irish novelist] Charles Lever, dirty, untidy, daring, and what Charles Lever, who loved more normal activities, might not have valued so highly, very imaginative and learned. . . . I think [Oscar Wilde] lived with no self-mockery at all, an imaginary life; perpetually performed a play which was in all things the opposite of all that he had known in childhood and early youth. . . . I think, too, that because of all that half-civilised blood in his veins he could not endure the sedentary toil of creative art and so remained a man of action, exaggerating, for the sake of immediate effect, every trick learned from his masters, turning their easel painting into painted scenes.[26]

Richard Ellmann points out that Yeats's theory of anti-self goes far beyond Wilde's concept of mask, as Yeats allows for an element of unconscious will as well as the consciously assumed pose, for an undirected will "which when evoked proves to have powers beyond those of the evoker."[27] That Wilde's career turned tragic would seem to confirm Yeats's more complex understanding of the artist's persona as being both willed and unwilled. In asserting the total power of the conscious will to transcend empirical life, Wilde left himself open to those other, less than conscious powers; he succumbed to the chaos of empirical life because he sought to escape it rather than reshape it. Perhaps as a result of his contact with Dowden, Yeats more clearly realized that the creating self remains dual, both empirical and transcendent, and that the living man requires the structure of art to achieve unity of being. George Wright puts it well:

For Yeats a man could attain a fuller realization of himself through art instead of through life; the poem could be the means of remolding the world somewhat nearer to the heart's austere desire. He accordingly developed a poetry that served as a realization of the man, a crystallization of the best and most fundamental part of him. . . . Although the mask is superior to the man, it cannot be presented in isolation. What the poet aspires to be can be realized in the poem, but only by emphasizing the conflict between aspiration and degradation. The contriving poet must present, for his own best expression, not only the idealized mask but also the "rag-and-bone shop" of the trivial quotidian personality out of which the mask grows and in relevance to which the mask is significant achievement.[28]

Long before encountering the concepts of persona advocated by Dowden and Wilde, Yeats was introduced by his father to the philosophy and poetry of William Blake; and not long after his initial exposures to Dowden and Wilde, Yeats began a systematic study of Blake with another of his father's friends, Edwin Ellis.[29] This study was to become their joint, three-volume edition, *The Works of William Blake: Poetic, Symbolic and Critical,* and to constitute Yeats's own most thorough exposure to the implications of a dual poetic self. Yeats and Ellis found a duality of identity in the empirical Blake as well as in his writings; the biographical "Memoir" that opens the study portrays the poet as experiencing both empirical and visionary or transcendent states of being: "A trance-like absorption of his whole nature . . . accompanied his finest writing, a mood from which he returned to the ordinary conversation of life as a man from another land. Feeling this keenly, he could not but attribute the authorship of his life's work to influences which his ordinary *self* did not contain."[30] Although such an interpretation of the creative process is relatively common, Yeats found it sufficiently provocative to extend this duality of the historical man to a theory of duality in poetic vision, in an essay in the same edition, "The Necessity of Symbolism":

> The mind or imagination or consciousness of man may be said to have two poles, the personal and impersonal, or, as Blake preferred to call them, the limit of contraction and the unlimited expansion. When we act from the personal we tend to bind our consciousness down as to a fiery centre. When, on the other hand, we allow our imagination to expand away from this egotistic mood, we become vehicles for the universal thought and merge in the universal mood. . . . The [personal] "genius" within us is impatient and law-breaking, and only becomes peaceful and free when it grows one with the "poetic genius"—the universal mood. It does so not by surrender of its own nature, but by expanding until it contains that which is the essence of all. Blake refuses to consider the personal as in itself evil for by it we obtain experience. It is continually feeding the universal life, as it were, with fuel of individual emotion. It becomes evil in the true sense of the word only when man invents a philosophy from reasoning upon it, asserts that its limited life is alone real, and that there is nothing but what is perceived by the five senses of the individual man. . . . Having denied the existence of that for which his bodily life exists, man begins an unceasing preoccupation with his own bodily life, neglecting to regard it as a symbol.[31]

Yeats expanded his own theory of the duality of self and refined his understanding of the interaction of the empirical and universal aspects of identity through his readings of Blake. In Blake, Yeats saw duality as not only productive but creative and not just in art, as with the "second self," or just in life, as with a mask or pose, but at all levels of thought and existence—the empirical, personal, perceiving self feeding the poetic, impersonal, visionary self, which in turn redeems the experiences of the empirical self by placing them within a structure of universal values. Yeats also grasped the relation of this creative duality to Blake's belief in the potential for an apocalyptic unification of humanity:

> The mood of the seer, no longer bound in by the particular experiences of his body, spreads out and enters into the particular experiences of an ever-widening circle of other lives and beings, for it will more and more grow one with that portion of the mood essence which is common to all that lives. . . . He who has thus passed into the impersonal portion of his own mind perceives that it is not a mind but all minds.[32]

To Blake, such an imaginative experience of the universal, the idealist realization that all that can be perceived or conceived is within oneself and is oneself, was absolute and irreversible, and would eventually mark the end of time and space and the symbolic function of all external reality as commonly known to the empirical mind.[33] To the young Yeats, such an imaginative unity of being was also conceivable but only if it remained anchored in the temporal world. Yeats did not follow Blake in awaiting an ontological apocalypse; he remained committed to art as the all-important process of achieving unity from the duality of self.

Several critics, notably Northrop Frye and Harold Bloom, evaluate Yeats's withdrawal from the apocalyptic goal of Blake's artistic philosophy as a poetic limitation, arguing that Yeats is incapable of finally transcending the world into the realm of universal identity that Blake symbolizes with his Eden.[34] Yeats, however, has made it quite clear that he doubted even Blake's ability to achieve a permanent ideal state and thus had no reason to attempt the impossible himself: "The limitation of [Blake's] view was from the very intensity of his vision; he was a too literal realist of the imagination."[35] Yeats thus devoted his poetic powers not to duplicating Blake's apocalyptic vision but to testing its implications. He assumed a position in relation to Blake that is analogous to Blake's own poetic characters: Urizen trapped in the material world, or Los laboring to create an imaginative order out of the empirical chaos. Yeats voluntarily subordinated himself to the man he once called "my master, William Blake,"[36] as Hazard Adams has most clearly described:

Blake and Yeats looked at the same world from different points of view. Yeats focussed upon the frustrations of this world from within this world, and Blake focussed upon the possibilities of this world from a position extremely difficult to pinpoint anywhere in the delusion we call space. . . . Blake absolutely rejects the age of intellect as delusory. . . . Yeats, though he mistrusts it, lives in it and follows its ways. Blake is putting words into the mouth of a trapped character.

In startling contrast, Yeats usually treats himself as the trapped character. . . . Dramatizing himself, he shows that he thinks Blake's view is right, but he also shows himself still struggling to attain a similar vision. He speaks with a baffled honesty which as his style matures makes a cold yet dramatic statement.[37]

At least part of the reason that Yeats assumed the role of Blake's pupil is, as Adams suggests, that Blake is not easily located in his poetry; he does not dramatize himself as a developing persona, as Yeats does. Because all of his creations are part of him, in his mind, Blake's entire poetic canon is a rough equivalent for the Blakean persona. The same cannot be said of Yeats, who carefully and continuously projects himself in his verse as the poetic "I," who is identifiably different from his other objectively drawn poetic characters.

If Yeats as poetic persona dramatizes Blake's poetic theories, he internalizes the quality of existence of Blake's poetic characters: the duality of self as projected in "spectre" and "emanation," and Blake's variation on the mask principle in the "covering cherub." Specter and emanation, state and space or "true intellect" and body of "experience and sense," are "divided from each other as active from passive, spirit from substance, and God from his mirror," a relationship that approximates Yeats's theory of the duality of poetic identity. The specter, or spiritual self in the fallen state, "accompanies" its emanation either "as a guard, or as a pursuer seeking to destroy its emanation, now become by separation its opposite, as thought separated from feeling wars upon feeling, the one depending for its life upon contraction the other upon diffusion." In the unfallen state, specter and emanation are united, complementary, one: "The space is a radiation or garment of the state, surrounding and flowing from it and containing it as the emotional nature contains the soul. The separation of one from the other and their final reunion is an aspect of the history of the fall and restoration of man."[38] Active specter, in falling, projects its emanation as external to itself, thereby relinquishing it as a complement of self and coveting or hating it insofar as it seems "other" and inaccessible. So the fallen spirit of man perceives nature, his own body, and even the products of his own toil or creation as outside and opposed to himself. Yeats correctly understood the reunion of specter and emanation to be an act of the "free" and "uncreated" imagination:

> By the imagination Blake means, among other things, the sympathetic will or love that makes us travel from mental state to mental state and surround ourselves with their personified images, for all imaginative perceptions are personifications of the impalpable expressed in terms of previous, no less personified feelings. We perceive the world through countless little reflections of our own image.[39]

Blake chastises fallen man for accepting the emanation as external or other, and his poetry is largely, as Yeats saw, a history of how man fell to this divided state and how he will reascend to unity. Blake's mythological history gave Yeats little help in reuniting the two aspects of self in his poetic persona, however, since Blake personifies these aspects as individual characters and not as psychological entities. According to Harold Bloom, though, Yeats used Blake's concept of "covering cherub" to build his own theory of mask, which, in turn, fed his conceptions of anti-self, daimon, and persona.[40] Yeats explicated Blake's "covering cherub" as the "mask of created form in which the uncreated spirit makes itself visible," in terms quite similar to the *prosopon* principle of the Greek Stoics—as the mask through which one gazes and assumes his role in the universal will. The "covering cherub" parallels the dual concept of persona to the extent that in it, "spectre and emanation are both contained . . . though not united into one, for when united they make up the Divine humanity."[41] "Covering cherub" as mask thus represented for Yeats the role of art in achieving unity of being and not Blake's final apocalyptic state of Eden. As an artistic concept, it not only harmonizes specter and emanation but also assimilates the states of human life into a structured whole:

> The Cherub is divided into twenty-seven heavens or churches, that is to say, into twenty-seven passive states through which man travels, and these heavens or churches are typified by twenty-seven great personages from Adam to Luther. . . . In these twenty-seven great personages, and in their lives as set forth in sacred and profane history, Blake found, wrapped up in obscure symbolism, the whole story of man's life, and of the life of moods, religions, ideas, and nations.

Moreover, each phase of the "covering cherub" can be alternately symbolic and representative of the "uncreated power" or a "satanic hindrance keeping our eager wills away from the freedom and truth of the Divine world."[42] Here, as Bloom has also seen, is the seed of the role of true and false masks in *A Vision*. Yeats thus found in Blake not only a poetic theory of the dual persona but a structure that contains its unity as well.

Although Yeats learned a philosophic idealism from Blake, Robert Snukal has cogently explained that Yeats's idealism is not the radical philosophic position that is generally denoted by the term:

> By "idealism" Yeats means the epistemological and metaphysical doc-
> trines which claim that the universe we discover about us is in some
> sense a product of the human mind. Any philosophical or quasi-
> philosophical position which seemed to imply that objective reality was
> mind-dependent, Yeats would call idealist. This is not quite the usual
> meaning of the word. The philosophical term "idealist" usually refers
> to someone who believes, as did Plato, that the ideal is the real. That is,
> Plato and others like Plato claimed that there are some things that differ
> from the ordinary things which are reported to us by our senses. These
> things are immaterial and in some way prior to, or above, material
> things. Or it may mean someone who believes, as did Berkeley, that all
> those things which seem real are ideas. According to Berkeley, these
> ideas were in the mind of God and were thus "objective." Hence Yeats
> says Berkeley is both realist and idealist alike. Both of these ideas
> displeased Yeats because they left the human mind a passive vehicle for
> perception—a camera or a mirror—in the same way as did most forms
> of realism. . . . Instead of the idealism of Plato and Berkeley, Yeats says
> that he is concerned with the idealism of Kant and Hegel and their
> successors.[43]

Snukal identifies Bradley, McTaggart, Croce, Gentile, Fichte, Schopenhauer, and Nietzsche as the philosophers who were of greatest interest to Yeats in his search for an ideal reality. Yeats's critics have considered the influence of most of these men on Yeats, in particular the effect of Nietzsche's opposing Apollonian and Dionysian aspects of human identity on Yeats's conception of self and anti-self.[44] To the extent that Yeats considered Berkeley fully an idealist and not part idealist and part realist, however, Berkeley's role for Yeats has not been adequately analyzed; and the subtle but very important influence of Giovanni Gentile as an "actual idealist" on Yeats's developing conception of the role of his poetic persona, or "I," has only begun to be explored. Yeats's fascination with both Berkeley and Gentile is evident in his epistolary philosophical debate with T. Sturge Moore.[45]

As Donald Torchiana points out, Yeats was as much interested in Berkeley's "personality, his inner biography,"[46] as in his philosophy, for the Irish Bishop provided Yeats (as he did Blake, from whom Yeats got his interest in idealism and Berkeley) with another intriguing example of the use of a mask.[47] Unlike Blake, however, Berkeley hid behind his mask rather than using it constructively to promote unity of being. This was not the Berkeley whom Yeats admired:

> I reject . . . the Berkeley who has come down to us in the correspondence of his day; the sage as imagined by gentlemen of fortune—a rôle accepted by Berkeley that he might not be left to starve in some garret by a generation terrified of religious scepticism and political anarchy, and loved because it hid from himself and others his own anarchy and scepticism.[48]

What Yeats describes here is a variation on Dowden's "second self," a self created in writing that gains independent being and social approval but that is nonetheless a false representation of the writer's higher self and thus a caricature rather than a persona. Yeats recognized the temptation to create such a false mask and even noted a similar didactic tendency in himself: "I spoke in the Irish Senate on the Catholic refusal of divorce and assumed that all lovers who ignored priest or registrar were immoral; upon education, and assumed that everybody who could not read the newspaper was a poor degraded creature."[49] But the self must deny its potential for unity of identity to serve such external and abstract ideas; such views are projections through a false mask that abstracts the outside world rather than uniting that world to the internal experience.

Yeats thus criticized Berkeley for being "idealist and realist alike" and for refusing continuously, in order to maintain his mask, to "define personality, and [to] say that Man in so far as he is himself, in so far as he is a personality, reflects the whole act of God. . . . It was the next step, and because [Berkeley] did not take it Blake violently annotated *Siris*."[50] However, Yeats continued to respect Berkeley for his original idealist position. When T. Sturge

Moore wrote to Yeats of Berkeley's "view being only verbally different from the common-sense scientific view," Yeats replied: "I agree with [you] about the later Berkeley, who was a Platonist. My Berkeley is the Berkeley of the *Commonplace Book*, and it is this Berkeley who has influenced the Italians. The essential sentence is of course 'things only exist in being perceived,' and I can only call that perception God's when I add Blake's 'God only acts or is in existing beings or men.' "[51] And in a poem written within this same period, Yeats openly expressed his admiration of, and approval for, Berkeley's early idealism:

> And God-appointed Berkeley that proved all things a dream,
> That this pragmatical, preposterous pig of a world, its farrow
>   that so solid seem,
> Must vanish on the instant if the mind but change its theme.
>
> (CP, 233)

Blake and Berkeley also provoked Yeats to an understanding of idealism that could encompass poets and philosophers alike and so include Yeats himself in both his roles of thinking man and poetic persona:

> The romantic movement seems related to the idealist philosophy; the naturalist movement, Stendhal's mirror dawdling down a lane, to Locke's mechanical philosophy, as simultaneous correspondential dreams are related, not merely where there is some traceable influence but through their whole substance. . . . When I speak of idealist philosophy I think more of Kant than of Berkeley, who was idealist and realist alike, more of Hegel and his successors than of Kant.[52]

Yeats's poetic persona is one of the self-proclaimed "last romantics" (CP, 240), and Yeats is one of the new idealists, one of the heirs of Kant and Hegel who respect Berkeley for the truths he hid behind his mask:

> It is plain . . . from [Berkeley's] later writings that he thought of God as a pure indivisible act, personal because at once will and understanding, which unlike the Pure Act of Italian philosophy creates passive "ideas"—sensations—thrusts them as it were outside itself.[53]

The "Pure Act of Italian philosophy," apparently a reference to the *Theory of Mind as Pure Act* by Giovanni Gentile, denies any externality or projection of mind by God or man, which is precisely the point at which Berkeley remained tied to realism. Yeats, however, was ready to transcend realism completely and to embrace the idealist concept of unity of being in the pure activity of thought:

> Only where the mind partakes of a pure activity can art or life attain swiftness, volume, unity; that contemplation lost, we picture some slow-moving event, turn the mind's eye from everything else that we may experience to the full our own passivity, our personal tragedy.[54]

Perhaps the greatest unrecognized influence on Yeats's developing ideas of persona is the work of Giovanni Gentile. Torchiana has noted that "foremost among those Yeats chose as allies against neorealism were the Italian idealist philosophers, Gentile and Croce," and Virginia Moore tells the story of Yeats's introduction to the work of Gentile,[55] but Yeats's poetic debt to this philosopher remains largely unexplored. Yeats first encountered the work of the Italian philosopher and minister of education when Yeats himself was an inspector of schools for the Irish Senate, and he enthusiastically endorsed both the ideas and the man, describing the latter as the "most profound disciple of our own Berkeley."[56] Gentile's book on educational theory probably attracted the idealist artist in Yeats with such arguments as "Art is the self-realization of the spirit as subject,"[57] but Gentile's philosophical treatise, *Theory of Mind as Pure Act*, spoke much more directly to Yeats's abiding interest in unity of being. Yeats praised Gentile's work to Moore for its "intensity of thought—which is Beauty" and later described the book, referring to it as "The Mind as Pure Art," to Olivia Shakespear as a "dry difficult beautiful book."[58] Yeats again mentioned Gentile's philosophical treatise in the second edition of *A Vision*, this time referring to it as "Theory of Mind as Pure Art."[59] In both these references Yeats tellingly misquotes the book's title, giving "art" for "act"—an intuitive application, perhaps, of Gentile's idealist philosophy to Yeats's own interest in the embodiment of philosophy in art. "Theory of Mind as Pure Art" is not an inappropriate description of Yeats's own philosophical book, *A Vision*, and not a bad title for the story of the development of Yeats's persona as a principle of poetic structure and unity of being.

It is little wonder that Yeats was attracted to Gentile's idealist philosophy, for it develops from a grounding in Berkeley in much the same way Yeats saw Blake as reforming Berkeley. Also, many of Gentile's beliefs sound strikingly like prose restatements of Blake's poetic dicta:

> If we think of ourselves empirically as in time, we naturalize ourselves and imprison ourselves within definite limits, birth and death, outside of which our personality cannot but seem annihilated. But this personality through which we enter the world of the manifold . . . is rooted in a higher personality, in which alone it is real. . . . This personality is outside every "before and after." Its being is in the eternal.[60]

For Gentile, as for Blake, the human mind has been falsely divorced from what it perceives, the subject separated from its object, whereas thought (and the "reality" that thought constitutes) is the dynamic interaction of subject and object, the constant and paradoxical urge to unify:

> Our whole experience moves between the unity of [the subject's] centre, which is mind, and the infinite multiplicity of the points constituting the sphere of its objects. . . . When we feel the difference, and only the difference, between ourselves and things, when we feel the affinity of things among themselves, and seem ourselves to be shut up as it were within a very tiny part of the whole, to be as a grain of sand on the shore of an immense ocean, we are regarding our empirical selves, not the transcendental self which alone is the true subject of our experience and therefore the only true self.

This argument recalls not only Blake's oft-quoted "To see a World in a Grain of Sand / . . . Hold Infinity in the palm of your hand," which views the particle of sand from Gentile's transcendent perspective of the all-encompassing self, but also the lesser-known proverb "One thought fills immensity."[61] Where Blake presents specters and emanations in his poetry as divorced aspects of the once-unified self, Gentile works in terms of empirical and transcendental identities. The empirical self, like Spitzer's "empirical 'I,' " is the historical being, the self perceived as object in an object-laden world, the sense of being as physical existence only. The transcendental self, like Spitzer's "poetic 'I,' " is the self as perceiving subject, that which *is* all it perceives because it perceives and thereby acts as the creating force in the universe. Where Blake chastises specters for contemplating their own projected emanations as alien, Gentile asks: "Seen from within your soul, is not this 'nature' your own non-being, the non-being of your own inward commotion, of the act by which you are to yourself? . . . It is . . . what you are not and must become."[62]

Gentile builds on the *"esse est percipi"* of Berkeley ("to be is to be perceived," thus the perceiver brings the external world into existence) and on the *"cogito ergo sum"* of Descartes ("I think therefore I am," thus thinking is existence) without accepting either as sufficient. What is missing from both, Gentile argues, is the recognition that what constantly connects mind and matter is not only perception or thought but the *act* of thought. Neither the transcendent nor the empirical self, therefore, constitutes the whole person; rather, the act of thinking, that continuous unification of subject and object, embraces both selves and constitutes, on another level entirely, the whole self. This reunited self is the product as well as the process of an act of conceptual discovery:

> The individual is the discovery which thought makes when it suddenly realizes that it has withdrawn from its original standpoint, and instead of having before it the ideas which it has constructed and projected before itself, has itself confronting its own self. The individual is the realization of the process in which the ideas arise and live the moment we turn from the abstract to the concrete. . . . In the "I" the particularity and the universality coincide and are identified by giving place to the true individual.[63]

That is, the mind, having contained and then projected ideas and things, realizes its own act and becomes self-conscious, conscious of itself creating itself, conscious of itself as both subject and object. In that act of consciousness lies the whole self, unity of being, the "I." Yeats thus found a philosophical rationale in Gentile for projecting his own persona, his "I," as the "hero" of a quest for unity of being, whereas he found only the abstract value of "centre" in place of "I" in Blake's mythology:

> The Centre is itself the hero, as it were, of a myth. Its story is a paradox. . . . Ulro, as the selfish Centre is outside Beulah, which is the true, holy, inner circumference and camp. . . . The apparent contradiction disappears when looked at in the light of Blake's religious belief in the essential brotherliness of Imagination . . . and the essential egotism and isolation of Reason. . . . Each is endowed with a centre and a circumference. The centre of brotherhood, or its essence, is its quality of expansiveness. But this is an inner expansiveness. Each man opens his own mind inwards into the field of Vision and there, in this infinite

realm, meets his brother-man. . . . The selfish centre which is "outside"
is outside in an unexpansive sense, for nonentity is not expanse, though
it be limitless as error. The selfish centre is made of the exterior reason
and the five senses. It is the mortal personality, that which death inevitably dissolves, but which it is life's business to destroy, for this is
"Salvation." Hence salvation is the opposite of morality, and the centre
is outside the circumference. The paradox turns out to be a symbol, not
a contradiction.[64]

The similarities between Gentile's "I" and that of the Greek
Stoics and between Gentile's "actual" concept of selfhood and the
Stoics' internal and external associations for persona are clear and
provocative. In particular, Gentile's analysis of the dual identity of
artist as both man and work recalls the external/internal focuses of
prosopon. The poet is both dead and alive, historical and spiritual:

> Horace as the man who was born and died is indeed dead, and his
> monument rises up in us, in an "us" who, in so far as we are subject and
> immanent act, are not different from Horace himself. For Horace,
> besides being an object among the other manifold objects compresent
> in history as we know it when we read it, is presented to us, not as
> something different from us, but as our brother and father, even as our
> very self in its inner transparence, in its self-identity. . . . The poet's
> true eternity, then, is not the poet in so far as he belongs to the
> manifold, but the poet in so far as he is one with the unity of the
> transcendental "I," with the immanent principle of every particular
> experience, in so far, that is to say, as the poet and we ourselves are
> one.[65]

The poet differs from most "I"s in that his act of unifying empirical
and transcendent selves is embodied in the processes of art and
therefore becomes an experience in the unifying thinking of other
minds, whose acts of thought are not made concrete in art. The life
of the poet is thus of exemplary interest in that the "most characteristic feature of art is the raising of self-consciousness in its abstract immediacy to a higher power," and in that the poet's life is
not only the accumulation of events but also the artistic embodiment of that accumulation: "This in substance is not two things,
the poem and its preparation taken together; it is one concrete
thing, the poem in its process of spiritual actuality." The poet
makes his act of unification, his persona, present to us in his
poetry; "the poet's 'life' is a subjective free creation detached from
the real, a creation in which the subject himself is realized and, as it

were, enchained, and posits himself in his immediate abstract subjectivity."[66] Yeats had come to this conclusion on his own many
years before reading Gentile: "A poet is by the very nature of
things a man who lives with entire sincerity, or rather the better his
poetry the more sincere his life; his life is an experiment in living
and those that come after him have a right to know it."[67] Gentile
merely clarifies and augments the reasoning behind the concept.

Gentile moves in his work from idealist philosophy in all its
implicit manifestations to its explicit applications in life and art; he
was, by this virtue, more accessible to the philosophy-hungry
Yeats than Blake, who "was a too literal realist of the imagination." Where Yeats learned from Blake primarily by reenacting the
experiences of Blake's poetic characters, Yeats assimilated and ap-
plied Gentile's theories to his own poetic beliefs and practices.
Gentile, in effect, provided Yeats with a system that is not unlike
Yeats's own *A Vision*, a philosophic structure from which to create
poetry. Indeed, Gentile conceived of his own book as a process of
self-discovery that is also self-expression, as he implies in his "Preface": "Here and there I find in [the book] several buds which I
perceive have since opened out in my thoughts and become new
branches. . . . But what of this? I have never led my readers or my
pupils to expect from me a fully defined thought, a dry trunk as it
were encased in a rigid bark. A book is the journey not the destination; it would be alive not dead."[68] So, too, Yeats as poetic persona
is always in the process of becoming within a poetic structure. "A
poet writes always of his personal life . . . . [he is] reborn as an
idea, something intended, complete."

In his lifelong study of unity of being, Yeats encountered many
perspectives on its embodied expression, the poetic persona. Participating in mystical rituals, Yeats experienced the apparent
unification of body and spirit. In Dowden's work, however, Yeats
saw the celebration of a "second self" arising from literature alone,
and in Wilde's life he saw the destructive results of assuming a
mask without assuming also the corresponding universal role. In
his extensive study of Blake, Yeats learned of duality as a mark of
fallen humanity and of the lifelong individual and collective struggle toward reunited being. In Berkeley, Yeats found a philosophic
reconciliation of mind and matter in idealism, and in Gentile he
saw that reconciliation carried to its natural fruition in the acts of
the thinking "I" in both life and art. No simple modern definition

of persona covers all these relevant influences. The "I" of Yeats's poetry is not the "implied author" of Wayne Booth's definition, for there is no ironic distance between the "I" that narrates and the "I" that writes Yeats's poetry. Leo Spitzer's distinction between "empirical" and "poetic" identities is somewhat more applicable to Yeats's persona, but only insofar as they can be united in the poetic persona, by its act of contemplating the concerns of empirical life within a poetic structure. If any definition is to come close to describing this process, it is that of the Greek Stoics, who saw the persona as both mask and role, together placing the individual will in the context of the greater universal will.

Several modern critics have nevertheless tackled the dilemma of defining Yeats's poetic persona. George Wright concludes that, for Yeats, "the poem, taken as a whole, is the mask through which he speaks, as poet, to his reader; the poem, not the 'I,' is his voice, his persona."[69] Wright arrives at this conclusion through a reading of Yeats's poetic roles as unrelated, fragmentary, and impersonal, so that only the poem as a whole grasps the totality of Yeats's protean identity. Ironically, this modern turn of attention toward fragmentation and away from the integrity of a poetic persona is exactly what Yeats criticized in his successors and tried to correct in his own poetry. Wright's conclusion may apply to such dialogue poems as "Ego Dominus Tuus," in which Yeats obviously portrays a limited aspect of self in each character. But Hic and Ille are just that—characters; neither is the poet's persona. In the majority of Yeats's poems, he speaks through the poetic "I," and that speaking, thinking "I" is the persona, the manifestation of Yeats's identity in the act of uniting empirical and transcendent, or object and subject, aspects of self. This unification of autobiography (empirical self) and poetic structure (transcendent self) is what Wright fails to see. No one poem embodies this unity; rather it occurs, as Gentile stresses it must, in the persona's act of development through the poetic canon. It is the ongoing assimilative nature of the "I," rather than the comprehensive quality of any one poem, that constitutes the persona of Yeats's poetic efforts.

In a much more recent study of Yeats's poetic identity, Robert Langbaum acknowledges the need to move the modern definition of persona beyond the sense of facade or "socially fixed self" in order to account for the mystical nature of Yeats's dual persona:

The passions we have excluded in order to make an identity return as an unconscious-conscious projection that challenges the old identity and helps us make a new one. Yeats calls this projection the antiself or Daimon. . . . For Descartes, thought was subjective and incorporeal; it went on entirely inside the head. For Yeats, thoughts are subtly corporeal and are out there "in the general vehicle of *Anima Mundi*"; instead of thoughts passing through us, we pass through thoughts, mirroring them "in our particular vehicle."[70]

Yeats had precedent for such an outside inside in both Blake's emanation and Gentile's self-conscious self. But Langbaum is quoting from "Per Amica Silentia Lunae," which Yeats wrote after much study of Blake but before he had any knowledge of Gentile —that is, before Yeats became conscious of the fact that he was, indeed, achieving unity of being in a particular poetic "I." Being more concerned with the theory than the technique, with product rather than process, Langbaum fails to see how the poetic persona achieves a unity from the dual aspects of his own identity.

Both Langbaum and Wright make the common mistake of not considering the empirical aspect of self in Yeats's persona. Wright focuses on poetic structure and Langbaum on the spiritual realm— both aspects of the transcendent identity. Even in "Per Amica Silentia Lunae," however, the "I" has an empirical identity, a history, and it undergoes empirical experiences that are not unrelated to Yeats's own. The prose is an appropriate starting point for an examination of Yeats's persona in action, where it cannot be, obviously, just the poetry or the spiritual realm. Rather than pursuing Langbaum's theoretical analysis of the persona, a study of the speaking "I" is in order, for only by observing the "I" in action can its role be properly assessed as a vehicle of unity of being for the poet Yeats.

2
"Subject-Matter":
Prose Developments of the Persona

IN section II of "A General Introduction for My Work" Yeats explores Irish literature, past and contemporary, as the "subject-matter" of, or "tapestry" behind, his work. This section also reveals that Irish literature does not constitute the whole tapestry, for Yeats writes: "Everything I love has come to me through English"; "Gaelic is my national language, but it is not my mother tongue."[1] In the literature he reads and writes as in the life he lives, Yeats discovers duality. He greatly admires Irish literature for the popular and mythological traditions it embodies and for its universal voice; English literature attracts him with the power of its individual minds: "I owe my soul to Shakespeare, to Spenser and to Blake, perhaps to William Morris, and to the English language in which I think, speak, and write." Conversely, Yeats sees Irish literature as an inadequate mode of expression for the individual, and he sees English literature as prone to becoming too individual in its conerns:

It was through the old Fenian leader John O'Leary I found my theme. . . . He gave me the poems of Thomas Davis, said they were not good poetry but had changed his life when a young man. . . . I saw even more clearly than O'Leary that they were not good poetry. I read nothing but romantic literature; hated that dry eighteenth-century rhetoric; but they had one quality I admired and admire: they were not separated individual men; they spoke or tried to speak out of a people to a people; behind them stretched the generations. I knew, though but now and then as young men know things, that I must turn from that modern literature Jonathan Swift compared to the web a spider draws out of its bowels; I hated and still hate with an ever growing hatred the literature of the point of view. I wanted, if my ignorance permitted, to

46

get back to Homer, to those that fed at his table. I wanted to cry as all men cried, to laugh as all men laughed, and the Young Ireland poets when not writing mere politics had the same want, but they did not know that the common and its befitting language is the research of a lifetime and when found may lack popular recognition.[2]

Irish literature, Yeats feels, excels in the concrete, in content and context, whereas English literature excels in the more abstract mechanics of expression. Separately, the limitations of each are apparent: Irish nationalist poets become mired in politics or sentimentality; Wordsworth, as a representative English poet, altogether ignores contemporary Irish nationalism and writes a sonnet on one man in a far-off land. Together, however, Irish tradition and English expression provide the context and structure that are essential to unity of being:

> I am convinced that in two or three generations it will become generally known that the mechanical theory has no reality, that the natural and supernatural are knit together, that to escape a dangerous fanaticism we must study a new science; at that moment Europeans may find something attractive in a Christ posed against a background not of Judaism but of Druidism, not shut off in dead history, but flowing, concrete, phenomenal.
>
> I was born into this faith, have lived it, and shall die in it; my Christ, a legitimate deduction from the Creed of St. Patrick as I think, is that Unity of Being Dante compared to a perfectly proportioned human body, Blake's "Imagination," what the Upanishads have named "Self": nor is this unity distant and therefore intellectually understandable, but imminent, differing from man to man and age to age, taking upon itself pain and ugliness, "eye of newt, and toe of frog."[3]

It is notably the "I" in this extract that facilitates the union of Irish and English characteristics, by standing "convinced" that an individual Christ "posed against a background . . . of Druidism" would represent unity of being. Even more importantly, this "I," as well as declaring its faith, embodies it: "I was born into this faith, have lived it, and shall die in it." Literally, Yeats was a union of Irish and English characteristics, being Anglo-Irish by heredity, by marriage, and by literary preference. He is still a living symbol of the propitious union of the English and Irish, much as the Christ he speaks of is a symbol of the union of the human and divine, for the ongoing process of Yeats's life in his writings constitutes the activity in which the complementary qualities are united. This act of union is best seen in the writings that deal most obviously with Yeats's desire to pose himself against, without losing himself to, the traditions embodied in Irish literature—his fictional prose. In the prose fiction, Yeats's persona both fears and is attracted to the unknown depths of Irish subject matter; he clings to his empirical identity while being tempted to sacrifice it to a transcendent identity. This ambivalence is first apparent in *John Sherman,* which structurally and thematically exploits the Irish/English duality, and is gradually resolved in *Mythologies,* which develops a persona that finally can dip in and out of the traditional realm of Irish supernaturalism at will.

Mythologies is an important manifestation of Yeats's act of unifying empirical and transcendent identities in the persona because it covers a wide range of the totality of Yeats's efforts at writing fictional prose: from the early Irish fairy tales in "The Celtic Twilight" and folklore in "The Secret Rose" and "Stories of Red Hanrahan"; through the contemporary original compositions that reflect Yeats's own occult activities, "Rosa Alchemica," "The Tables of the Law," and "The Adoration of the Magi"; to the work which is generally viewed as the precursor of *A Vision,* "Per Amica Silentia Lunae." The volume is also important in Yeats's development of a persona as an embodiment of unity of being insofar as Yeats himself seems to have arranged the book as an aesthetic whole from the numerous discrete tales it comprehends. Although published posthumously, *Mythologies* is substantially a reworking of the 1925 *Early Poems and Stories,* with the addition of "Per Amica Silentia Lunae," which did not appear in the earlier work. The "Note" at the beginning of *Mythologies* is reprinted from that earlier volume and provides an important summary of the histories of, and connections among, the individual tales. Richard Finneran has further identified a set of page proofs for a volume of the unpublished "Coole edition" of Yeats's collected works that bears the title *Mythologies* and appears to be the precursor of the present volume, although these proofs still do not include "Per Amica Silentia Lunae."[4] Intentionally arranged in whole or in part, however, *Mythologies* demonstrates a progressive development in Yeats's conception of the persona: from the barely augmented autobiographical presentation of self in "The Celtic Twilight," to the part-fictional, part-autobiographical persona of the "Rosa Alchemica" group, to the artistically fully autonomous but empirically grounded thinking "I" of "Per Amica Silentia Lunae."

Richard Finneran wonders a little at the exclusion of Yeats's *Dhoya* from *Mythologies,* arguing that it would not be "out of place" among the numerous Irish tales in the collection.[5] Yeats was, however, uncomfortable with this very early effort at fiction, as he was with *John Sherman,* and dismissed both in 1904 as "written when I was very young & knew no better."[6] From the viewpoint of the development of a persona, these two tales are indeed outside the achievement of *Mythologies,* in which the "I" is the primary persona. Both *Dhoya* and *John Sherman* are told from the perspective of an omniscient narrator, and the characters are fully objective presentations, pieces of that narrator's knowledge. By contrast, even those objective characters which do appear in *Mythologies,* in "The Secret Rose" and "Stories of Red Hanrahan," are presented not from without but from within; the internal conflicts of the characters are the focus of the tales rather than their actions. In order to understand Yeats's movement toward a personal persona in *Mythologies,* however, it is valuable first to note his original narrative standpoint outside the tale, and *John Sherman* is exemplary of this stance in its structured presentation of objective characters, which constitutes Yeats's original concern with duality of identity in literature.

As Richard Ellmann reads the novel, "it is clear that [Yeats's] real subject matter is himself, and that he has cut himself definitely into two parts," Sherman representing Yeats's youthful, dreaming self and Howard the self Yeats thought he would have to become to survive in London and win the respect of Maud Gonne.[7] Although no critic disputes the autobiographical element, Richard Finneran interprets the duality on a more abstract, philosophical plane:

> John Sherman is not . . . simply Yeats's autobiographical sketch of himself. Rather Sherman and the Reverend William Howard together present an early illustration of that division of personality which Yeats was later to treat by means of such terms as the Self and the Anti-Self. That is, both characters represent segments of what was, at least for Yeats, an unattainable total or complete personality. . . . In the largest terms of this division it is clear that Sherman represents the Self, Howard the Anti-Self: Sherman is subjective, Howard objective; Sherman is introverted, Howard extroverted; Sherman is the man of the country, a Romanticist, Howard the man of the city, a Classicist. . . . Howard

desires a life which is intellectualized, controlled, and static; Sherman
desires a life which is unintellectualized, loosely controlled, and active.[8]

Since this list employs many of the terms that Yeats uses in "A
General Introduction for My Work," it is worth noting that Sherman is Irish and Howard English.[9] This observation concerning
the opposing male characters of *John Sherman* carries the book
beyond autobiography and into literary theory, specifically into
the theory and practice of conceiving literary characters. Admit-
tedly, Yeats does not succeed in this novel in uniting the two
aspects of personality, or even in deftly portraying their opposing
characteristics, but *John Sherman* is a remarkable first attempt at
bringing these antitheses into conscious expression, and, in itself,
the novel does not imply that their unification is forever "unattain-
able." However, when the dual qualities of one whole being are
projected into two separate characters, obviously they cannot be
unified, except in a Blakean, apocalyptic sense. So Yeats, as author, grants John Sherman some success at novel's end, but the
character has not substantially changed from his original subjective
stance; his contacts with the complementary, antithetical William
Howard have not raised him to some attainment of unity of being.
     Yeats does not create a single unified persona in *John Sherman,*
that thinking "I" or act of mind in Gentile's philosophy that unites
internal and external identities, although the act is certainly implied in Yeats's writing of, and, therefore, in his thinking through,
the novel. In "The Celtic Twilight," an "I" begins to emerge amid
a great variety of objectively drawn characters, not very sure of
itself at first but moving tentatively forward. The autobiographical
source of Yeats's literary concerns now becomes explicit in contrast to the markedly traditional nature of his subject matter, Irish
mythology. In a friend's copy of the original edition Yeats has
incribed, "All real stories heard among the people or real incidents
with but a little disguise in names and places,"[10] and in the preface
to the first edition Yeats describes his intentions in recording the
tales:

> Next to the desire, which every artist feels, to create for himself a little
> world out of the beautiful, pleasant, and significant things of this
> marred and clumsy universe, I have desired to show in a vision some-
> thing of the face of Ireland to any of my own people who care for
> things of this kind. I have therefore written down accurately and can-
> didly much that I have heard and seen, and, except by way of commen-

tary, nothing that I have merely imagined. I have, however, been at no pains to separate my own beliefs from those of the peasantry, but have rather let my men and women, dhouls and faeries, go their own way unoffended or defended by any argument of mine. The things a man has heard and seen are threads of life, and if he pull them carefully from the confused distaff of memory, any one who will can weave them into whatever garments of belief please them best.[11]

As in "A General Introduction for My Work," Yeats here sees Irish story as providing the material for transcendent "vision" and "garments of belief," and Yeats's role of directly relating the stories is his means of raising himself from empirical concerns to transcendent vision. By presenting himself autobiographically, as the empirical W. B. Yeats, but in the act of retelling traditional tales, Yeats functions as the thinking "I" that unites empirical and transcendent realms. What this thinking, mediating role does to Yeats's artistic presentation of himself is to raise the "I" to the status of persona.

Yeats may protest that he has "been at no pains to separate my own beliefs from those of the peasantry," but the self Yeats presents in "The Celtic Twilight" is obviously quite uncomfortable in his stance toward folk beliefs.[12] The opening tale, in fact, serves to disabuse Yeats of responsibility for the veracity or rationality of the tales that follow by attributing many of them to "one Paddy Flynn, a little bright-eyed old man," with the "visionary melancholy of purely instinctive natures" (M, 5).[13] Yeats is projecting another intuitive self in Paddy Flynn, as he has in John Sherman, so it is not surprising that the stance Yeats himself takes as reteller of the tales in "The Celtic Twilight" is quite similar to that of the cosmopolitan rationalist, William Howard. But Paddy Flynn is never heard from again after this one mention of his role, and Yeats, or the narrative "I," assumes the role of storyteller. Because he has established himself as once removed from the tales themselves, however, Yeats can allow himself the luxury of commenting on the tales as well as telling them. He participates, that is, in both the intuitive subjective nature of such peasant folk as Paddy Flynn, with whom the tales originate, and the rationalistic objective nature of those educated men and women of the world who are likely to be the book's audience. That Yeats himself felt both natures to be conflicting parts of his own he had already demonstrated in writing *John Sherman.*

In the first tale proper, suggestively titled "Belief and Unbelief,"

Yeats takes no stance toward his subject matter but seems to find some comfort in the opening line: "There are some doubters even in the western villages" (M, 7). The persona is warming up, as it were, and merely repeats the attitudes of the peasants toward their supernatural experiences: "I have met also a man with a Mohawk Indian tattooed upon his arm, who held exactly similar beliefs and unbeliefs. No matter what one doubts, one never doubts the faeries, for, as [he] said, 'they stand to reason' " (M, 7). In short order, however, the persona himself tackles the question of "belief and unbelief" by assuming progressively a more flexible role, sometimes as a character in a tale, sometimes far removed from a story as an evaluator. Because he fluctuates between participation and criticism, or belief and unbelief, the persona never settles in one position but rather actively connects the two by continuously comparing and contrasting them. Some tales the "I" merely relates, one "just as it was told," accepting the impersonal effect of "those old rambling moralless tales" (M, 125) without protest; in others, the persona reluctantly speaks of supernatural experiences of his own:

> I fell, one night some fifteen years ago, into what seemed the power of Faery. . . . We saw it all in such a dream, and it seems all so unreal, that I have never written of it until now, and hardly ever spoken of it, and even when thinking, because of some unreasonable impulse, I have avoided giving it weight in the argument. Perhaps I have felt that my recollections of things seen when the sense of reality was weakened must be untrustworthy. (M, 81–82)

In yet another story, the narrator worries about a friend: "I am not certain that he distinguishes between the natural and supernatural very clearly" (M, 61).

It thus becomes high priority for the persona to distinguish between the empirical and the transcendent in these tales, even as his act of telling them joins the two realms. This is the paradoxical essence of unity of being—two fully individual characteristics or states in a complementary as well as opposing tension. That the persona himself is not always successful in distinguishing the two indicates their ultimate complementarity. The persona indeed occasionally loses consciousness of his empirical self and enters a transcendent state of vision, as in the preceding extract on the "power of Faery" from "The Old Town." In large part, however, Yeats depicts the persona as heroically standing his empirical ground before the supernatural, a somewhat reductive position that is occasionally almost comic. In "Regina, Regina Pigmeorum, Veni," for instance, the "I" invokes the presence of a fairy queen: "I too had by this time fallen into a kind of trance, in which what we call the unreal had begun to take upon itself a masterful reality, and I had an impression, not anything I could call an actual vision, of gold ornaments and dark hair" (M, 55). In the midst of his trance or quasi vision, however, he chooses to interrogate the queen in empirical terms: "I asked her other questions, as to her nature, and her purpose in the universe, but only seemed to puzzle her. At last she appeared to lose patience, for she wrote this message for me upon the sands—the sands of vision—'Be careful, and do not seek to know too much about us'" (M, 56). Yeats himself does not fully learn this lesson until years later when, near death, he realizes that "Man can embody truth but he cannot know it."[14] In this classic confrontation of empirical and transcendent natures, as in *John Sherman*, the two do not unite, but the persona takes a step closer to such a unity by learning to adjust his thought processes so that he avoids alienating the supernatural world by trying to understand it rationally and rather accepts it as part of life and thus part of self, as surely Paddy Flynn would do.

"The Sorcerers," which is in many respects a prelude to "Rosa Alchemica," is the most explicit tale on the interrelations of the two realms of the empirical and the spiritual and on their connection with the duality of identity. At a séance, a sorcerer employs his considerable powers to invoke the supernatural realm, and as he succeeds, the persona finds himself struggling against a trance and fearing that the "influence which was causing this trance was out of harmony with itself, in other words, evil" (M, 39). The persona succeeds in resisting supernatural influence, but as he departs he cannot resist a little curiosity and asks, "'What would happen if one of your spirits had overpowered me?'" The sorcerer responds, "'You would go out of this room . . . with his character added to your own'" (M, 40). This brush with the supernatural is the fictional precursor of Yeats's theory of anti-self in "Per Amica Silentia Lunae," and the persona's response to it here, one of distrust, anticipates the reactions of the persona in the later prose work and in "Rosa Alchemica." It is a complementary relationship of equals that Yeats's persona seeks in telling tales of the supernatural realm, not a wholesale loss of empirical identity to the transcendent.

The developing duality of the persona in "The Celtic Twilight" surfaces not only in the intrusion into the traditional tales of his

own empirical and supernatural experiences but also in the tension
between the tales and their footnotes, which were added by an
older and surer Yeats when he edited the actions of the persona
created in his youth. The notes include phrases to the effect of "I
know better now" (M, 37n), and they assert the more solid reality
of the mature Yeats in his achieved identity as an accomplished
poet. The castle of Ballylee in "'Dust Hath Closed Helen's Eye,'"
for instance, becomes Thoor Ballylee, "now my property," in a
note appended in 1924. The footnotes function, then, as an
affirmation of the possibility of a unity of empirical and transcendent identities that is only glimpsed as a potentiality by the
persona of "The Celtic Twilight"; the notes function also to put
the persona of the early prose into perspective, as an early manifestation of the desire for unity of being in a lifelong quest. At an
even later age, Yeats would disparage "The Celtic Twilight" as a
"bit of ornamental trivial needlework sewn on a prophetic fury got
by Blake and Boehme,"[15] but there is no denying the significance
of this persona's role of vigilant distinguisher of natural and supernatural, which constitutes paradoxically an unwitting act of unifying the two. It is not inappropriate to regard the persona of "The
Celtic Twilight" in terms of the girl in a later poem, "The Double
Vision of Michael Robartes" (CP, 168), who dances between the
Sphinx and Buddha (as manifestations of objective and subjective
realms, respectively), not bringing them any nearer in a physical
sense but achieving some sort of personal unity of being in her
dance between them.

The persona of "The Celtic Twilight," like that dancer, also
gains some subconscious comprehension of his dual nature. In
"Dreams That Have no Moral," the persona gets directly involved
in the story despite claiming to "tell [it] just as it was told"
(M, 125). At one point the "I" walks into the tale, as it were, to
drink some milk (M, 130), and again at the tale's end, "I was
passing one time myself, and they called me in and gave me a cup
of tea" (M, 137). (It may also be significant to the empirical aspect
of identity that there are two brothers in this tale named Bill and
Jack.) The persona has come to accept the supernatural world as
another level of reality and to enter into it without fear of losing
forever his empirical identity. In the last story, the persona has
come far enough to be able to verbalize his new understandings:

Folk-art is, indeed, the oldest of the aristocracies of thought, and
because it refuses what is passing and trivial, the merely clever and

pretty, as certainly as the vulgar and insincere, and because it has gathered into itself the simplest and most unforgettable thoughts of the generations, it is the soil where all great art is rooted. . . . In a society that has cast out imaginative tradition, only a few people . . . favoured by their own characters and by happy circumstance, and only then after much labour, have understanding of imaginative things, and yet, "the imagination is the man himself."[16] (M, 139)

Significantly, Yeats does not use the first-person pronoun here to articulate his findings; it is rather as if the truth were greater than the individual and speaks through the archetypal man. Thus, the persona that begins as the empirical Yeats comes to embody a universal truth, an achievement of unity of being worth the "labour" of mediating between the natural and supernatural realms of "The Celtic Twilight."

"The Secret Rose," the collection of tales immediately following "The Celtic Twilight" in *Mythologies,* shows the results of the development of Yeats's persona from the particular empirical "I" of "Mr. Yeats," the poet (M, 36), to the archetypal "man." There is no narrative "I" in the tales of "The Secret Rose." There are several fully drawn objective characters, variations on the archetypal "man," such as the knight in "Out of the Rose" and the old man of "The Heart of the Spring," but Yeats does not project himself into any particular character. These characters do, however, function in a fashion somewhat similar to that of the "I" of "The Celtic Twilight"; that is, they struggle to unite the natural and supernatural realms. The knight, for instance, has "the face of one of those who have come but seldom into the world, and always for its trouble, the dreamers who must do what they dream, the doers who must dream what they do" (M, 157). Similarly, the gleeman of "The Crucifixion of the Outcast" proclaims proudly near the end of his life, " 'I ask no more delays, for I have drawn the sword, and told the truth, and lived my dream, and am content' " (M, 154).

Philip Marcus senses Yeats's own developing sensitivity to portraying the duality of natural and supernatural orders in this collection of objective characters in the manner in which Yeats has arranged the tales in the volume:

Yeats decided to arrange his stories in chronological order of the action. The seventeen stories span a period from the earliest times to the period at which Yeats was writing ["Rosa Alchemica"]. . . . Such an arrangement has thematic significance, for it gives historical perspective to the war between spiritual and natural order, illustrates its persistence through the centuries of Irish civilization. . . . Considering its irregular manner of evolution, *The Secret Rose* is a remarkably well-unified collection.[17]

Marcus is evaluating the 1897 edition of *The Secret Rose,* which encompasses those tales about Red Hanrahan and "Rosa Alchemica" which are presented as separate entities in *Mythologies.* Marcus's comment on the "war between spiritual and natural order" refers to Yeats's "Dedication" to Æ (Yeats's friend George Russell) in that early volume, which has been omitted, along with the preface to "The Celtic Twilight," from *Mythologies.* Structurally, these omissions are logical, for they allow the first two volumes of prose to blend together and with the other collections to constitute one large integrated volume of prose "mythologies" rather than remaining a mere conglomeration of individual volumes on different themes. Nevertheless, an important thematic link is lost with the omission of the "Dedication" to "The Secret Rose," a theme that ties the Yeatsian persona to the poem which opens the collection and to the prose tales as a unit. That theme is, as Marcus notes, the "one subject" of the tales, the "war of spiritual with natural order." Yeats dedicated the original volume to Æ because he felt sure that the mystical Æ would "sympathize with the sorrows and the ecstasies of its personages, perhaps even more than I do myself." Yeats so qualified his own involvement in "The Secret Rose" apparently because he composed it in part to "interest a certain people among whom he has grown up" or to fulfill a "duty towards them." Indeed, the "Dedication" reads almost like an apologia for straying from the central concern of unity of being of the self in the development of a poetic "I":

My friends in Ireland sometimes ask me when I am going to write a really national poem or romance, and by a national poem or romance I understand them to mean a poem or romance founded upon some moment of famous Irish history, and built up out of the thoughts and feelings which move the greater number of patriotic Irishmen. I on the other hand believe that poetry and romance cannot be made by the most conscientious study of famous moments and of the thoughts and feelings of others, but only by looking into that little, infinite, faltering, eternal flame that one calls one's self.[18]

Richard Finneran reads this "Dedication" as heralding a turn in the prose "from the folk and fairy to the esoteric and the occult," a movement Finneran takes to be consciously designed to appeal "not to the populace but to the initiate."[19] In support of his conclusions Finneran cites a letter in which Yeats says of *The Secret Rose:* "It is at any rate an honest attempt towards that aristocratic esoteric Irish literature, which has been my chief ambition. We have a literature for the people but nothing yet for the few."[20] This letter, however, anticipates in its phrasing the much later "A General Introduction for My Work," in which Yeats emphasizes the complementary relationship of the individual man and the tradition of men. The heroes of the tales in "The Secret Rose" are not so much superior to the masses of men as "aristocratic" in the sense of embodying the best, archetypal aspects of mankind. They are, more specifically, heroic questers, seeking that unity of being to which all men aspire, consciously or otherwise.

The poem that functions as a bridge between the thematically explicit "Dedication" and the tales which enact the themes characterizes these heroic questers quite clearly and also demonstrates Yeats's relation to them. "To the Secret Rose" (M, 145–46) celebrates such mythological heroes as Cuchulain and Fergus for their quests for unity of being, which is symbolized by the rose, and it depicts the Yeatsian "I" desiring to follow their lead. Yeats exhorts the rose: *"Enfold me in my hour of hours; where those / Who sought thee in the Holy Sepulchre, / Or in the wine-vat, dwell beyond the stir / And tumult of defeated dreams."* The poem ends with the persona desiring to be within the apocalyptic context of his heroes' completed quests:

> *. . . I, too, await*
> *The hour of thy great wind of love and hate.*
> *When shall the stars be blown about the sky,*
> *Like the sparks blown out of a smithy, and die?*
> *Surely thine hour has come, thy great wind blows,*
> *Far-off, most secret, and inviolate Rose?*

Yeats thus recalls the lives of Irish mythological heroes as examples and inspirations to himself but has not yet personally made the leap into the realm in which earthly heroes embody spiritual truths; the tales that follow do create such heroes, but not at the personal level of the "I."

Six tales of the herioc quester Red Hanrahan also originally appeared in the 1897 volume, *The Secret Rose*, and were incorporated into the more general stories of that volume. Yeats subsequently reorganized and virtually rewrote the series of related stories, republishing them as an independent collection. "Stories of Red Hanrahan," as it appears in *Mythologies*, thus represents Yeats's realization of how a heroic character commands the literature that gives him birth, to the point, eventually, of giving that work its structure. As Richard Finneran and F. A. C. Wilson have shown, the Hanrahan tales conform to the structure of a romantic quest: "If we look at the six stories as a unified whole, it seems clear that Yeats had in mind a basic pattern of sin, suffering, repentance, and redemption—though those terms must be understood not in their Christian but rather in their Romantic sense."[21] It is important to note this early example of the expression of a character in quest for unity of being in an artistic structure that embodies that quest, for it is a phenomenon that Yeats reenacts in his own quest for unity of being in the poetic persona, as Michael Sidnell has seen: "The *Stories of Red Hanrahan*, like 'The Wanderings of Oisin' and the stories of Robartes and the encompassing narrative of the collected poems, comprise a version of the poet's life that Yeats first imagined and subsequently embodied: the story of a poet who has glimpsed an otherworld and remains, firmly, in this one."[22]

The successful union of character and structure in "Stories of Red Hanrahan" sheds light on Yeats's first attempts to create his own heroic "I" in the three tales of deferred or incomplete quest that follow in *Mythologies*. "Rosa Alchemica," "The Tables of the Law," and "The Adoration of the Magi" each employ the personal Yeatsian "I" from "The Celtic Twilight" but in a relationship with one or several objective characters against which that persona reacts. Robert O'Driscoll describes these characters, including the narrative "I," as "caught between dream and vision . . . characters who have renounced the joy of the mortal world but who have not been able to accept the tragic ecstasy of the immortal world to which they have half-awakened."[23] Frank Lentricchia sees a similar dilemma in Red Hanrahan, [24] although Hanrahan's dilemma is only temporary and is eventually resolved in the visions he experiences at death. The persona of the "Rosa Alchemica" group suffers failures of the quest for unity of being analogous to Hanrahan's original refusal to accept the fairy world as an aspect of his own identity:

> "It is a pity for him that refuses the call of the daughters of the Sidhe, for he will find no comfort in the love of the women of the earth to the end of life and time, and the cold of the grave is in his heart for ever. It is death he has chosen; let him die, let him die, let him die." (M, 233)

There is considerable critical disagreement over the identity of the "I" in "Rosa Alchemica." Richard Ellmann unquestioningly identifies him specifically as Owen Aherne, the focal character of "The Tables of the Law" and a self-professed past associate of Michael Robartes, the character in "Rosa Alchemica" who lures the narrator to the Temple of the Alchemical Rose. Richard Finneran more cautiously refers to the "I" as an "unnamed narrator." John Lester assumes that the narrator of the three tales is one and the same, an assumption which is supported by Yeats's revelation, in the "Note" reprinted from the 1925 edition of *Early Poems and Stories*, that he originally intended "The Tables of the Law" and "The Adoration of the Magi" to be printed along with "Rosa Alchemica" in *The Secret Rose* but that the arrangement was vetoed by his publisher. Despite his grasp of the personae's common identity, however, Lester judges that it "serves little artistic purpose" and finds in it a "mark of Yeats's distrust in his powers of presentation."[25] Lester assumes, that is, that the "I" is the open expression of Yeats as an empirical writer struggling with his craft rather than the artistic expression of an independent identity arising from, but finally free of, the empirical Yeats. This raises the question of ironic distance between Yeats and his fictional persona; is the "I" of "Rosa Alchemica" a transcendent persona, an augmentation of Yeats's empirical self, or a reductive persona, a concrete projection of one weak or incomplete aspect of the author's identity that Yeats projects in order to expose its insufficiency?[26]

Although the "I" of "Rosa Alchemica" is not as positively identified with Yeats himself as the "I" of "The Celtic Twilight," certain characteristics of the later persona link it also to the empirical Yeats: he lives in Dublin and has a strong interest in the occult, he is more artist than mystic, and he has published a book titled *Rosa Alchemica*. What the "I" of "Rosa Alchemica" says he has done, the writer Yeats is in the process of doing; it is an interesting and paradoxical relationship. Otherwise, this persona has a lifestyle that is portrayed in concrete detail and that is not given the persona of "The Celtic Twilight" or entirely an autobiographical rendition of Yeats's own experiences. This "I" has an autonomous existence in the fiction, at least in part. Like the "I" of "The Celtic Twilight," however, the "I" of "Rosa Alchemica" is somewhat unsure in his relationship to the subject matter of his narration, which has shifted from supernatural fairies to mystical spirits. This persona also freely and consciously dramatizes his own inner conflicts over the desire to unite natural and supernatural realms and the fear of being consumed by transcendent powers greater than his empirical ones. Horatio Krans has praised this open portrayal of conflict for its compelling style: "The touch of awe is in its tense, nervous style, excitement in the hurried accents of the narrator, and the air of the whole is electric with terror. A thrill goes out from it that is a new literary experience."[27] Much of the awe and thrill proceed from the persona's agonized self-portrait of the duality of identity:

> When I pondered over the antique bronze gods and goddesses, which I had mortgaged my house to buy, I had all a pagan's delight in various beauty and without his terror at sleepless destiny and his labour with many sacrifices; and I had but to go to my bookshelf . . . to know what I would of human passions without their bitterness and without satiety. I had gathered about me all gods because I believed in none, and experienced every pleasure because I gave myself to none, but held myself apart, individual, indissoluble, a mirror of polished steel. I looked in the triumph of this imagination at the birds of Hera, glittering in the light of the fire as though of Byzantine mosaic; and to my mind, for which symbolism was a necessity, they seemed the doorkeepers of my world, shutting out all that was not of as affluent a beauty as their own; and for a moment I thought, as I had thought in so many other moments, that it was possible to rob life of every bitterness except the bitterness of death; and then a thought which had followed this thought, time after time, filled me with a passionate sorrow. All those [art] forms . . . belonged to a divine world wherein I had no part; and every experience, however profound, every perception, however exquisite, would bring me the bitter dream of a limitless energy I could never know, and even in my most perfect moment I would be two selves, the one watching with heavy eyes the other's moment of content. I had heaped about me the gold born in the crucibles of others; but the supreme dream of the alchemist, the transmutation of the weary heart into a weariless spirit, was as far from me as, I doubted not, it had been from him also. (M, 268–69)

In consciously recognizing and verbalizing the duality of identity in himself and in man generically, the "I" of "Rosa Alchemica" has taken a great stride beyond the capacities of the persona of "The Celtic Twilight," who sees this duality mainly as an external phenomenon, between himself as rationalist and an outer spiritual world, and beyond the heroic characters of "The Secret Rose" and "Stories of Red Hanrahan," who enact the duality but cannot express it in thought as well as in act. In "Rosa Alchemica," the persona portrays himself as wavering, mentally and physically, between the two realms associated with the duality of self, the empirical and spiritual. He vacillates from a dreamy rationalism in part I, to belief in a mystical unity of being under the influence of Michael Robartes in part II, to a state of tempered or reformed rationalism in III and then temptations toward and subsequent flight from mystical union in IV, to a consciously willed, empirically based unity of being founded on Roman Catholicism in part V. The persona, in contemplating that "little, infinite, faltering, eternal flame" of self, is fully engaged in his own story. Rather than re-creating himself, however, as Yeats argues in "A General Introduction for My Work" that a poet must do, the "I" of "Rosa Alchemica" is redramatizing his past experiences. He is, after all, more a critic than an artist. His *Rosa Alchemica* is a study of alchemical doctrines and not a creative work, and the artworks he so admires are all the creations of other men in other times. Not a committed and self-defined artist, this persona is a critical dabbler, one of those critics characterized in a later poem who "but half create" (M, 321).

Robert O'Driscoll criticizes this persona, not only for his passive attitude toward the arts but for his ignorance of the inadequacy of that attitude as well:

> On the one hand he attempts to shut out the external world, but on the other hand he wishes to experience all human activity vicariously through the art he has collected. He is . . . a *collector* of art . . . rather than an artist himself. What he does not realize is that it is only through the constant activity of art, not merely surrounding oneself with works of art, that ecstasy can be experienced and a changing heart transmuted for a moment into a changeless work of art.[28]

Where the persona is satisfied to redramatize his experiences of conflict in the desire for unity of being and to maintain a passively wishful attitude toward the arts, Yeats is in fact engaging in the "constant activity of art" by re-creating himself, in part, in terms of this limited persona. From this perspective, the relationship of poet and persona is an ironic one. Frank Lentricchia, however, considers the persona to be a sincere and whole re-creation of Yeats and sympathizes with what he sees to be the persona's genuine dilemma:

> In "Rosa Alchemica," [Yeats's] latent fears about a supernaturally sanctioned aesthetic were suggested in his image of the magical poet as a puppet whose artistic will is controlled and directed by beings of a higher order. The transcendental promises of Robartes' philosophy, certainly attractive to Yeats, are overshadowed by the implicit compromise of artistic autonomy.
>
> The magical imagination . . . implicitly postulates transparency and therefore a severe compromise of the artist's autonomy. I think we may go so far as to say that the quest for radical artistic freedom is the underlying continuity of Yeats's complex thought . . . . The quest for a free imagination led Yeats into time and a finite world, toward a theory of impersonality, the mask of liberation, and away from the mask of magic, the mask of imprisonment.[29]

Robert Langbaum disagrees. He sees the persona lagging behind in the "direction of Yeats's development," as Robartes in "Rosa Alchemica" and later Aherne in "The Tables of the Law" represent it, and he argues that the mystical masks that Robartes, Aherne, and the persona feel themselves at times become are beneficial, successful inversions of the "Western into an Oriental sense of identity."[30]

So the question remains, is the persona of "Rosa Alchemica" an embodiment of Yeats's transcendent poetic self or a satiric projection of the lesser, conservative aspects of the empirical self? Specifically, is the narrator's turn to Roman Catholicism a retreat into an unthinking, passive role, or can it be defended as the superior of two approaches to the spiritual world? Robartes's approach, that of invoking spirits to overcome and occupy the empirical mind and body, is quite frightening to the persona, who counters one of Robartes's spells "with forced determination, 'You would sweep me away into an indefinite world which fills me with terror; and yet a man is a great man just in so far as he can make his mind reflect everything with indifferent precision like a mirror'" (M, 276). If this is the persona's understanding of unity of being, it sounds perilously similar to Yeats's later criticism of the naturalist movement in literature in terms of "Stendhal's mirror dawdling down a lane."[31] On the other hand, there is not much in the way of unity of being to be found in Robartes's spells, either. Immediately on defending the mirror concept of mind, the persona succumbs to a trance and hears voices chanting: " 'The mirror is broken in two pieces,' . . . 'The mirror is broken in four pieces,' . . . 'The mirror is broken into numberless pieces' " (M, 276). The persona in fact loses control of his mind as a focus of reality and is reduced to a collection of random perceptual fragments; he describes the experience later as being "no more, as man is, a moment shuddering at eternity, but eternity weeping and laughing over a moment" (M, 278–79).

At the height of the mystical dance of union in the Temple of the Alchemical Rose, the devotees of the cult and the persona seem to achieve a unity of empirical and spiritual realms, as "every mortal foot danced by the white foot of an immortal" (M, 289). This consummation results in a general swooning, a loss of empirical consciousness, from which the persona is the first to awaken, and the ecstasy of unity is followed by an equally powerful threat from the empirical world, in the form of a mob of peasants. The persona flees, leaving Michael Robartes and his fellow mystics to their uncertain fate.[32] In retrospect, the persona finds neither extreme, ecstasy or violence, to be a viable approach to unity of being, since either seems to necessitate the abdication of the other aspect of identity. He consequently embraces the controlled and time-tested unity of being symbolized by Christ, a unity that he, ironically, first perceives in the Temple, where the dancers have tried to " 'trouble His unity with their multitudinous feet' " (M, 288). Christ is a traditional symbol of unity of being, in terms of his incarnation of spirit, but the persona seems to use Christ as a shield against threats of disorder from either empirical or spiritual worlds rather than respecting his symbolic integrity:

There are moments even now when I seem to hear those voices of exultation and lamentation, and when the indefinite world, which has but half lost its mastery over my heart and my intellect, seems about to claim a perfect mastery; but I carry the rosary about my neck, and when I hear, or seem to hear them, I press it to my heart and say, "He whose name is Legion is at our doors deceiving our intellects with subtlety, and flattering our hearts with beauty, and we have no trust but in Thee"; and then the war that rages within me at other times is still, and I am at peace. (M, 292)

The persona is blameless in rejecting both the threatening physicality of the crowd and the consuming spirituality of mysticism, but he is somewhat shortsighted in assuming that only Christ can unite the two. He fails to see, as O'Driscoll points out, that the "war that rages within" him is the process of unification itself, what Gentile calls "mind as pure act," and that Christ is a symbol of this unity because he is the archetype of the ongoing process of such unifying efforts and not because he is altogether different from all mortal men. The Yeatsian persona in "Rosa Alchemica" has neither the sophisitcation nor the self-consciousness necessary to envision himself as an embodiment of unity of being; he still feels obliged to project that potential onto others, much as Yeats himself has done in creating the heroes of "The Secret Rose."

The autonomy of the "I" of "Rosa Alchemica" and the two related tales, "The Tables of the Law" and "The Adoration of the Magi," is thus somewhat suspect because of his dependence on the symbols of Roman Catholicism, but this persona is also rather admirable for his rejection of extremes of behavior in the pursuit of unity of being, whether that rejection arises from cowardice or virtue. In addition, the persona makes progress in these three tales, away from his extreme aestheticism in "Rosa Alchemica" and toward greater self-consciousness concerning the symbolic value of his own acts. Just as the extreme spiritualism in the Temple of the Alchemical Rose tempers the persona's original aestheticism, so Aherne's radical conversion to Roman Catholicism in "The Tables of the Law" gives the persona a new perspective on his own religious dependency. In Aherne the persona at first recognizes a rather undisciplined state of mind that is not unlike his own at the opening of "Rosa Alchemica":

> He was to me . . . the supreme type of our race, which, when it has risen above, or is sunken below, the formalisms of half-education and the rationalisms of conventional affirmation and denial, turns away . . . from practical desires and intuitions towards desires so unbounded that no human vessel can contain them, intuitions so immaterial that their sudden and far-off fire leaves heavy darkness about hand and foot. (M, 293–94)

Interestingly, the persona feels obliged to qualify his judgment of Aherne's impracticality with a phrase that acknowledges his own recently adopted religious views: "unless my hopes for the world and for the Church have made me blind." This remark of self-evaluation sets the views and acts of Aherne and the persona in opposition, and a comparison of the outcomes of their opposing stances may be taken as an implicit evaluation of the attitudes toward unity of being they represent.

Aherne has a revolutionary zeal for imposing the spiritual order on the empirical. He aspires to travel widely, " 'that I may know all accidents and destinies,' " and in order to further the " 'Kingdom of the Holy Spirit' " by recording " 'my secret law upon those ivory tablets, just as poets and romance-writers have written principles of their art in prefaces' " (M, 301). The results of his efforts, are, however, the reversal of his expectations, for Aherne, unlike Robartes, is unable to release himself fully from consciousness of external law and empirical reason:

> "At first I was full of happiness . . . and it was as though I was about to touch the Heart of God. Then all changed and I was full of misery; and in my misery it was revealed to me that man can only come to that Heart through the sense of separation from it which we call sin, because I had discovered the law of my being, and could only express or fail to express my being. . . . I have seen the whole, and how can I come again to believe that a part is the whole? I have lost my soul because I have looked out of the eyes of angels." (M, 304–6)

Aherne's despair is on the surface rather puzzling; he seems to deny his own success at achieving a unity of being. He says that the "whole" is not enough because humankind can approach God only through the "sense of separation" in sin. Perhaps Aherne has discovered that man is not created to experience a spiritual wholeness or unity but to strive constantly to achieve a complementary relationship between the dual aspects of self by seeking to and failing to overcome that separation. Comprehension of this dynamic duality might well have defeated his carefully wrought conception of the " 'Kingdom of the Holy Spirit.' " Where Robartes escapes all recognition of the duality involved in unity of being through the ecstasy of submitting his empirical being to the control of a spiritual power, Aherne is struck by his recognition of duality so forcefully that he is virtually paralyzed by it.

The persona pities Aherne and attributes his downfall to Catholicism having "seized him in the midst of the vertigo he called philosophy" and failing "to do more than hold him on the margin" (M, 305). This is a crucial recognition for the persona—that Catholicism presents Christ as the embodiment of unity of being but does not necessarily assist mortal individuals to a similar attainment. He might well have recalled at this point one of Blake's

pronouncements on religion that he might have encountered in the
Temple of the Alchemical Rose: "Thus men forgot that All deities
reside in the human breast."[33] Instead, the persona again feels
threatened by spirits surrounding Aherne and unthinkingly retreats into Catholic doctrine in an effort to defend his integrity.
Robert O'Driscoll concludes from a comparison of Aherne and the
"I" of "Rosa Alchemica" that Aherne represents the more advanced position:

> In *The Tables of the Law*, Owen Aherne, like the narrator of *Rosa
> Alchemica*, has shut himself off from the material world and sur-
> rounded himself with art in the hope of attaining to "vision and ec-
> stasy." . . . But Owen Aherne has more capability for vision than the
> narrator of *Rosa Alchemica*, and is more capable of grasping the impli-
> cations of the knowledge revealed to him; his inability, therefore, to
> live by the light of this knowledge has more tragic consequences.[34]

Granted, Aherne, like Robartes, represents an extreme capacity
for vision, but this capacity is not necessarily more a virtue than
the persona's comparative moderation. Indeed, a greater capacity
for vision may only indicate an incapacity to achieve the complementary duality of a unified identity. O'Driscoll does recognize
such a limitation in Aherne:

> Aherne is caught in the irresolvable dilemma between instruction and
> instinct, between his orthodox Catholic teaching and the truth he has
> discovered in his own heart. What he does not realize is that instinct is
> a condition of truth, that mortality is a condition of immortality, that it
> is only by the recognition of the presence of the mortal and immortal
> elements in the porcelain vessel called man that the apparently irresolv-
> able paradox can be accepted.[35]

In this respect, the persona is superior to Aherne; he at least ap-
preciates the symbolic value of Christ, much as Yeats does in "A
General Introduction for My Work," whereas Aherne fails in desiring to approach God directly. Aherne succumbs to his own
apocalyptic hopes, but the persona survives to go on thinking and
struggling for a unity of being.
    In "The Adoration of the Magi," the persona reveals yet another
strength, as he retells another story in the manner of his very early
predecessor, the "I" of "The Celtic Twilight." The persona is still
shaken by his confrontation with the spiritual world of Robartes
and Aherne, and he still retreats behind his faith when fearing that

"immortal demons" have "put an untrue story into my mind for some purpose I do not understand" (M, 314–15). Richard Ellmann has noted that Yeats uses Catholicism in these stories as a "convenient symbol of conventional and prudent belief, an example of a traditional refuge."[36] But the persona steps beyond this refuge in "The Adoration of the Magi"; he finds relief as well in thinking and in writing. If he has been gradually educated out of his original role of aesthete, he has never abandoned the habit of writing; indeed, the three stories of the "Rosa Alchemica" group represent his ongoing desire to record, clarify, and understand. Specifically, the act of writing counteracts the danger of ideas degenerating into illusions:

> I have let some years go by before writing out this story, for I am always in dread of the illusions which come of that inquietude of the veil of the Temple . . . and only write it now because I have grown to believe that there is no dangerous idea which does not become less dangerous when written out in sincere and careful English. (M, 309)

This persona, who fears loss of control and craves the wholeness of identity that "sincerity" implies, has judged Robartes and Aherne as evil because they embody absolutes which are too extreme. The persona is also, however, capable of clearly describing both their characteristics and their effects on him; that is, the persona actually embodies the contrary implications of Robartes and Aherne in his writings and, in effect, unites them in his thought. The prose "I" is thus not, after all, a weak or untrustworthy character but a dramatization of the very position Yeats, as empirical author, takes toward his characters Robartes and Aherne—that they are "part of the phantasmagoria through which I can alone express my convictions about the world."[37] In a rather confusing diary entry in 1908, Yeats discusses the prose persona and Christ in the three tales of the "Rosa Alchemica" group and appears to approve of the similarity between the two:

> The hero [of "The Tables of the Law"] must not seem for a moment a shadow of the hero of "Rosa Alchemica." He is not the mask but the face. He realizes himself. He cannot obtain vision in the ordinary sense. He is himself the centre. Perhaps he dreams he is speaking. He is not spoken to. He puts himself in place of Christ. He is not the revolt of multitude. What did the woman in Paris reveal to the Magi? Surely some reconciliation between face and mask? Does the narrator refuse this manuscript, and so never learn its contents? Is it simply the doc-

trine of the Mask? The choosing of some one mask? Hardly, for that
would but be the imitation of Christ in a new form. Is it becoming
mask after mask? Perhaps the name only should be given, "Mask and
Face." Yet the nature of the man seems to prepare for a continual
change, a phantasmagoria, one day one god and the next another.

The imitation of Christ as distinguished from the self-realization of
the "Tables of the Law." What of it? Christ is but another self, but he is
the supernatural self.[38]

Aherne is apparently the "hero" of "The Tables of the Law," who
finds himself and not God, who puts himself in Christ's place
rather than "imitating" him. The "I" of "The Adoration of the
Magi" is seeking "some reconciliation between face and Mask," or
between empirical and created selves; and he is struggling between
the "choosing of some one mask," which is the "imitation of
Christ in a new form" and the random succession of masks, the
"phantasmagoria," represented in Robartes, Aherne, and the magi.
At this point, the persona elects to emulate the unity of being in
Christ, not by being Christ but by working to achieve a similar
personal unity through expressing his doubts in "sincere and careful English."

An unpublished early version of "Per Amica Silentia Lunae"
reveals a developmental connection between this theoretical piece
and "Rosa Alchemica," a connection that affirms both the artistic
propriety of "Per Amica Silentia Lunae" as the conclusion of
Mythologies and the continuity of identity of the persona among
the latter pieces in the volume:

After I had written "Rosa Alchemica" I became restless. I was
dissatisfied with its elaborate style where there is little actual circumstance, nothing natural, but always an artificial splendour. . . . I must
find a tradition, that was part of actual history, that had associations in
the scenery of my own country, and so bring my speech closer to that
of daily life. . . . Could I not found an Eleusinian Rite, which would
bind into a common symbolism, a common meditation, a school of
poets and men of letters, so that poetry and drama would find the
religious weight they have lacked since the middle ages perhaps since
ancient Greece? I did not intend it to be a revival of the pagan world,
how could one ignore so many centuries, but a reconciliation, where
there would be no preaching, no public interest. I could not like a
Frenchman look for my tradition to the Catholic Church for in Ireland
to men of my descent, organized Catholicism . . . does not seem

traditional; and in the cottages I found what seemed to me medieval Christianity, now that of Rome, now that of the Celtic Church, which turned rather to Byzantium, shot through as it were with perhaps the oldest faith of man. Could not a poet believe gladly in this country Christ. . . .[39]

In "Per Amica Silentia Lunae" the Yeatsian "I" thus steps beyond the sincere but self-limiting Roman Catholicism of the persona of the "Rosa Alchemica" group and toward a unity of being in a Christ that more concretely assimilates empirical and spiritual aspects of self—a "Christ posed against a background not of Judaism but of Druidism, not shut off in dead history, but flowing, concrete, phenomenal," as Yeats writes in section II of "A General Introduction for My Work." In essence, the "I" of "Per Amica Silentia Lunae" is a re-creation of the meaning of the Christ symbol in Yeats's own image, whereas the earlier persona aspires to adapt himself to the abstract, symbolic Christ of Roman Catholicism. This taking on of the Christ image is not blasphemy but another reincarnation of the ideal unity of all being that is God, and the result is a more self-assured persona, one finally in touch with the spiritual world as an aspect of himself and not an external threatening power. The persona of "Per Amica Silentia Lunae," like his early predecessor in "The Celtic Twilight," assumes the particular identification of "W. B. Yeats" in the prologue and of "W. B. Y." in the epilogue as a succinct expression of concrete identity, but this later persona is much more than the empirical Yeats. The persona remains nameless within the main text of the work, which consists of the two essays "Anima Hominis" and "Anima Mundi," reflecting the fact that the act of the thinking "I" of Yeats brings about the actual unification of empirical and spiritual aspects of being and not the limited historical identity of the thinker.

Yeats's conscious assimilation in this work of concrete personality and abstract thought is first evident in "Ego Dominus Tuus" (M, 321–24), the poem that opens "Per Amica Silentia Lunae." The two speakers of the dialogue anticipate the bipartite structure of the prose work and are, as Harold Bloom notes, akin to characters with whom the persona has dealt previously: Hic is a *"primary,* objective soul or Owen Aherne-figure," and Ille "has inherited the magic book of Michael Robartes [and] does not deny that he is 'enthralled by the unconquerable delusion, / Magical shapes.' "[40] The particular "I" of "Per Amica Silentia Lunae" thus prefaces his own internal monologue with a dramatic dialogue of external, independent beings who speak for the dual aspects of identity. Because they are complementary and mutually illuminating, the persona need not become involved with them as equal empirical characters, as he does with the fairies in "The Celtic Twilight" and with the spirits in the "Rosa Alchemica" group; he is now free to transcend their duality and encompass them as internally expressive voices. The title of the poem confirms this relationship of whole and parts; it is a reference to a statement in Dante's *Vita Nuova*, "I am your lord," where the "I" is the voice of the Lord of Love and the "you" the empirical man, Dante.[41] The transcendent divine "I" of this reference thus assimilates the empirical part, the "you"; the same may be said of the relationship of Yeats to Hic and Ille. The title "Ego Dominus Tuus" also points to the importance of the pronouns of this poem. Hic, the "objective soul," speaks almost solely in second or third person, as if projecting aspects of himself into objective existence outside himself; Ille speaks primarily in first person, singular and plural, as if all that can be perceived or conceived is made part of himself. Hic is an empiricist, seeking self-definition in empirical terms; Ille is an idealist, interested in reducing all that is not himself into an anti-self and then uniting with that opposite.

Perhaps because Ille closes the poem with his theory of anti-self or because that theory resembles the specter / emanation construct Yeats so admired in Blake's poetry, Robert Langbaum assumes, along with many other critics, that Ille speaks wholly and solely for Yeats.[42] Yeats's comment on needing to create a "country Christ," however, and his equally objective presentation of the two poetic voices argue for a more restrained reading of Ille and perhaps a more respectful reading of Hic. In his deprecation of Hic's "modern hope" of achieving personal sincerity, "We are but critics, or but half create," Ille does voice a rather sophisticated insight—that unity of being is an act of creation, for it requires the projection and subsequent assimilation of an image least like one's given self, and that it is this act of mind that unites the internal and external, empirical and transcendent. Ille similarly responds to Hic's protest that Dante "utterly found himself": "And did he find himself / . . . and is that spectral image / The man that Lapo and that Guido knew? / I think he fashioned from his opposite / An image. . . . / He set his chisel to the hardest stone." The artist, Ille implies, achieves unity of being by creating a persona that assimilates the "you" of otherness, just as God creates all objective being in the subjective act of the Word. Ille thus has the theory right but not the practice. Hic is also justified in believing that the artist's identity is "utterly found" in his art and in assuming that empirical artists can achieve the happiness of unity of identity "and sing when they have found it." Ille sees no such continuity of life and art, preferring the formal aesthetic unity of the latter and desiring to escape the labor involved in the former: "art / Is but a vision of reality. / What portion in the world can the artist have / Who has awakened from the common dream / But dissipation and despair?" Although Ille's argument here is persuasive, it is all thought and no life; Yeats in fact reprints this passage from "Ego Dominus Tuus" in *The Autogiography* to characterize the disastrous disunity of being in the lives of his fellow artists of the "tragic generation."[43] Ille's empirically unanchored transcendence would likely bring him to a similarly tragic end, were he a human being and not an objective characterization of an abstract quality.

Where Hic somewhat naively accepts the artist's ability to achieve self-knowledge in his art and Ille rather too fanatically engages himself in the details of achieving unity of being, the "I" of "Per Amica Silentia Lunae" avoids both extremes, much as the earlier persona of the "Rosa Alchemica" group learns to distrust both Aherne and Robartes. Because the characters have become internal qualities rather than external entities, this "I" can unite the technical theories Ille voices and Hic's assumption that identity inheres in art and then evolve between them a coherent personal theory of mask, anti-self, and unity of being. And the theory itself cannot be divorced from the dramatized, ongoing thinking of the persona, creating his own context, "utterly" finding himself; the end is the means. In fact, the "I" of this work escapes self-conscious autobiography only as long as it speaks in an unconsciously dramatic fashion, continuously experiencing the duality of self and yet not reflecting consciously on that experience.

In the opening pages of "Anima Hominis," for instance, the persona seems at first, Hic-like, concerned to define his own identity among the externally imposing selves of others, and then, like Ille, convinced of a perfect transcendent identity, but He finally comes to the realization that both experiences together comprise the self, one aspect empirical and one transcendent but both "I":

> When I come home after meeting men who are strange to me, and sometimes even after talking to women, I go over all I have said in gloom and disappointment. Perhaps I have overstated everything from

a desire to vex or startle, from hostility that is but fear; or all my
natural thoughts have been drowned by an undisciplined sympathy.
. . . But when I shut my door and light the candle, I invite a marmorean
Muse, an art where no thought or emotion has come to mind because
another man has thought or felt something different, for now there
must be no reaction, action only, and the world must move my heart
but to the heart's discovery of itself, and I begin to dream of eyelids
that do not quiver before the bayonet: all my thoughts have ease and
joy, I am all virtue and confidence. When I come to put in rhyme what
I have found it will be a hard toil, but for a moment I believe I have
found myself and not my anti-self. It is only the shrinking from toil,
perhaps, that convinces me that I have been no more myself than is the
cat the medicinal grass it is eating in the garden.

How could I have mistaken for myself an heroic condition that from
early boyhood has made me superstitious? That which comes as complete, as minutely organized, as are those elaborate, brightly lighted
buildings and sceneries appearing in a moment, as I lie between sleep-
ing and waking, must come from above me and beyond me. (M, 325–
26)

Solitude and contemplation, which comprise a withdrawal from
the empirical world, and the toil of writing poetry, which represents an effort to attain a transcendent state, here seem to produce
a voluntary, temporary, un-self-conscious unity of being in the
persona. It is only when the "I" disengages from creative activity
that it perceives the unity to be in actuality the spontaneous conjunction of a transcendent power with the empirical self. The
means may be consciously calculated, that is, but the experiential
product is uncontrolled. In such manner are the unquestioning
assumptions of creative unity in Hic, and which characterize
"Anima Hominis," related to the self-conscious critical technical
theories of Ille and "Anima Mundi"—as two perspectives on a
common, irreducible experience.

Once the persona realizes that it is meditation and artistic creation that facilitate the experience of unity of being in himself, he
can recognize a pattern in the alternating experiences of unity in
the art and duality in the lives of his artistic peers and predecessors:
"When I think of any great poetical writer of the past . . . I
comprehend, if I know the lineaments of his life, that the work is
the man's flight from his entire horoscope, his blind struggle in the
network of the stars" (M, 328). Art is the activity of invoking a
transcendent identity, in reaction to the externally imposed fate of
the empirical being, his "struggle in the network of the stars." The

artistic identity is in one sense the truer self, because it is spiritually self-created and self-enhancing and not passively inherited from impersonal natural law. The most successful artist is, then, the one who most fully achieves or experiences the transcendent visitation of universal identity within the given framework of the empirical facts of his life. Unity of being is an intimate interrelation of auto-biography and spiritual autonomy, as the example of Dante best illustrates for Yeats: "While reading Dante, we never long escape the conflict, partly because the verses are at moments a mirror of his history, and yet more because that history is so clear and simple that it has the quality of art" (M, 329). Dante's art reflects the framework of his life, and the life assumes the archetypal quality of art.

The Yeatsian "I" occupies an undefined but important position among the other artists who are examined in "Anima Hominis." As the originator of the self/anti-self theory and the assigner of other artists into certain illustrative roles within that theory, Yeats's persona, by implication, mentally encompasses or em-bodies all the details of the theory, as the "I" or "ego" that is "Lord" of all others. Peter Ure has described "Per Amica Silentia Lunae" and the later *A Vision* in terms of a "parable which sys-tematizes a conflict seen even in the poet's search out of subjectiv-ity for an objective art."[44] The overtones of morality and religion in the word *parable* are in themselves an appropriate gloss on Yeats's Christ-like concerns for unity of being and culture. In the opening four sections of "Anima Hominis," Yeats establishes his persona as *homo*, an archetypal ideal man like Christ, and in the remaining section the thought processes of this ideal, unified man display a great mind in "pure act," to use Gentile's concept, in expressions marked by such phrases of immediate mental dis-covery or creation as "I think" and "I find." In these sections of dramatic, creative thought, the "I" necessarily meditates in a social vacuum, neither addressing an audience nor creating other charac-ters in his internal drama: "There must be no reaction, action only." The "I" of "Anima Hominis" is an act of internal commun-ion of empirical and transcendent identities. Many of its utter-ances, such as the following that conceives the theory of anti-self, proceed in a rhythm of increasing transcendence, from rational theories of the empirical mind to emotional expectations of the transcendent. Notably, portrayal of self in these passages develops also in degrees of increasing unity: from "one," to "we," and then to "I":

The other self, the anti-self, or the antithetical self, as one may choose to name it, comes but to those who are no longer deceived, whose passion is reality. . . . We must not make a false faith by hiding from our thoughts the causes of doubt, for faith is the highest achievement of the human intellect, the only gift man can make to God, and therefore it must be offered in sincerity. Neither must we create, by hiding ugliness, a false beauty as our offering to the world. He only can create the greatest imaginable beauty who has endured all imaginable pangs, for only when we have seen and foreseen what we dread shall we be rewarded by that dazzling, unforeseen, wing-footed wanderer. We could not find him if he were not in some sense of our being, and yet of our being but as water with fire, a noise with silence. He is of all things not impossible the most difficult, for that always which comes easily can never be a portion of our being; "soon got, soon gone," as the proverb says. I shall find the dark grow luminous, the void fruitful when I understand I have nothing, that the ringers in the tower have appointed for the hymen of the soul a passing bell. (M, 331–32)

The empirical self thus has the power of invoking the transcendent anti-self "by turning from the mirror to meditation upon a mask" (M, 333–34), from a naturalist philosophy ("Stendhal's mirror dawdling down a lane") that is content to register empirical data, to an idealist philosophy that allies role with mask and challenges the empirical self to fit the universal role. Harold Bloom denigrates this theory by reading emphasis into the externality and objectivity of the mask: "Our efforts, in feeling or in thought, are doomed unless we learn to meditate upon the Mask, which means we must renounce mere *primary* experience, even with its saving epiphanies."[45] Bloom ignores, however, the continuing presence of the primary self, which meditates on, then gazes through the mask. The persona nowhere discovers in "Anima Hominis" that the mask or anti-self obliterates the primary self; he finds rather that unity of being is a meeting of the two through contemplation and not the wholesale takeover of one by the other. Indeed, within this same section of "Anima Hominis," Yeats quotes himself from "an old diary,"[46] and this act of communing with an earlier identity, as well as the clear meaning of the words, confirms the ongoing, dynamic, and creative activity of the primary self seeking and assuming a mask:

"I think all happiness depends on the energy to assume the mask of some other life, on a re-birth as something not one's self, *something created* in a moment *and perpetually renewed*. . . . If we cannot imagine ourselves as different from what we are, and try to assume that second self, we cannot impose a discipline on ourselves though we may accept one from others. Active virtue, as distinguished from the passive acceptance of a code, is therefore theatrical, consciously dramatic, the *wearing of a mask*." (M 334; italics added)

Yeats, in this passage, alludes again to William Blake, his "master" on the theory of a dual persona: "I must Create a System, or be enslav'd by another Man's / I will not Reason & Compare: my business is to Create."[47] Robert Langbaum recalls Yeats's understanding of the classical concept of mask:

> Masks are not false, because we *know* they are artifices. Great acting is obviously artificial; it is stylized and cold. . . . Our deepest passions in sex, art, religion are felt and articulated by selves that seem to be using our bodies to play out a personal and historical drama of which we are ignorant. . . . The cold expressionless artifice of the mask is a sign that it prefigures the identity we have not yet achieved. Its very deficiency invokes the Daimon, who descending into us completes our identity by making us act out the unknown drama.[48]

Giovanni Gentile similarly characterizes mask or anti-self in terms of internal nature, as "what you are not and must become" to be whole.[49]

The persona's act of imagining the uses of masks in "Anima Hominis" also recalls classical concepts of the mask; the "I," in fact, comes quite close to rediscovering the origins of the word *mask* in the sense of the Greek *prosopon* and Latin *persona,* by envisioning it as a means of altering identity, not from without as an object that hides the face of an actor but from the internal perspective of the person wearing the mask, whose vision is being altered by the archetypal shape and historical associations of the mask:

> I thought the hero found hanging upon some oak of Dodona an ancient mask, . . . and that he changed it to his fancy, . . . that when at last he looked out of its eyes he knew another's breath came and went within his breath upon the carven lips, and that his eyes were upon the instant fixed upon a visionary world: . . . but now I add another thought: the Daimon comes not as like to like but seeking its own opposite, for man and Daimon feed the hunger in one another's hearts. Because the ghost is simple, the man heterogeneous and confused, they are but knit together when the man has found a mask whose lineaments permit the expression of all the man most lacks, and it may be dreads, and of that only. (M, 335)

The persona's imagination of mask is strikingly similar to Adolf Trendelenburg's summation of the concept of mask developed by the Greek Stoics: "For everything is as it should be and the course of life is beautiful when the will of the universal disposer and the *daemon* of the individual are in harmony."[50] Assuming the mask of an identity that is most opposite one's own invokes the daimon, which completes the natural self by supplying all that it lacks, the resulting unified being is not only in harmony with the universal, it is one expression of the universal. Indeed, "it is not permitted to a man who takes up pen or chisel, to seek originality, for passion is his only business, and he cannot but mould or sing after a new fashion because no disaster is like another" (M, 339). Yeats has, in effect, achieved his understanding of a transcendent mask by freeing his identity, in the form of an artistic persona, to participate in universal concepts that are not ordinarily available to the empirical mind. What the historical Yeats apparently never chanced on in his studies—the classical concept of mask—the artistic persona discovers by unselfconsciously participating in archetypal imaginings that are available only through the universal language of art.

At the end of "Anima Hominis," however, the thinking "I" recedes, and Yeats portrays the self objectively, in the third person, as a "poet . . . growing old" and seeking to establish "his mask and his vision without new bitterness, new disappointment" (M, 342). This dramatic collapse of the artist back into empirical consciousness can have some highly deleterious results if this objective, empirical self is newly accepted as the norm:

> We need no protection, but [the vision] does, for if we become interested in ourselves, in our own lives, we pass out of the vision. Whether it is we or the vision that create the pattern, who set the wheel turning, it is hard to say, but certainly we have a hundred ways of keeping it near us: we select images from past times, we turn from our own age and try to feel Chaucer nearer than the daily paper. (M, 341)

The key to maintaining vision is mental movement. When one has reached the top of the ladder of transcendence, one can only start from the bottom again, "in the foul rag-and-bone shop of the heart" (CP, 336); when the wheel of interaction comes to rest, it must be set turning once again. For it is only in the movement of thought, in that active virtue of assuming a mask in the toil of artistic creation, that empirical and transcendent identities merge and unity of being is attained.

As in "Anima Hominis" the persona embodies archetypal characteristics of man, or *homo,* so in "Anima Mundi" the persona functions as a vehicle of the Great Memory. The "I" appears much less frequently in the latter essay, occasionally replaced by "we" but largely rendered unnecessary by the artist's omniscient presentation of the Great Memory. The focus of "Anima Mundi" is not on the activity of the unifying mind via the persona but on defining the universal realm from which the daimon or transcendent self emerges. When he speaks at all, the persona takes the stance of an admiring and awed but self-consciously inferior mind; Yeats is in effect peering at the mask from without, rather than from within, in an effort to provoke the "Anima Mundi" into revelation. His persona in this part is consequently didactic rather than dramatic and speaks in descriptive, past tenses: "I have always sought," "I therefore invented," "I came to believe," "I had always to compel myself." One passage in particular captures the radical change in style from "Anima Hominis" to "Anima Mundi": "At one time I thought to prove my conclusions by quoting from diaries where I have recorded certain strange events the moment they happened, but now I have changed my mind—I will but say, like the Arab boy that became Vizier: 'O brother, I have taken stock in the desert sand and of the sayings of antiquity'" (M, 343). The role of the persona has been reduced, when it appears at all, from one of self-discovery to one of self-effacement:

> Before the mind's eye, whether in sleep or waking, came images that one was to discover presently in some book one had never read, and after looking in vain for explanation to the current theory of forgotten personal memory, I came to believe in a Great Memory passing on from generation to generation. But that was not enough, for these images showed intention and choice. They had a relation to what one knew and yet were an extension of one's knowledge. . . . The thought was again and again before me that this study had created a contact or mingling with minds who had followed a like study in some other age, and that these minds still saw and thought and chose. Our daily thought was certainly but the line of foam at the shallow edge of a vast luminous sea. (M, 345–46)

Robert Langbaum reads this projection of creative beings outside the self as a recognition that the Great Memory is the personal unconscious mind, created by the individual in the process of defining his empirical self:

> The passions we have excluded in order to make an identity return as an unconscious-conscious projection that challenges the old identity and helps us make a new one. Yeats calls this projection the antiself or Daimon. . . . *Per Amica Silentia Lunae* (1917) makes the large, bold statement that our unconscious mind lies outside us; hence our identity comes from without. We discover who we are by looking outside not inside.[51]

Such an assessment squares with the Jungian account of *anima* as opposed to *persona,* but it contradicts Yeats's avowed adherence to idealism, which he has by now learned from Blake and will later admire in Berkeley and Gentile. The whole thrust of Blake's philosophical poetry, as Yeats has seen it, is to bring about the reunion of specter and emanation, or self and all that the self has banished during its fall from unity, so that the "centre is outside the circumference."[52] Langbaum's reading of "anima mundi" as an exterior unconscious mind would thus represent, in the ideal terms of Yeats's inheritance from Blake, a failure to achieve unity of being and, worse, an acceptance of that failure as inevitable and even ingrained in the human mind. And yet, "Anima Mundi" does portray the empirical self not as the circumference of all but as helpless before all: "Our animal spirits or vehicles are but, as it were, a condensation of the vehicle of *Anima Mundi,* and give substance to its images in the faint materialisation of our common thought, or more grossly when a ghost is our visitor" (M, 350); "Though images [in *Anima Mundi*] appear to flow and drift, it may be that we but change in our relation to them, now losing, now finding with the shifting of our minds" (M, 351).

Part of the problem is that in shifting his perspective on the mask from personal and internal to impersonal and external, Yeats has made a change in vocabulary as well—from concrete to abstract concepts and images. Man and his daimon are abstracted, for instance, into the "terrestrial condition" and the "condition of fire," respectively (M, 356–57). Their relationship is likewise presented not in particular terms of "active virtue" and the "wearing of a mask" but in terms of an organic development of "thoughts":

> I think of *Anima Mundi* as a great pool or garden where [a logical process] moves through its allotted growth like a great water-plant or fragrantly branches in the air. . . . The soul by changes of "vital congruity," More says, draws to it a certain thought, and this thought draws by its association the sequence of many thoughts, endowing them with a life in the vehicle meted out according to the intensity of

the first perception. A seed is set growing, and this growth may go on apart from the power, apart even from the knowledge of the soul. (M, 352–53)

As the use of "soul" in this passage implies, it is the daimon, or transcendent self, that initiates this organic interaction, knowingly or not, and participates in it; the role of empirical being has been entirely subjected to the daimon:

When all sequence comes to an end, time comes to an end, and the soul puts on the rhythmic or spiritual body or luminous body and contemplates all the events of its memory and every possible impulse in an eternal possession of itself in one single moment. That condition is alone animate, all the rest is fantasy, and from thence come all the passions and, some have held, the very heat of the body. (M, 357)

In a section of *The Autobiography* published after "Per Amica Silentia Lunae," Yeats recalls the period of his life during which he discovered and experimented with the "anima mundi." Yeats says he purposefully avoided creating rituals and choosing images "deliberately, like a poem," because he wanted the true "Unity of Image, which I sought in national literature" to reveal itself,[53] much as the organic branching of thoughts described in "Anima Mundi" were expected to result someday in an apocalyptic unity of being. Yeats in *The Autobiography* is willing to reveal his own sufferings under such a self-effacing philosophy, however, which the scantily drawn persona of "Anima Mundi" does not do. Yeats finds that he has been wandering in a "labyrinth," a " 'darkly splendid world wherein lieth continually a faithless depth and Hades wrapped in cloud, delighting in unintelligible images,' " that he has strayed onto the "Path of the Chameleon, upon *Hodos Chameliontos*," where "image called up image in an endless procession, and I could not always choose among them with any confidence; and when I did choose, the image lost its intensity, or changed into some other image." Yeats thus "began to feel . . . not only solitary but helpless" and concludes: "I now know that revelation is from the self, but from that age-long memoried self, that shapes the elaborate shell of the mollusc and the child in the womb, that teaches the birds to make their nest; and that genius is a crisis that joins that buried self for certain moments to our trivial daily mind."[54]

In "Anima Mundi" the submerged persona makes a similar discovery and at the end reemerges to anchor the abstract in concrete terms again: "The mask plucked from the oak-tree is but my imagination of rhythmic body. . . . I begin to study the only self that I can know, myself, and to wind the thread upon the pern again" (M, 364). With this reappearance of the "I," the empirical self regains its part in the process of attaining unity of being, for it is the empirical self that dons the mask that invokes the daimon. In more general terms, it is only through the empirical self (as long as it is not taken as the whole self) and through the art that the self can create that an individual has access to that "age-long memoried self," the archetypal human life:

> At certain moments, always unforeseen, I become happy, most commonly when at hazard I have opened some book of verse. . . . I am in the place where the Daimon is, but I do not think he is with me until I begin to make a new personality, selecting among those images, seeking always to satisfy a hunger grown out of conceit with daily diet; and yet as I write the words "I select," I am full of uncertainty, not knowing when I am the finger, when the clay. (M, 364–66)

The "I" once again dramatizes or embodies a union of empirical and transcendent identities, the experience of that "age-long memoried self" in the particular lineaments of an individual personality. The persona of "Per Amica Silentia Lunae" is finally more self-conscious and self-possessed than its predecessors in "The Celtic Twilight" and the "Rosa Alchemica" group, by virtue of its loss and rediscovery of a dual identity. It is an "I" that, like Red Hanrahan, has asserted its empirical identity, then faced the abyss of an incomprehensible and independent spiritual world, and finally forged a composite identity between the two.

Ultimately, "Anima Hominis" and "Anima Mundi" stand as separate but complementary essays, neither doctrinal truth but each a piece of the truth, much as Hic and Ille in "Ego Dominus Tuus" act as counterbalancing forces. An analogy may even be drawn between the direct, primary concerns of the empirical Hic to find the self and the power of the empirical "I" in "Anima Hominis" to invoke the daimon via masking, and between the antithetical, otherworldly interests of Ille and the enigmatic revelations in "Anima Mundi." In such a reading, even the names of the poetic characters assume added significance: Hic, "this one," is grounded in an empirical human reality; Ille, "that one," is further off, transcendent, somewhere out there in the world of spirit. In "Per Amica Silentia Lunae," unlike " Ego Dominus Tuus," however, the framing narrative of a composite persona clarifies the interdependence of the two aspects of being presented in the two essays and the two characters. The "Prologue" identifies the "I" as the author, Yeats, and sets the whole work that follows in the context of an actual conversation between friends, a context that section I of "Anima Hominis" reinforces by presenting the persona returning home from another conversation before invoking his transcendent identity. The final section of "Anima Mundi" reestablishes an image of the persona at home, treading up and down his stairs (between upper and lower levels of identity as well) and speculating on his future. Will he take to poetry again and again manipulate the daimon through assuming a mask, or will he grow old, simple, and pious, and passively receive what the spiritual world will offer him? It is nearly the same dilemma as that depicted in the old poet at the end of "Anima Hominis," but here there is no answer given or implied. This "I" is rather active and dramatic, embodying his own resolution in his symbolic movements and in the "pure act" of his thought; he is not a static image of an old man. Finally, the "Epilogue" reestablishes the "I" as Yeats, a specific individual with a certain history and with certain hopes for his work:

> Last summer you . . . spoke much of the French poets young men and women read today. . . . It was no longer the soul, self-moving and self-teaching—the magical soul—but Mother France and Mother Church.
> Have not my thoughts run through a like round, though I have not found my tradition in the Catholic Church, which was not the Church of my childhood, but where the tradition is, as I believe, more universal and more ancient? (M, 368–69)

As Yeats makes clear later in "A General Introduction for My Work," the identity he seeks is that of the unified being against a background of concrete cultural history, "Christ posed against a background . . . of Druidism," as he puts it. What comes clear in the development of the persona through *Mythologies* is that the individual poet can be such a unified being, a Christ posed against the structure of his own art. In "The Celtic Twilight" the persona is attracted to the supernatural beliefs of Irish folk but also jealously guards his individuality in terms of empirical rationality. In "Rosa Alchemica," "The Tables of the Law," and "The Adoration of the Magi" the persona again feels a need to belong to a tradition that encompasses more than his own individuality but fears the world of mystical spirits and finds comfort in the tradition of Roman Catholicism, particularly in the symbol of Christ. In "Per Amica Silentia Lunae" the persona confronts the fact that he cannot sublimate his needs in Christ, because a "vast luminous sea" of thoughts and images are connected to the empirical self and continuously challenge it, and the "I" must assimilate that transcendent realm by assuming a mask of opposition, thereby creating a greater identity from the interactions of empirical and transcendent identities. The "how" is not given in *Mythologies*, just the knowledge that it is some interaction of "finger" and "clay"; but the "who" is discovered to be the self, W. B. Yeats, in the "more universal and ancient" sense of his identity.

Richard Finneran and Frank Lentricchia both remark that Yeats's turn from fictional prose to autobiography had great significance in the development of his career. Lentricchia sees "Anima Mundi" as a profession of belief but of a belief that is "unimportant for the making of poetry" and finds that it is in *The Autobiography*, surprisingly, that Yeats deals most successfully with the need for an impersonal, traditional self.[55] Yeats did turn to autobiography at about the same time he was composing "Per Amica Silentia Lunae,"[56] and the empirical foundation of the persona in "Per Amica Silentia Lunae," as well as the close relationship of "Anima Mundi" to "Hodos Chameliontos" in *The Autobiography*, suggests that the transition in genres was a movement to allow Yeats to contemplate his own composite self free of any fictional contexts. Peter Ure reads the later prose, from "Per Amica Silentia Lunae" to *A Vision*, including several books of *The Autobiography*, as a modern version of the "growth of a poet's mind":

> This body of prose writings, worthy to rank with Keats's *Letters* as one of the most remarkable and explicit accounts of the "growth of a poet's mind" which we possess, has been strangely neglected by students of twentieth-century poetry. Yeats's art is that of "a nature, that never ceases to judge itself," and in the prose writings we have, as one would expect, many anticipations and echoes of the verse, which help to illuminate and explain much that is obscure.[57]

Perhaps the prose has been so neglected precisely because it is the complex and paradoxical record of a nature continuously reevaluating and remaking itself and not the presentation of a consistent literary self. It is just as precisely this characteristic of the prose that most illuminates the poetry, however, by helping to define the Yeatsian persona. *Mythologies* represents Yeats's development of a fictional "I," or a projection of self within fictional contexts; but *Mythologies* also records Yeats's discovery that the created self, the persona, must operate from the context of the empirical life and not a fictional plot, if the emphasis is to be on the unification of the self rather than the story. *The Autobiography* and *A Vision* explore both the empirical life and the transcendent identity that accompanies the empirical life. These later prose works thus analyze the "I" more systematically than does the fictional prose. *The Autobiography* records the development of the empirical self to see what form it takes, and *A Vision* projects abstract life structures to see how particular empirical lives evolve and fit together into composite wholes. The two works in essence parallel "Anima Hominis" and "Anima Mundi" in their complementary unilateral perspectives on the unified persona, but the later works are more successful in their developing realization of the transcendent as life experience in artistic forms, particularly the archetypal form that structures Yeats's own life and art in his poetry, the romantic quest. In *The Autobiography* and *A Vision*, however, the persona's characteristic activity of mediating between empirical and transcendent identities continues unabated, as that act of mind which is the essence of unity of being.

3
"Style and Attitude":
Aspects of Life and Art

WHEREAS *Mythologies* establishes the integrity, continuity, and developmental nature of Yeats's persona, *The Autobiography* and *A Vision* explore its dualistic foundation in the empirical man and in the artistic work. "Style and attitude" are the terms Yeats uses in section III of "A General Introduction for My Work" to identify these empirical and artistic aspects of the persona. Although Yeats does not explicitly define these terms, his discussion indicates that they participate in the dialectical relationship of empirical, or personal, and transcendent, or universal, aspects of identity.

Style is a technical characteristic that is continually in the process of becoming during the act of writing; it is so closely linked to the individual's personality that the writer is probably less aware of his style than are his readers:

> Style is almost unconscious. I know what I have tried to do, little what I have done. . . . I tried to make the language of poetry coincide with that of passionate, normal speech. I wanted to write in whatever language comes most naturally when we soliloquise, as I do all day long, upon the events of our own lives or of any life where we can see ourselves for the moment.[1]

Style, then, is the mark of that poet, described in section I of "A General Introduction for My Work," who "writes always of his personal life" and of that tradition of individual expression in English literature described in section II; it expresses what is inherited, the empirical self. Attitude, on the other hand, is, like a pose or a mask, a willed and deliberate assumption of an identity that is more universal or archetypal than the empirical self; it is thus related to the "reborn," "intended, complete" identity and to the Irish literary culture, as they are discussed in the previous sections of Yeats's essay. In section III, attitude is presented in terms of the "ice or salt" that preserves the personal identity from decay through time:

> If I wrote of personal love or sorrow in free verse, or in any rhythm that left it unchanged, amid all its accidence, I would be full of self-contempt because of my egotism and indiscretion, and foresee the boredom of my reader. I must choose a traditional stanza, even what I alter must seem traditional.

The traditional knowledge that is implicit in attitude involves a transcendence of self-awareness: "Talk to me of originality and I will turn on you with rage. I am a crowd, I am a lonely man, I am nothing. Ancient salt is best packing."[2] A merging of empirical and transcendent selves can, however, be achieved by the incorporation of individual characteristics into a universal structure, a union Yeats discusses in terms of the adaptation of his own lyric rhythms to the more traditional blank verse form in his "dance plays":

> When I speak blank verse and analyse my feelings, I stand at a moment of history when instinct, its traditional songs and dances, its general agreement, is of the past. I have been cast up out of the whale's belly though I still remember the sound and sway that came from beyond its ribs. . . . The contrapuntal structure of [my] verse . . . combines the past and the present. . . . What moves me and my hearer is a vivid speech that has no laws except that it must not exorcise the ghostly voice. I am awake and asleep, at my moment of revelation, self-possessed in self-surrender.[3]

"Self-possessed in self-surrender" is an appropriate description of the experience of the Yeatsian persona in *The Autobiography* and *A Vision*. The "I" is necessarily self-possessed in the former work, as autobiography commits its practitioner to a purposeful reshaping of empirical experience into an artistic whole; and self-possession inevitably involves the evolution of a style. The early books of *The Autobiography* attribute Yeats's immature lack of direction to a want of style, and the later books celebrate the power of an achieved style: "The self-conquest of the writer who is not a man of action is style"; "Style, personality—deliberately adopted and therefore a mask—is the only escape from the hot-faced bargainers and the money-changers."[4] The development of style that eventually helps Yeats to define himself, as these quotes demonstrate, borders on the archetypalism of attitude; at some point the unconscious struggle for style becomes a conscious assumption of an attitude. In *A Vision,* Yeats depicts himself in self-surrender to his spiritual "instructors," and as their instrument in the development of a cosmic system that does not center on himself. An attitude has, in effect, been forced on the empirical self. Assuming this attitude, however, expands the mind of the individual to comprehend all that has passed through it, which results, paradoxically, in a self-possession built on universal or archetypal knowledge. The general outlines of attitude are, as a result, fleshed out with the personal details of style: "All that is laborious or mechanical in my book is finished. . . . Descartes went on pilgrimage to some shrine of the Virgin when he made his first philosophical discovery, and the mountain road from Rapallo to Zoagli seems like something in my own mind, something that I have discovered."[5]

In both *The Autobiography* and *A Vision,* therefore, style and attitude are inevitably interrelated; style leads to attitude in the former, and attitude leads to style in the latter. As in Yeats's intermixture of lyric and blank verse meters, empirical self-possession and artistic self-surrender interact in these two works in the development of a persona that is both individual and archetypal. The significant difference between the two works is one of approach to that unity of being which is the result of the successful merger of style and attitude.

In the "Preface" to his first volume of autobiography, "Reveries over Childhood and Youth," Yeats confesses some discomfort concerning the merging of present and past identities that is involved in the genre:

> I have changed nothing to my knowledge; and yet it must be that I have changed many things without my knowledge; for I am writing after many years and have consulted neither friend, nor letter, nor old newspaper, and describe what comes oftenest into my memory.
> I say this fearing that some surviving friend of my youth may remember something in a different shape and be offended with my book. (A, viii)

Although certain friends of Yeats's youth have disagreed with his self-portrait,[6] it is of more concern that some of Yeats's current critics also suspect that the mature writer has misrepresented the maturing youth. David Lynch regrets that the "story of the boy who did not become a grocer remains untold."[7] Marjorie Perloff takes this objection a step further, charging that the omission of any open discussion in *The Autobiography* of Yeats's long-lasting affair with Maud Gonne substantiates the artificiality of his "masking process":

> Because he is playing the role of the temperate, reflective man in *Autobiographies*, the poet must convey the impression that he was, all along, moving toward the wisdom of maturity. The treatment of Maud Gonne in ["The Trembling of the Veil"] is thus an excellent example of the degree of fictionality autobiography can attain.[8]

Even Richard Ellmann, Yeats's preeminent biographer to date and usually a sympathetic reader of Yeats's works, disparages the autobiographical writings: "Because he was a myth-maker his autobiography was never pure. Another difficulty was that he wrote about himself late in life." In general, Ellmann worries also over the artificiality of "masking":

> [Yeats] wrote a great deal about himself, but the autobiographical muse enticed him only to betray him, abandoning him to ultimate perplexity as to the meaning of his experiences. He spent much of his life attempting to understand the deep contradictions within his mind. . . . Unsure what qualities were purely Yeatsian, he posed and attitudinized, then wondered whether pose and attitude were not more real than what they covered over. Afraid of insincerity, he struggled unsuccessfully to fuse or to separate the several characters by whom he felt himself to be peopled. . . . Autobiography did not come easy to a man who had grown to literary maturity with Villiers de l'Isle-Adam's epigram running in his ears, "As for living, our servants will do that for us."[9]

At first, Perloff's charge of "fictionality" in Yeats's autobiographical treatment of Maud Gonne might appear to be justified. The "First Draft" of Yeats's second volume of autobiography, "The Trembling of the Veil," shows in full Yeats's obsessive emotions for this woman.[10] Memoirs are of a different genre from autobiography, however, and any comparison of the two genres must take into account their differing intentions. Memoirs are only a slightly formalized refashioning of the diary form; they are written for the purpose of recording facts for posterity and not ostensibly to record judgments of those facts and events.[11] Yeats has, in fact, labeled the "First Draft" of his autobiography, "Private. A first rough draft of Memoirs made in 1916–17 and containing much that is not for publication now if ever."[12] The entries in this work are abrupt in style and lacking in artistic structure, but these are not the only reasons the "First Draft" is not autobiography. As to Perloff's concern with Yeats's feelings for Maud Gonne, the "First Draft" shows that the "I" which is recording memories has not yet resolved the issue of his relationship with Maud Gonne nor fathomed its implications; the relationship is, in essence, still unresolved at the time of writing:

> I was twenty-three years old when the troubling of my life began. . . . I remember nothing of her speech that day except that she vexed my father by praise of war, for she too was of the Romantic movement and found those uncontrovertible Victorian reasons, that seemed to announce so prosperous a future, a little grey. As I look backward, it seems to me that she brought into my life in those days—for as yet I saw only what lay upon the surface—the middle of the tint, a sound as of a Burmese gong, an overpowering tumult that had yet many pleasant secondary notes. . . . I felt in the presence of a great generosity and courage, and of a mind without peace, and when she and all her singing birds had gone my melancholy was not the mere melancholy of love. I had what I thought was a "clairvoyant" perception but was, I can see now, but an obvious deduction of an awaiting immediate disaster.[13]

It is clear that it would have been difficult for Yeats to evaluate this relationship and its effects on him in his autobiography, but for him to do so would also have involved a mixing of the genre of autobiography, which is an artistically structured and resolved remembering of things past, with the genre of memoirs, which is a comparatively casual recording of things past the better to come to terms with them. Denis Donoghue, the editor of *Memoirs*, has accurately portrayed the Yeats of the "First Draft" as a "man who thought psychology vulgar . . . peering into his own motives, accusing and forgiving himself by turns, knowing himself morbid."[14] This is not the assured, "selective 'I'" that Francis Hart has identified as the locus of "truth" in autobiography:

> To seek the personal focus of an autobiographical truth is to inquire what kind of "I" is selected, how far the selected "I" is an inductive

invention and how far an intentional creation, and whether one single or one multiple "I" persists throughout the work. Moreover, the autobiographer's relation to the pastness or historicity of his selected "I" invokes his sense and manipulation of the problem of continuity and discontinuity of identity and perspective. . . . By whatever criteria chosen, the selective "I" plays one or more of a number of structural roles: the "I" that has been hidden or misconstrued; the "I" that has been lost, or gained, regained or sought after in vain; the "I" that has been cultivated, imposed, preserved, developed.[15]

Yeats's turn from memoirs to autobiography is not an act of fictionalizing but an act of shaping his life, which, because it is a deliberate act, must overlook those aspects of life that are so persistently immediate as to be unresolved and thus unshapable. Yeats recognizes the difference between autobiography and memoirs in a letter he wrote to his father on completing "The Trembling of the Veil" and while he was considering the continuation of his autobiography up to the present moment: "There would be too many living people to consider and they [memoirs] would have besides to be written in a different way. When I was immature I was a different person and I can stand apart and judge. Later, I should always, I feel, write of other people. I dare say I shall return to the subject but only in fragments."[16] Perloff's and Ellmann's objections betray less an intention to evaluate Yeats's performance in the genre of autobiography than an impatience with Yeats for not writing an accurate history of himself, which would speak much more directly to critics who are concerned to evaluate Yeats's development as a poet and the events and persons that influenced that development. Yeats was not, however, interested in recording all the facets of his empirical identity for posterity; that would be egotism, indeed. He was, rather, dedicated to exploring the process by which the empirical identity is joined to a transcendent identity and achieves unity of being. Autobiography rather than memoirs is thus the more relevant genre for it offers, in its process of a present identity shaping the past, a means of defining the empirical identity and locating its transcendent implications:

Autobiography is a shaping of the past. It imposes a pattern on a life, constructs out of it a coherent story. It establishes certain stages in an individual life, makes links between them, and defines, implicitly or explicitly, a certain consistency of relationship between the self and the outside world. . . . This coherence implies that the writer takes a particular standpoint, the standpoint of the moment at which he re-

views his life, and interprets his life from it. . . . It is his present
position which enables him to see his life as something of a unity,
something that may be reduced to order.[17]

Other critics, while accepting the generic integrity of *The Autobiography*, question its structural integrity. Certainly, *The Autobiography* has evolved in a rather erratic fashion. "Reveries over
Childhood and Youth" was published first, and then reprinted
with "The Trembling of the Veil" in 1926 as *Autobiographies*. In
1938, Yeats added "Dramatis Personae," "Estrangement," "The
Death of Synge," and "The Bounty of Sweden" and changed the
title to *The Autobiography*. Some critics prefer the earlier edition,
arguing, as Dillon Johnston does, that *Autobiographies* covers the
same ground as *The Autobiography* (a biblical progression from
Edenic youth to near Apocalypse in maturity) but does so more
succinctly and in a "more unified and controlled fashion." Johnston finds that the last section of *Autobiographies*, "The Stirring of
the Bones," achieves the same apocalyptic anticipation of unity of
culture in the "elite coterie" in Lady Gregory's home that Yeats
claims in "The Bounty of Sweden," the final section of *The Autobiography*, to have found in the court of Sweden: "The pattern of
self-seeking and self-creating is complete in *Autobiographies*, and
its recurrence in 'The Bounty of Sweden' . . . suggests its per-
petuity."[18] Johnston's analysis is supported not only by the somewhat thematically repetitive nature of "Dramatis Personae" and
"The Bounty of Sweden" but also by the radically different,
meditative perspective of "Estrangement" and "The Death of
Synge." Joseph Ronsley defends the integral value of these latter
volumes of *The Autobiography* by citing Yeats's own alteration of
the title from the plural *Autobiographies*, which suggests a collection of independent entities, to the singular *Autobiography*, which
implies a unity. Ronsley defines the element of unity in *The Autobiography* as Yeats's "main purpose" of "bolster[ing] his assertion
of the artist's totality by making known his own 'experiment in
living' ":

> And if understanding individual experiences is helpful, putting these
> experiences together to see what larger patterns of thought and feeling
> they form would be even more helpful. To do so would not be
> generalization, but rather a method of achieving keener insight into the
> meaningful patterns taking form in the course of his life.[19]

Toward this end, the journallike quality of "Estrangement" and

"The Death of Synge" provides the framework of "understanding individual experiences" on which *The Autobiography* as a whole rests. Both "Estrangement" and "The Death of Synge" derive from the "Journal" Yeats maintained in 1909;[20] the entries have been edited but not reworked into a cohesive autobiographical structure. They are like the "First Draft" in recording empirical events but resemble the revised first books of *The Autobiography* in presenting only items that are of more than everyday interest. The entry that opens "Estrangement" suggests something of Yeats's intention in including these revised "Journal" notes within the more formal structure of an autobiography:

> To keep these notes natural and useful to me I must keep one note from leading on to another, that I may not surrender myself to literature. Every note must come as a casual thought, then it will be my life. Neither Christ nor Buddha nor Socrates wrote a book, for to do that is to exchange life for a logical process. (A, 311)

Yeats has apparently chosen to incorporate a portrait of the subjective "I" in his autobiography, the "I" which represents the viewpoint from which the other, more traditional, books of autobiography have been written. Curtis Bradford, who has studied the "Journal" and its metamorphosis into "Estrangement" and "The Death of Synge," reports that the changes Yeats makes are more quantitative than qualitative, serving to protect others from undue publicity, to minimize ill-considered opinions, and to achieve some stylistic clarity.[21] Yeats says, in another letter to his father, "One goes on from year to year gradually getting the disorder of one's mind in order and this is the real impulse to create";[22] "Estrangement" and "The Death of Synge" show this process of ordering the mind that then creates the other parts of *The Autobiography*. Composition dates bear out this relationship. The "Journal" entries date from 1909 for the most part, and Yeats refashioned them into "Estrangement" and "The Death of Synge" in 1926 and 1928, respectively. The finished forms of "Reveries over Childhood and Youth" and "The Trembling of the Veil" date from 1914 and 1922, and "Dramatis Personae" and "The Bounty of Sweden" date from 1934 and 1925—all within the general period in which Yeats wrote and revised these "Journal" entries.

Notwithstanding Ellmann's concern for the advanced age at which Yeats wrote his autobiography, the fact that Yeats "wrote about himself late in life" is an asset, as Pascal points out; the subject must reach a plateau of maturity or of self-knowledge from which he can review and evaluate his early experiences and form them into an artistic whole. In any event, Yeats can hardly be described as being "late in life" when he began to write "Reveries over Childhood and Youth" in 1914, at the age of forty-nine. This middle-age plateau, which is preserved in "Estrangement" and "The Death of Synge," affords Yeats the perspective of a self-consciously successful artist. Ian Fletcher describes the period:

> In 1908 the appearance of Yeats's *Collected Works* must have seemed to the poet to mark an era, as though his achievement were already in the past. At this time we find him in letters referring to himself as "belonging to the fabulous ages" and "becoming mythical even to myself." . . . The pressures in such circumstances were towards the organization of an attitude; documentation and self-clarification; an attempt to stabilise the present.[23]

Pascal says of the great people who write the "best auto-biogaphies" that they display a "certain power of the personality over circumstance . . . in the sense that the individual can extract nurture out of disparate incidents and ultimately bind them together in his own way, disregarding all that was unusable."[24] Yeats's extraction from national concerns of personal interests is immediately apparent in "Estrangement." He speaks of a "new ill-breeding in Ireland," which manifests itself in "thoughts never really thought out in their current form in any individual mind, but the creation of impersonal mechanism," and seeks to oppose this wayward state with a very personal act: "I can only set up a secondary or interior personality created out of the tradition of myself, and this personality (alas, only possible to me in my writings) must be always gracious and simple. It must have that slight separation from interests which makes charm possible, while remaining near enough for passion" (A, 312–13). This proposed artistic personality operates on the same basis as that union of classical attitudes and personal style that creates an archetypal being: "I am a crowd, I am a lonely man, I am nothing." Thinking to redeem his race, Yeats reaches inside for a personality in the "tradition of myself" and finds that he contains the whole race within:

> All my life I have been haunted with the idea that the poet should know all classes of men as one of themselves, that he should combine the greatest possible personal realisation with the greatest possible knowledge of the speech and circumstances of the world. . . . The artist grows

more and more distinct, more and more a being in his own right as it were, but more and more loses grasp of the always more complex world. Some day setting out to find knowledge, like some pilgrim to the Holy Land, he will become the most romantic of characters. He will play with all masks. (A, 318)

In a very real sense, the quest for knowledge in this metaphor is the structure of *The Autobiography*—an early conceived and ongoing search for self, as it is both unique and universal. In part, this personal-national self acts through the Abbey Theatre in establishing a national drama based on individual personalities. Yeats learns from Synge "that we must renounce the deliberate creation of a kind of Holy City in the imagination, and express the individual. . . . You can only create a model of a race to inspire the action of that race as a whole, apart from exceptional individuals, when you and it share the same simple moral understanding of life" (A, 335). Ironically, Yeats's involvement in the establishment of a national theater frustrates his internal development of a universal identity, by occupying all his time and diverting his energies and imagination outwardly rather than internally: "I often wonder if my talent will ever recover from the heterogeneous labour of these last few years. . . . Virtue has come upon me and given me a nation instead of a home. Has it left me any lyrical faculty? Whatever happens I must go on that there may be a man behind the lines already written; I cast the die long ago and must be true to the cast" (A, 328–29). Already implicit in this note of despair, however, is an acceptance of Yeats's "heterogeneous" theater experiences for their anchoring of his verse in the complexity of his life:

> I cry continually against my life. I have sleepless nights, thinking of the time that I must take from poetry—last night I could not sleep—and yet, perhaps, I must do all these things that I may set myself into a life of action and express not the traditional poet but that forgotten thing, the normal active man. (A, 333)

In the meditations he records at the time of the death of John Millington Synge, Yeats continues his debate on the relative virtues of the lives of artist and "normal active man." He muses that contemplation and the related estrangement of emotions may result in their becoming "fantastic" and so "create the strange lives of poets and artists" (A, 354). The laboring poet may see no unity in his work or life: "Our own acts are isolated and one act does not buy absolution for another. They are always present before a strangely abstract judgment. We are never a unity, a personality to ourselves" (A, 340). The empirical self suffers in fragments, yet the transcendent self maintains the potential for a unity of personality. Perhaps that "strangely abstract judgment" which demands perfect unity is an aspect of it, but Yeats sees the transcendent personality most clearly in Synge himself, in Synge's self-sufficient character while he was alive and in his persona after his death:

> He had no need of our sympathies. It was as though we and the things about us died away from him and not he from us. . . .
>   He had that egotism of the man of genius which Nietzsche compares to the egotism of a woman with child. Neither I nor Lady Gregory had ever a compliment from him. . . . He had under charming and modest manners, in almost all things of life, a complete absorption in his own dream. . . . For him nothing existed but his thought. He claimed nothing for it aloud. He never said any of those self-confident things I am enraged into saying, but one knew that he valued nothing else. He was too confident for self-assertion. . . . I do not think he disliked other writers—they did not exist. One did not think of him as an egotist. He was too sympathetic in the ordinary affairs of life and too simple. In the arts he knew no language but his own. . . . Can a man of genius make that complete renunciation of the world necessary to the full expression of himself without some vice or some deficiency? You were happy or at least blessed, "blind old man of Scio's rocky isle." (A, 346–47)

Synge is being idolized or at least idealized here, but for a purpose. Yeats uses the completed structure of Synge's life as a projection of the meaning of his own incomplete life and that of his nation, both of which seem highly disparate to him at the time.

Several months later Yeats "dreams" a thought that sheds some light on his sufferings in the empirical world: " 'Why should we complain if men ill-treat our Muses, when all that they gave to Helen while she still lived was a song and a jest?' " (A, 353). Empirical life is incapable of producing its own value or meaning, for it is never complete. Only through the memories and imaginations of creative people are the lives of others transformed into something symbolic, something ideal. Yeats thus restructures Synge's life after his death to preserve its ideal expression in the artistic form of literature. And in doing so for Synge, in reviewing and redeeming that man's life, Yeats comes to understand even more clearly the relations of life and art in his poetic persona. Nine years later, Yeats would return to his ideal reconstruction of Synge's life in composing "In Memory of Major Robert Gregory," a poem that takes for its structure the poetic act of remembering a real man, projecting his ideal image, and participating in that projected unity of being.[25] As a more immediate response to Synge's death and memory, Yeats began within five years to write his autobiography, in an attempt to remember and restructure his own life toward some symbolic value.

Roy Pascal identifies Wordsworth as the first artist to perceive and practice autobiography as the revelation of a life structure that amounts to a personal myth, that is, to create a poetic persona based on the artist's own empirical life experiences:

> Wordsworth is the first autobiographer to realise—and the poetic form of his autobiography is the realisation—that each man constructs out of his world a unique framework of meaningful events, and that the deepest purpose of autobiography is the account of a life as a projection of the real self (we call it personality but it seems to lie deeper than personality) on the world.[26]

The structured life, or persona, that emerges from a selective and symbolic remembrance of experience is the "real" self in that it is the realization, paradoxically, of the ideal archetype of the empirical self. In "Reveries over Childhood and Youth," Yeats recalls one characteristic of immaturity to be the lack of this structured identity:

> I did not care for mere reality and believed that creation should be deliberate, and yet I could only imitate my father. . . . I was still very much of a child, sometimes drawing with an elaborate frenzy, simulating what I believed of inspiration, and sometimes walking with an artificial stride in memory of Hamlet and stopping at shop windows to look at my tie gathered into a loose sailor-knot and to regret that it could not be always blown out by the wind like Byron's tie in the picture. I had as many ideas as I have now, only I did not know how to choose from among them those that belonged to my life. (A, 55)

The volume as a whole, however, imposes on the child's experiences the structure that Ronsley and Johnston have identified as biblical. Yeats refers to this formal structure at several points in "Reveries over Childhood and Youth." The opening paragraph, for instance, characterizes his memory as chaotic, "as though one remembered some first moments of the Seven Days. It seems as if time had not yet been created, for all thoughts connected with emotion and place are without sequence" (A, 1). The imagistic structure of these opening pages depicts the semi-conscious state of the child; events are recalled as if through the child's eyes rather than through those of the adult writer. Slowly, order emerges from this confusion, as during Creation, as the child's mind grows to encompass and control by evaluation those sensory stimuli that bombard him: "Indeed I remember little of childhood but its pain. I have grown happier with every year of life as though gradually conquering something in myself, for certainly my miseries were not made by others but were a part of my own mind" (A, 5).

Soon, the internal orderings of the mind become more interesting than the chaotic events of the external world: "Because I had found it hard to attend to anything less interesting than my thoughts, I was difficult to teach" (A, 14). Childhood becomes a time of conflict between the internal ideal and outer obligations of mundane existence:

> Often instead of learning my lesson, I covered the white squares of the chessboard on my little table with pen and ink pictures of myself, doing all kinds of courageous things. . . . I was vexed and bewildered, and am still bewildered and still vexed, finding it a poor and crazy thing that we who have imagined so many noble persons cannot bring our flesh to heel. (A, 25)

In addition, there is a growing consciousness of being "an artist's son" and so of having the responsibility, beyond the normal aims which other children pursue of "becoming well off and living pleasantly" (A, 27), to tame that flesh, to locate somehow the ideal within the real:

> When I look at my brother's picture, "Memory Harbour" . . . I recognise in the blue-coated man with the mass of white shirt the pilot I went fishing with, and I am full of disquiet and of excitement, and I am melancholy because I have not made more and better verses. I have walked on Sinbad's yellow shore and never shall another's hit my fancy. (A, 33)

The Edenic landscapes of Yeats's memory of childhood suggest its glory, but the emergence of self-consciousness and a sense of responsibility puts the ideal life not in the past but in some ill-defined future, to be attained through art.

Dillon Johnston points to the development of Yeats as constituting another structure within the overall narrative progression from Creation to Apocalypse, a structure that plots the mental struggle toward unity of being from crisis of identity. Johnston identifies four stages in this structure, "infancy, negative identity, self-definition, and self-identification," and notes that it is a common structure for autobiographies. In Yeats's case, the stages encompass these life experiences:

> First, the child inherits an identity from his West Ireland ancestors; secondly, he loses direct possession of this inherited identity as a consequence of his father's uprooting of the family, and he achieves a negative identity by reacting to his father and then to the modern forces ultimately responsible for his father's and his deracination; and, thirdly, he defines himself in terms of six groups in Dublin and London. The fourth phase, in which Yeats separates himself from each group and develops a unique self-image, is only suggested in the direct narration of the events of Yeats's life.[27]

Yeats does not recall his development through these periods simply by presenting himself in the throes of each stage of development. Rather, he consistently presents growth and events through the eyes of the developing youth, so that development is continuous and no stages are sharply demarcated. The developmental structure of the volume is most clearly seen in terms of those others onto whom Yeats projects his own ideals, as he does with Synge in the "Journal" entries; that is, the heroes whom Yeats discovers at different periods of his life reflect the development of his own mental growth, along the lines of the general structure outlined by Johnston.

Yeats's first hero is his grandfather, who represents a godlike, dominant personality to Yeats as a child; all life seems to revolve around his grandfather as its central figure of authority. Yeats's father is hero of the second stage of growth, in his role as dissenter from all current cultural authority. From his father's very independence of all complacent definition, however, Yeats learns that no one dominant identity is sufficient, that his grandfather would be an anachronism in the modern societies of Dublin or London. If Yeats were to become an artist he would have to encounter life at its fullest, and this demanded contact with numerous identities:

> I was about to learn that if a man is to write lyric poetry he must be shaped by nature and art to some one out of half a dozen traditional poses, and be lover or saint, sage or sensualist, or mere mocker of all life; and that none but that stroke of luckless luck can open before him the accumulated expression of the world. And this thought before it could be knowledge was an instinct. (A, 57–58)

At this point, Yeats does not choose to embody any one or few of these poses; rather he allows several heroes or heroines of "nature and art" to epitomize various poses for him in this third stage of his life. Yeats idolizes Maud Gonne as a lover, John O'Leary and Madame Blavatsky as sages, George Russell and William Morris as saints, and Oscar Wilde as a sensualist. Yeats's contacts with these people and the movements they represent—national politics, national literature, the occult, mysticism, aestheticism—comprise, in effect, "that stroke of luckless luck" which "can open before him the accumulated expression of the world." But for a long while these myriad interests and heroes impose themselves on Yeats with such authority that he suffers a dispersal of identity, as disconnected ideas overload his sensibility and prevent the artistic personality from ordering life:

> My father would hear of nothing but drama; personal utterance was only egotism. I knew it was not, but as yet did not know how to explain the difference. I tried from that on to write out of my emotions exactly as they came to me in life, not changing them to make them more beautiful. . . . Yet when I re-read those early poems which gave me so much trouble, I find little but romantic convention, unconscious drama. It is so many years before one can believe enough in what one feels even to know what the feeling is. (A, 68–69)

"The Trembling of the Veil" records the dispersal of Yeats's creative energies and of the heroes projected from them, his awakening recognition that such confusion is a symptom of the culture and the age, and his response of imposing a mental structure on the social chaos, much as he did in childhood by turning his attention inward. Yeats recalls: "A conviction that the world was now but a bundle of fragments possessed me without ceasing" (A, 128). Not only the world was wearing thin but Yeats himself as well: "It was many years before I understood that I had surrendered myself to the chief temptation of the artist, creation without toil" (A, 135). Yeats's pursuit of his many varied interests is to all appearances quite productive, but Yeats realizes that it distracts his energies from his chief concern of writing poetry. One of his first instincts toward a reconciliation of the fragments is to evoke images of unity through knowledge of the occult. This willed movement toward unity results, however, in greater fragmentation, as Yeats's mind is drawn into the indefinite realm of imagery rather than drawing one cohesive image from it; this is the frightening experience of "*Hodos Chameliontos*":

> To that multiplicity of interest and opinion, of arts and sciences, which had driven me to conceive a Unity of Culture defined and evoked by Unity of Image, I had but added a multiplicity of images. . . . I asked no help of books, for I believed that the truth I sought would come to me like the subject of a poem, from some moment of passionate experience, and that if I filled my exposition with other men's thought, other men's investigation, I would sink into all that multiplicity of interest and opinion. That passionate experience could never come—of that I was certain—until I had found the right image or right images. . . . But now image called up image in an endless procession, and I could not always choose among them with any confidence; and when I did choose, the image lost its intensity, or changed into some other image. . . . I was lost in that region a cabbalistic manuscript, shown me by Macgregor Mathers, had warned me of; astray upon the Path of the Chameleon, upon *Hodos Chameliontos*. (A, 180–81)

Immediately on depicting this crisis of identity in his youth, Yeats shifts the viewpoint of the "I" from past to present and imposes on the past confusion a present confidence of comprehension. He speaks of self and anti-self, and of "our trivial daily mind" (A, 183) and "that age-long memoried self" (A, 182), and of how they are united in men of genius, such as Villon and Dante:

> The two halves of their nature are so completely joined that they seem to labour for their objects, and yet to desire whatever happens, being at the same instant predestinate and free, creation's very self. We gaze at such men in awe, because we gaze not at a work of art, but at the re-creation of the man through that art, the birth of a new species of man. (A, 183)

The section of "The Trembling of the Veil" that Yeats has called "Hodos Chameliontos" thus portrays the youthful Yeats in the throes of an identity crisis that parallels similar crises in his nation and in Western literary tradition. It then portrays the mature Yeats in possession of a psycholiterary theory that grants him the hope of unity of being as it has been embodied in such literary geniuses of the past as Villon and Dante. Here is an instance of the transcendent "I" of the Journal sections of *The Autobiography* conferring a structure and a meaning on the empirical "I" of the early sections, a process inherent in autobiography itself but also quite similar to that state of being simultaneously "predestinate and free" that Yeats ascribes to the two poets he so admires or of being "self-possessed in self-surrender," as Yeats puts it in "A General Introduction for My Work." Autobiography, as the "realisation of an inner self that is as much compulsion as it is freedom,"[28] through the reevaluation and restructuring of the empirical identity by the transcendent, is thus one possible path to a retrospective type of unity of being. Yeats suggests as much in his "Preface" to "The Trembling of the Veil," when he defends his intimate analysis of fellow poets of his youth:

> They were artists and writers and certain among them men of genius, and the life of a man of genius, because of his greater sincerity, is often an experiment that needs analysis and record. At least my generation so valued personality that it thought so. I have said all the good I know and all the evil: I have kept nothing back necessary to understanding. (A, 74)

The life of artist or genius is an "experiment" in the struggle toward unity of being. Yeats discovers and affirms this struggle and the attainability of unity through memory in *The Autobiography* by openly analyzing his own life, past and present simultaneously. He also exposes, through contemplating the lives of his dead friends, the tragic alternative to creative autobiography.

If "sincerity" in autobiography or in life implies the recollection or recognition of crises and the willingness to face those crises openly in order to struggle toward unity of being, the members of the "tragic generation" were unfortunately insincere. "The Rhymers had begun to break up in tragedy, though we did not know that till the play had finished" (A, 199); Yeats is not sure why but suspects the profound aesthetic influence of Walter Pater:

> I began to wonder if [*Marius the Epicurean*], or the attitude of mind of which it was the noblest expression, had not caused the disaster of my friends. It taught us to walk upon a rope, tightly stretched through serene air, and we were left to keep our feet upon a swaying rope in a storm. Pater had made us learned; and, whatever we might be else-

where, ceremonious and polite, and distant in our relations to one another. (A, 201)

That is, Pater has preached a development of the transcendent self but not the unity of that self with the empirical self that suffers the conflicts of everyday life. The Rhymers take Pater's doctrine overly seriously and are soon split into fragmented personalities. Lionel Johnson writes pious Catholic verse and speaks of profound encounters with distinguished people, while in reality keeping almost entirely within his rooms and drinking excessively. Ernest Dowson, "who seemed to drink so little and had so much dignity and reserve, was breaking his heart for the daughter of the keeper of an Italian eating house, in dissipation and drink" (A, 201–2). Perhaps the most energetic apostle of Pater and the most spectacular in demise is Oscar Wilde[29]: "I might have known that Wilde's fantasy had taken some tragic turn, and that he was meditating upon possible disaster, but one took all his words for play—had he not called insincerity 'a mere multiplication of the personality' or some such words?" (A, 189). Wilde's words, in the context of his theory on masks, as noted in chapter 1, are highly ominous in their implications. If sincerity involves a recognition of personal disunity and a heroic artistic attempt at unity, Wilde's "mere multiplication of the personality" is an acceptance of disunity in a playful attitude toward artistic posing that veils great despair over the impossibility of unity in the empirical personality:

> He understood his weakness, true personality was impossible, for that is born in solitude, and at his moon one is not solitary; he must project himself before the eyes of others, and, having great ambition, before some great crowd of eyes; but there is no longer any great crowd that cares for his true thought. He must humour and cajole and pose, take worn-out stage situations, for he knows that he may be as romantic as he please, so long as he does not believe in his romance, and all that he may get their ears for a few strokes of contemptuous wit in which he does believe. (A, 195)

Yeats is not clear, as his analysis of Wilde betrays, whether the individual himself or the age he inherits is to blame for the downfall of so many gifted men: "Was it that we lived in what is called 'an age of transition' and so lacked coherence, or did we but pursue antithesis?" (A, 202). Yeats's previous discovery in "Hodos Chameliontos" that transition is immanent in all life and that "genius is a crisis that joins that buried self for certain moments to our trivial daily mind" (A, 182–83) suggests, however, that the best minds forge unity from the greatest challenges. Those poets of the 1890s who "but pursue antithesis" do so to cover the "thesis" of empirical existence and all its inelegance rather than to utilize crisis as a spur to achieving unity of life and art or body and mind, unity of being. Yeats's excuse for Wilde, that "at his moon one is not solitary," betrays also his own method of dealing with the crisis of age and personality. Elsewhere in *The Autobiography* Yeats refers to this method as his "Lunar metaphor" (A, 221) and his "Lunar parable" (A, 231), which is, of course, fully developed in *A Vision*. This "lunar metaphor" is a psychological system that recognizes and categorizes all possible characteristics of cultural age and individual personality and their conflicts and unions. In so stepping back from the turmoil of his friends and society, Yeats can accept the tragedy and then struggle for the unification of the potentialities their lives have come to represent for him. It is, in one sense, an act of abstraction, which Yeats so dreads, but so far as it remains anchored in the concrete realities of his friends' lives, the system remains relevant:

> I can no more justify my convictions in these brief chapters than Shake-speare could justify within the limits of a sonnet his conviction that the soul of the wide world dreams of things to come; and yet I have set out to describe nature as I see it, I must not only describe events but those patterns into which they fall, when I am the looker on. (A, 221)

It is a bit of exaggeration on Yeats's part to suggest that he sees the pattern in events as they occur; certainly he does not have his "lunar metaphor" handy as he witnesses the demise of a whole generation of poets,. nor does he, by his own admission, realize fully the demise of that generation "till the play had finished." But insofar as his system has grown out of witnessing and realizing such a tragedy, and insofar as Yeats, in effect, rewitnesses events in remembering and recording them, it is a legitimate imposition of system on events. The words that should be stressed are "when I am the looker on." The "patterns" reflect Yeats's development and his concerns more than those of his unfortunate friends. With his system, Yeats can unite fact and figure, life and artistic structure, both in the history he tells and in the persona he creates. In assuming responsibility for explaining or at least recording the chaos of a fallen generation, Yeats, must take on the failures of his fellows in a theoretical sense; he must encompass in his own imagination that which he seeks to recognize and describe. This is a step toward unity of being in the persona, for it joins event and idea in a structure that eventually must reshape the life of the recorder:

> [Yeats] was compelled, not to abuse the sense of "transition" by formulating the theory of responsibility which is the usual mark of such creative periods as the Nineties, but to resolve antithesis in decision, in moral choice, in a conception of man and of history that looks beyond transition to the immutable laws of nature and of mind. . . . He found his life assuming, partly by force of conscious egoism, partly by force of circumstance, that collaboration between Will and the Body of Fate which manifests itself in a structure of phases or cycles: the pattern of growth. It was a growth from sensation to speculation, from revery to action . . . from immediacy of experience and emotion toward the universals of knowledge and value.[30]

Morton Zabel's analysis of Yeats's growth in *The Autobiography* anticipates *A Vision* in its terminology, but his findings are firmly rooted in the conceptual discoveries Yeats makes in "The Tragic Generation" and elsewhere in "The Trembling of the Veil."

When Yeats does not seek order in terms of his own "lunar metaphor" in *The Autobiography,* he studies structures that have been utilized by poets of the past: "Shakespeare leaned, as it were, even as craftsman, upon the general fate of men and nations, had about him the excitement of the playhouse" (A, 209). Shakespeare, however, in Yeats's vision of literary history, does not embody the greatest artistic expression of unity of culture; this high praise is reserved for Chaucer:

> Though I preferred Shakespeare to Chaucer I begrudged my own preference. Had not Europe shared one mind and heart, until both mind and heart began to break into fragments a little before Shakespeare's birth? . . . If Chaucer's personages had disengaged themselves from Chaucer's crowd, forgot their common goal and shrine, and after sundry magnifications became each in turn the centre of some Elizabethan play, and had after split into their elements and so given birth to romantic poetry, must I reverse the cinematograph? . . . A nation or an individual with great emotional intensity might follow the pilgrims as it were to some unknown shrine, and give to all those separated elements and to all that abstract love and melancholy, a symbolical, a mythological coherence. Not Chaucer's rough-tongued riders, but rather an ended pilgrimage, a procession of the Gods! (A, 129–31)

Yeats rewrites the story of the "tragic generation" as a failed pilgrimage of sorts, and he is finally left alone on the path to unity of being and turns to his poetic predecessors as role models of the lonely pilgrim. Dante, like his successor Chaucer, is extolled by Yeats not only for writing of unity of being but also for achieving it, but then he too is in part the product of a unified culture. Blake is mentioned for the impact of his philosophy but not as a poet enacting his life's efforts in his work. Yeats singles out only one poet-companion in *The Autobiography* as a predecessor, albeit an imperfect one, in the extremely difficult modern effort toward achieving unity of being in poetry—Percy Bysshe Shelley. As a man, Shelley is citicized by Yeats for being too ethereal, for pursuing the transcendent too far removed from the concrete reality of everyday life. But for his poetic characters, Shelley is greatly admired; Yeats speaks of Shelley "assuming" wisdom and beauty as he dons the masks of Ahasuerus and Athanase (A, 166–67).

Yeats remembers first being impressed as a youth with one of Shelley's early poetic characters, the Poet of "Alastor":

> I began to play at being a sage, a magician or a poet. I had many idols, and as I climbed along the narrow ledge I was now Manfred on his glacier, and now Prince Athanase with his solitary lamp, but I soon chose Alastor for my chief of men and longed to share his melancholy, and maybe at last to disappear from everybody's sight as he disappeared drifting in a boat along some slow-moving river between great trees. (A, 41–42)[31]

Shelley's Poet is haunted by a vision of ideal love and beauty and travels through a landscape that charts the structure of his own mind, into deeper and deeper realms of solitude and introspection, ultimately meeting unity and death. This poet-figure is thus the ultimate conception of the visionary who sees nothing in life to distract him from his internal drama; it is little wonder he attracts the young Yeats, who "found it hard to attend to anything less interesting than my thoughts" (A, 14). Athanase intrigues the youth for similar reasons; this poetic prince, like the Poet of "Alastor," confronts two images of his desire, one natural and the other spiritual. Unlike his predecessor, though, Athanase is more philosopher than poet:

> His soul had wedded Wisdom, and her dower
> Is love and justice, clothed in which he sate
> Apart from men, as in a lonely tower,
> Pitying the tumult of their dark estate.[32]

Finally, Yeats finds great attraction in Shelley's Ahasuerus, the wise Jew of the dramatic poem "Hellas," from which Yeats quotes at length in *The Autobiography*. Ahasuerus is a step beyond Athanase, that "young man, his hair blanched with sorrow, studying philosophy in some lonely tower" (A, 115). Ahasuerus is an "old man, master of all human knowledge, hidden from human sight in some shell-strewn cavern on the Mediterranean shore" (A, 115–16), and Yeats comes to appreciate him as representing the wisdom of the world, as a source of universal knowledge that is somewhat similar to what he calls elsewhere *"anima mundi."*

Where the Poet of "Alastor" resembles the portrait of his own youth that Yeats draws in *The Autobiography*, Athanase prefigures the middle-aged philosophic Yeats, living in Thoor Ballylee and working at his systematic philosophy, *A Vision*. And Ahasuerus, who proclaims, "Nought is but that which feels itself to be,"[33] is not unlike the Yeats of old age who took for his motto, "Man can embody truth but he cannot know it."[34] George Bornstein refers to this trio as a "subjective hierarchy"[35] for Yeats, and Dillon Johnston identifies their common element of attraction for Yeats as the attitude of a quest for self-knowledge in the form of self-unity:

> Yeats's integral self is not his anti-self, not Ahasuerus the cold savant, but Yeats in search of this mask, or Ahasuerus the Wandering Jew. . . . The page-length excerpt [in *The Autobiography*] . . . describes not Ahasuerus but the search for Ahasuerus by Mahmud who must go through an elaborate *passage duré* to encounter his symbol of wisdom and experience. . . . Yeats supports this self-image with other literary images—Hamlet, Athanase, Alastor, Manfred—which represent the perpetual wanderer or the divided self seeking a unity.[36]

Although, as Johnston also notes, Harold Bloom fails to notice this Shelleyan quest motif in Yeats's autobiography, Bloom does make careful note of Shelley's profound influence on Yeats's development of the concept of anti-self, and not solely in terms of Shelley's poetic characters:

> The *antithetical* solitude of the young Shelley, with his gentleness and humanitarian character, who yet creates as the heroes of his early poetry the isolated figures of sage, magician, violent revolutionary, and proudly solitary noble and poet, is very clearly the ultimate origin of Yeats's later theories of the mask and the antithetical self.[37]

Bloom's intuition, that it is the relation of Shelley to his own poetic characters that interests the mature Yeats and not merely the poetic characters themselves, is borne out by Yeats's two independent essays on Shelley: "The Philosophy of Shelley's Poetry" and "Prometheus Unbound." In the former essay, Yeats speculates that "Alastor" originated with an actual experience in Shelley's life:

> When Shelley went to the Continent with Godwin's daughter in 1814 they sailed down certain rivers in an open boat, and when he summed up in his preface to *Laon and Cythna* the things that helped to make him a poet, he spoke of these voyages: "I have sailed down mighty rivers, and seen the sun rise and set, and the stars come forth, whilst I have sailed night and day down a rapid stream among mountains."[38]

Yeats believed this experience to be potentially redemptive, an antithetical experience that, if sought by the primary self, would yield to unity of being:

> There is for every man some one scene, some one adventure, some one picture that is the image of his secret life . . . and that this one image, if he would but brood over it his life long, would lead his soul, disentangled from unmeaning circumstance and the ebb and flow of the world, into that far household where the undying gods await all whose souls have become simple as flame, whose bodies have become quiet as an agate lamp.

But Shelley projects this experience into dramatized, objective poetic characters rather than expanding his own identity in verse, speaking as "I," to encompass it. The result, as Yeats sees it, is a sacrifice of life for art, rather than a union of the two: "He was born in a day when the old wisdom had vanished and was content merely to write verses, and often with little thought of more than verses."[39] Thirty-two years later, in his Ahasuerus stage, as it were, Yeats writes even more openly in "Prometheus Unbound" of Shelley's compromised poetic life:

> Shelley's art shows that he was an unconverted man though certainly a visionary. . . . He was the tyrant of his own being, nor was it in all likelihood a part of the plan that it should find freedom, seeing that he worked, as did Keats and Marlowe, uncorrecting and unhesitating, as though he knew the shortness of his life. That life, and all lives, would be unintelligible to me did I not think of them as an exfoliation prolonged from life to life; he sang of something beginning.[40]

Shelley's life thus takes on a symbolic value for Yeats; from Shelley's very failure, as Yeats sees it, to join art and life, Yeats becomes aware of such a need and perhaps even of how to satisfy it. Yeats subsequently develops an autobiographical persona in his poetry, an "I" that merges both life and art as the focal point of the two by progressing through each stage of growth, rather than projecting questing heroes, as Shelley does, to embody each stage independently and to relieve the poet of making the same quest himself. At the plateau of identity from which he writes his autobiography, Yeats looks back on Shelley as a crucial influence during an earlier period of great challenge:

> When in middle life I looked back I found that [Shelley] and not Blake, whom I had studied more and with more approval, had shaped my life, and when I thought of the tumultuous and often tragic lives of friends or acquaintance, I attributed to his direct or indirect influence their Jacobin frenzies, their brown demons.[41]

Shelley is a major figure in *The Autobiography*, though only implicitly; he appears as a standard of evaluation. Yeats's friends and fellow poets of the "tragic generation" follow in Shelley's path, projecting poetic characters or masks rather than pursuing an integrated internal identity that embraces both their lives and their art. As Yeats evaluated the situation in 1892, "The typical young poet of our day is an aesthete with a surfeit, searching sadly for his lost Philistinism, his heart full of an unsatisfied hunger for the commonplace. He is an Alastor tired of his woods and longing for beer and skittles."[42] Yeats, who in his youth fantasizes becoming an "Alastor" Poet or an Athanase, eventually realizes the necessity of internalizing those poses and others as aspects of an integrated, continuous poetic persona, so that he would grow in wisdom and integrity, akin to Ahasuerus.

In "The Stirring of the Bones," the sequel to "The Tragic Generation" in *The Autobiography*, Yeats briefly summarizes his feelings on the possibility of a unity of culture along the lines he has laid for the individual's unity of being. The essay recalls Yeats's meeting with Lady Gregory and his first visits to her estate at Coole as "initiated through preternatural intervention."[43] Whether supernaturally ordained or not, Lady Gregory's employment of Yeats as a colleague in collecting Irish folklore and the healing atmosphere of her estate are shown to help rescue Yeats from the psychological chaos of the "tragic generation," the emotional exhaustion of his love for Maud Gonne, and the artistic impotence of *"Hodos Chameliontos."* Consequently, "Dramatis Personae," written twelve years after "The Trembling of the Veil," was also appended to the autobiography to eulogize Augusta Gregory (it was originally to be titled "Lady Gregory") and to attest to the creative power of an integrated identity in her and by implication in Yeats himself. The essay was conceived as a response to George Moore's reductive portrayals of Yeats, Lady Gregory, and their theater-building efforts in Moore's autobiography, *Hail and Farewell.*[44] "Dramatis Personae" is thus also a study of the relative artistic strengths of a diffuse, objectively oriented personality in George Moore, "more mob than man" (A, 289), which could never "attain the discipline of style" (A, 271), and those of an integrated, subjective personality in Lady Gregory, which employs style to unite life and art:

> A writer must die every day he lives, be reborn, as it is said in the Burial Service, an incorruptible self, that self opposite of all that he has named "himself." George Moore, dreading the annihilation of an impersonal bleak realism, used life like a medieval ghost making a body for itself out of drifting dust and vapour. . . . Lady Gregory, in her life much artifice, in her nature much pride, was born to see the glory of the world in a peasant mirror. (A, 307)

In the final part of *The Autobiography,* "The Bounty of Sweden," Yeats expands his vision of a unity of culture at Coole to encompass the greater realm of society—not that of Ireland, which has not succeeded in uniting its antinomies—but the monarchy of Sweden, which is the setting of that great social appreciation of lifetime achievements, the Nobel Prize awards. The structure and style of this essay are diaristic; and much as Yeats arranges for the "Journal" persona to exist amid the more structured whole of *The Autobiography,* he presents in this essay an image of the act of mind that expresses itself in poetry:

> Every now and then, when something has stirred my imagination, I begin talking to myself. I speak in my own person and dramatise myself. . . . Occasionally, I write out what I have said in verse, and generally for no better reason than because I remember that I have written no verse for a long time. . . . When I begin to write I have no object but to find for ["my soliloquies"] some natural speech rhythm and syntax, and to set it out in some pattern, so seeming old that it may seem all men's speech, and though the labour is very great, I seem to

have used no faculty peculiar to myself, certainly no special gift. I print the poem and never hear about it again, until I find the book years after with a page dog-eared by some young man, or marked by some young girl with a violet, and when I have seen that I am a little ashamed, as though somebody were to attribute to me a delicacy of feeling I should but do not possess. What came so easily at first, and amidst so much drama, and was written so laboriously at the last, cannot be counted among my possessions. (A, 359)

Here is a triumph of "attitude," as Yeats uses that term in "A General Introduction for My Work"—a transcendence of individual personality through style to an archetypal identity. Yeats has lived his life in the role of a poet so fully that it is no longer a role but an archetype; the symbolic mystique Yeats grants to Synge in "The Death of Synge" he is now capable of assuming himself. Yeats has found a transcendent poetic persona during life, through the effort at restructuring his life with memory and art in *The Autobiography*. On receiving the Nobel Prize in Literature, it all seems clear:

All is over, and I am able to examine my medal. . . . It shows a young man listening to a Muse, who stands young and beautiful with a great lyre in her hand, and I think as I examine it, "I was good-looking once like that young man, but my unpractised verse was full of infirmity, my Muse old as it were; and now I am old and rheumatic, and nothing to look at, but my Muse is young. I am even persuaded that she is like those Angels in Swedenborg's vision, and moves perpetually 'towards the day-spring of her youth.'" (A, 365)

Yeats closes his autobiography, however, not with this analysis of himself but with praise for others, for "all those workers, obscure or well-known, to whom I owe much of whatever fame in the world I may possess" (A, 373): Lady Gregory and John Synge, other colleagues in the Irish Dramatic Movement, such cultural unities as the Swedish court. Yeats redirects attention from himself to these others because in a very real sense, as a poet of universal voice, he speaks for them, he comprehends them. But Lady Gregory and John Synge, in particular, serve to symbolize the triumph of a unification of art and life; in his Nobel lecture, Yeats recalls: "When I received from the hands of your King the great honour your Academy has conferred upon me, I felt that a young man's ghost should have stood upon one side of me and at the other a living woman sinking into the infirmity of age" (A, 387). Between this specter of unity of being and this matron of unity of culture, Yeats stands as a representative of these twin unities to the world. Joseph Ronsley speculates, "Perhaps, even, by imagining himself standing between them, he envisages the qualities of both his friends symbolically coming together in himself."[45] It is certainly an artistic triumph and, so far as Yeats came to express himself through the role of a poet, a personal triumph as well; but above all, it ratifies the empirical, stylistic roots of the poetic persona. Morton Zabel puts it well:

> When a poet submits his life to allegorical interpretation, he implies a symbolic theory of experience; when he extends that interpretation to the lives of others and makes a system of his findings, his codification becomes a theory of history. What began by being private, privileged, prejudiced in the interests of individuality, becomes public, universal, a law of natural or human processes. The task which Yeats assumed in becoming a poet superior to the subjective limitations of aestheticism was soon discovered to be a task which would test the ability of his moral and intellectual capacities to rise superior to personal taste and interest, to the peculiar conditions of his egocentric personality. Yeats's autobiographies gain their most dramatic qualities from the urgency he shows this extension of vision to have exercised on all his faculties.[46]

Whereas *The Autobiography* represents an artistic structuring of empirical experience, *A Vision* is an abstract elaboration of that structure. The complementarity of the two works runs deep; Yeats frequently employs the "lunar metaphor" that is the foundation of *A Vision* as an analytical tool in "The Tragic Generation" and elsewhere in *The Autobiography*, and the bare skeleton of that metaphor in *A Vision*, the Great Wheel, is rendered meaningful and comprehensible by Yeats's application to it of the lives of many of the poets of that "tragic generation," among other prominent figures. Nietzsche calls philosophy a "species of involuntary and unconscious auto-biography," and Yeats himself has speculated, "We may come to think that nothing exists but a stream of souls, that all knowledge is biography."[47] Indeed, in his "Dedication" to the first edition of *A Vision*, Yeats reveals, "Perhaps this book has been written because a number of young men and women . . . met nearly forty years ago in London and in Paris to discuss mystical philosophy," some of the same young men and women Yeats discusses in *The Autobiography*:

Some were looking for spiritual happiness or for some form of un-known power, but I had a practical object. I wished for a system of thought that would leave my imagination free to create as it chose and yet make all that it created, or could create, part of the one history, and that the soul's. The Greeks certainly had such a system, and Dante . . . and I think no man since. . . . Swedenborg and Blake preferred to explain them figuratively, and so I am the first to substitute for Biblical or mythological figures, historical movements and actual men and women.[48]

The friends and acquaintances who are examined as aspects of Yeats's life in *The Autobiography* thus instigate and exemplify the aspects and phases of *A Vision*. The correlation extends even into Yeats's own life, as *A Vision*, in both editions, provides some autobiographical information on periods of Yeats's life not given in *The Autobiography*. Richard Ellmann goes so far as to characterize *A Vision* as a "huge projection of [Yeats's] own life, filled with autobiography and rationalization of his personal crises and tem-perament, his own soul sitting model for all the twenty-eight phases."[49]

Ellmann's observation is both subtly true and manifestly false, for Yeats is one figure from *The Autobiography* who does not appear in any of the phases of the Great Wheel. Moreover, other than the personal confession of the "Dedication" to the first edi-tion and the revelation in the second edition that the system has evolved from the automatic writings of his wife, Yeats makes a great effort to present the system as being objective and impersonal in nature. In the first edition, which is subtitled *An Explanation of Life Founded upon the Writings of Giraldus and upon Certain Doctrines Attributed to Kusta Ben Luka,* Yeats resurrects Owen Aherne and Michael Robartes to have them discover the system among ancient writings and tribal beliefs and to bring it to his attention. Yeats then poses as a transcriber and interpreter of a preexisting system, recalling the role of the "I" in "The Celtic Twilight," though the fictional nature of the system's origins is coyly reemphasized in Aherne's remarking that the portrait of Giraldus that Yeats includes in his edition remarkly resembles Yeats himself.[50] Even in the second edition, which offers an auto-biographical source for the system and speculates that it has evolved from the "personalities of a dream shared by my wife, by myself, occasionally by others . . . a dream that can take objective form" (V, 22–23), Yeats retains the story of Robartes's finding a book by Giraldus and tracing the system it contains back to Kusta

Ben Luka, thereby granting the philosophy both mythological coherence and a sort of historical precedent. In both editions,
moreover, Yeats presents the system itself as it has been revealed to
him—passively. Much as in "Anima Mundi," the Yeatsian persona, the "I," has very little to do with the main body of *A Vision;*
the transcendent aspect of art is present and functioning, but apparently not the empirical aspect of life.

Yeats is aware of this departure from the persona-based, personal norm of his writings and tries to defend the system and to
urge fair consideration of it in both versions. In the first edition,
Yeats admits the system's great abstractness but hopes that his
readers "will master what is most abstract there and make it the
foundation of their visions" and that thus the "curtain may ring up
on a new drama."[51] In the second edition, Yeats is less sure of his
audience, perhaps in part as a result of the reactions to the first
edition, but he is nonetheless confident in the ultimate value of the
system he presents:

> Some, perhaps all, of those readers I most value, those who have read
> me many years, will be repelled by what must seem an arbitrary, harsh,
> difficult symbolism. Yet such has almost always accompanied expres-
> sion that unites the sleeping and waking mind. . . . William Blake . . .
> remains himself almost unintelligible because he never drew the like.
> We can (those hard symbolic bones under the skin) substitute for a
> treatise on logic the *Divine Comedy,* or some little song about a rose,
> or be content to live our thought. (V, 23–24)

Yeats is describing a universal, archetypal structure that underlies
all works of mind; at one point, he describes the Great Wheel as
representing "every completed movement of thought or life" (V,
81). Once identified and explored, this structure should thus facilitate a variety of interpretations and understandings; it should be
what Yeats refers to as the "foundation" of his readers' own "visions." Many of Yeats's readers and critics, however, have been
repelled by this abstract system, and almost all have criticized
Yeats for what they see to be a largely incoherent effort. David
Lynch says, for instance: "On one hand it is the record, unchecked
by aesthetic considerations, of his hunger for structure, for the
artifice that would render as something 'intended, complete' not
just the lyric moment but the whole of experience. On the other
hand, it accurately reproduces, in its bewildering proliferation of
distinctions and 'geometrical' relationships, something of the inci-

pient chaos of that experience."[52] And yet, each reader of *A Vision* interprets it differently, and all together affirm the success of Yeats's venture—in essence take their places within the Great Wheel.

Cleanth Brooks, one of the earliest defenders of *A Vision*, sees the system as an "attempt to make a coherent formulation of the natural and the supernatural," without the aid of science. The result, according to Brooks, "allows Yeats to see the world as a great drama, predictable in its larger aspects (so that the poet is not lost in a welter of confusion), but in a pattern which allows for the complexity of experience and the apparent contradictions of experience (so that the poet is not tempted to oversimplify)."[53] Brooks sees a mythic drama that encourages artistic creation, the act of writing poetry reflecting the meaningfulness of life. Helen Vendler, another proponent of the system, reads *A Vision* as a "series of metaphorical statements about poetry," an aesthetic treatise in symbolic language. Vendler's interpretation is perhaps the most sympathetic of those published to date, as it views *A Vision* squarely within the traditional consensus that Yeats is a poet first and foremost and because it ties this difficult system to Yeats's life as well:

> In a strange way *A Vision* is one answer to Walter Pater. The Conclusion to *The Renaissance* had laid an enormous burden on the poets of the nineties, and many of them exhausted themselves and their art in trying to "maintain that ectasy" of constant awareness. Yeats had sense enough to provide a multiplicity of lives (metaphorically speaking) for the accomplishing of understanding. Creation, for Yeats as well as for Wordsworth, springs from emotion recollected in tranquillity. The purgatorial state of suspension in which emotion is relived and contemplated is called in *A Vision* "the period between death and birth" or "the period between lives," and though Yeats speaks about it in terms of knowledge, we are to realize that his essay is the conceptualizing of a chaotic and for the most part unconscious experience.[54]

From this perspective, *A Vision* is an act of symbolically redeeming the "tragic generation" because it arises from that experience and identifies its archetypal significance. Insofar as Yeats was a member of this group, *A Vision* also represents an integration of his life and work.

In contrast to Brooks's mythic and Vendler's symbolic readings of *A Vision*, Harold Bloom takes a quasi-Freudian approach to the work and comes away disappointed and discomfited. Bloom at-

tempts to read the work literally, as describing actual reincarna-
tions of the soul, for instance, and his dissatisfaction reflects the
necessary incapacity of any critic to evaluate claims for knowledge
that is much greater than any one life or mind can experience
personally. The result is an assessment of Yeats as pontifical and
wrong-headed:

> A Vision is technically an apocalypse; that seems to me its actual genre,
> rather than cosmology or anatomy or aesthetic treatise. Whether Yeats
> generates the moral authority to match his undoubted rhetorical au-
> thority is problematic, but A Vision does try to pass a Last Judgment
> on its own age, and its own poet.[55]

Bloom's psychoanalytic reading blinds him to the efforts that
Yeats makes in A Vision to present an objective (in the sense of
archetypal) structure which may be fleshed out by each individual
according to his own experiences and interests, his own "vision."
Whereas Bloom is actually projecting his own interests onto the
"bones" of Yeats's system and thereby confirming Yeats's hopes
for it, Bloom sees himself as revealing Yeats's true interests, which,
because they are so narrowly conceived, greatly compromise the
value of the system. In some unused notes for A Vision, Yeats
makes the plea, "For the present I but ask my reader to accept my
dream as he would accept the play of Hamlet when the curtain is
up."[56] Critical interpretations of Hamlet are at least as numerous,
at least as conflcting, and at least as justified as those of A Vision;
the point is that there can be and should be no definitive interpretation of such an archetypal structure.

Further evidence that Yeats intended no one correct reading of A
Vision inheres in his own absence from any phase in the Great
Wheel. Most critics have assumed Yeats to be a man of phase 17,
"The Daimonic Man" (V, 140), based apparently on Richard Ellmann's account of Mrs. Yeats's saying that her husband saw himself in that phase and on Cleanth Brooks's reasoning that Yeats's
poetic efforts and images place him there.[57] Even though all evidence and reason point to Yeats's being a representative of phase
17, he nowhere assigns himself to a phase, and any discussion of
how Yeats fits into A Vision should take this curious absence into
account. Certainly Yeats's description of phase 17 echoes phrases
and concerns from Yeats's writings as a whole: "Unity of Being,
and consequent expression of Daimonic thought, is now more easy
than at any other phase"; "The Will, when true to phase, assumes,

in assuming the *Mask*, an intensity which is never dramatic but always lyrical and personal, and this intensity, though always a deliberate assumption, is to others but the charm of the being" (V, 141–42). In *The Autobiography* Yeats demonstrates a change in personality, from the lonely introspection of early youth to the "gregariousness" of maturity,[58] which phase 17 of *A Vision* does seem to describe, in terms of primary Mask and antithetical Will, respectively:

> Because of the habit of synthesis, and of the growing complexity of the energy, which gives many interests, and the still faint perception of things in their weight and mass, men of this phase are almost always partisans, propagandists and gregarious; yet because of the *Mask* of simplification, which holds up before them the solitary life of hunters and of fishers and "the groves pale passion loves", they hate parties, crowds, propaganda. (V, 143)

Nonetheless, Yeats's examples for phase 17 are Shelley, Dante, and Landor, and not himself.

Placing himself outright in phase 17 of *A Vision* would have skewed the whole structure toward that phase instead of toward phase 15, the perfect phase of "complete beauty" (V, 135) and toward a larger perspective on the whole system, as indeed Bloom skews it in focusing on Yeats's personality alone: "The personal as opposed to the structural center of *A Vision* is Phase 17 rather than 15, and Yeats's imagination asserts itself always when he is most personal."[59] Again, Bloom is making a deduction rather than an observation; Yeats does not speak in the first person in his description of phase 17 and rarely in his discussion of the Great Wheel as a whole. Yeats treats the system objectively, as a revelation of spirits, and not his own, much as he analyzes all his peers in "The Tragic Generation" according to his "lunar metaphor" while he "alone has no crisis,"[60] no objective placement within the system. Only in the introductory and concluding matter of *A Vision* and in transitional discussions within the work does the "I" assert itself and relate itself to the system personally. In the subjective passages, Yeats presents himself not as a creature of one phase but as a representative of all phases. So Yeats may have seen his empirical aspect of self in phase 17, but as creator of the system, in his transcendent aspect of identity, Yeats could not place himself in any part of the system; he rather comprehends it all. He has, after all, held all of the system in his mind, between receiving and transmitting it, and he has supplied the biographies of people of his own acquaintance or from his own readings to exemplify the phases of the Great Wheel—concrete detail without which the purely abstract system of the communicators would have withered from starvation (V, 12).

Something of the significance of this experience to Yeats is conveyed in a comment at the end of Book II, "The Completed Symbol":

> I have now described many symbols which seem mechanical because united in a single structure, and of which the greater number, precisely because they tell always the same story, may seem unnecessary. Yet every symbol, except where it lies in vast periods of time and so beyond our experience, has evoked for me some form of human destiny, and that form, once evoked, has appeared everywhere, as if there were but one destiny, as my own form might appear in a room full of mirrors. (V, 213–14)

An archetypal structure that is common to all unites all in the mind that beholds it; Yeats comprehends (in both senses of the word) all the lives he fits into the Great Wheel from his perspective of a detached observer of life. Wilde, Synge, Dowson—anyone else in the Wheel presumably might also abstract himself from it and regard the rest of the world as a structure, Yeats in his aspect of empirical personage in phase 17 included. Thus, A Vision encourages a dual perception of personality, in both its empirical and transcendent aspects, as Yeats argues in his conclusion to the first edition:

> A book of modern philosophy may prove to our logical capacity that there is a transcendental portion of our being that is timeless and spaceless, and therefore immortal, and yet our imagination remain subjected to nature as before. . . . It was not so with ancient philosophy because the ancient philosopher had something to reinforce his thought. . . . He could assume, perhaps even prove, that every condition of mind discovered by analysis, even that which is timeless, spaceless, is present vivd experience to some being, and that we could in some degree communicate with this being while still alive, and after death share in the experience. . . . That we may believe that all men possess the supernatural faculties I would restore to the philosopher his mythology.[61]

Because Yeats has successfully restored a mythology of sorts,

Brooks, Vendler, Bloom, and others can argue equally their individual interpretations of the system of *A Vision*. It is rather surprising, in this light, that Northrop Frye, who might be expected to be most interested in Yeats's development of an archetypal structure, is highly suspicious of *A Vision*. Frye characterizes what he takes to be the endless, fatalistic cycle of history and life in *A Vision* as "Yeats's *Inferno*, his demonic or Thanatos vision," thus separating it qualitatively from the main concerns of the poetry; he even compares such an attitude on Yeats's part to thoughts of other, "insane" individuals.[62] At other times, Frye more generously accepts that Yeats tries to forge a union between empirical and transcendent, or what Frye calls physical and hyperphysical, worlds but concludes nevertheless that Yeats fails:

> The *Vision* begins by dividing all human types among twenty-eight phases, and even this, for all its arbitrary straight-jacketing, might have become the sub-conscious foundation of an art-form like the one represented in Chaucer's company of twenty-nine pilgrims, who evidently seem to be something of a perfect circle of planetary and humorous temperament. It is a pity that the qualities which enabled Chaucer to transform his perfect circle into great art were qualities that Yeats felt he ought to distrust—characterization and comedy.[63]

The analogy with Chaucer is revealing. Yeats was familiar with an archetypal interpretation of Chaucer's pilgrims from his study of Blake, who has described them as "characters which compose all ages and nations" and the "physiognomies of lineaments of universal human life, beyond which Nature never steps."[64] Yeats should also have known from his readings that, excepting three undescribed priests and Geffrey, Chaucer's self-portrait, and including the Host, there are twenty-eight pilgrims accounted for in the "General Prologue" of *The Canterbury Tales*. Chaucer characterizes his Geffrey, the removed observer of the other pilgrims, as a thoroughly empirical being, who believes no more than he sees or hears, a gullible transmitter of empirical data.[65] The transcendent perspective inheres only in the reader's awareness of Chaucer, the poet, behind his limited persona. Yeats, always striving for unity of being, is not interested in a comic rendition of the separation of transcendent and empirical aspects of identity; he declines to portray himself as an objective character in the structure to avoid just such self-reduction.

Chaucer also provides for a break in the structure of his system,

in the unpredictable arrival of a new pilgrim near the end of the
journey, the Canon's Yeoman. This gesture of recognition that no
structure is self-sufficient or whole resembles the Thirteenth Cone
in Yeats's *A Vision*, the radical element of miracle or freedom. Frye
is most interested in this element of Yeats's system, and he associates it with the power of art, specifically with the "dialectical
element in symbolism, where man is directly confronted by the
greater form of himself which challenges him to identify with it."
Frye thus feels that the Thirteenth Cone redeems *A Vision*, even if
it does render its voluminous mechanics largely unnecessary:

> The image is a product of the imagination: in the imaginative world the
> relation of subject and object is that of creator and creature. In this
> perspective the whole cycle of nature, of life and death and rebirth
> which man has dreamed, becomes a single gigantic image, and the
> process of redemption is to be finally understood as an identification
> with Man and a detachment from the cyclical image he has created.
> This ultimate insight in Yeats is the one expressed in his many
> references (one of which forms the last sentence of *A Vision*) to a
> passage in the *Odyssey* where Heracles, seen by Odysseus in hell, is
> said to be present in hell only in his shade, the real Heracles, the man in
> contrast to the image, being at the banquet of the immortal gods. Here
> we come to the heart of what Yeats had to say as a poet. The vision of
> Heracles the man, eternally free from Heracles the shadowy image
> bound to an endless cycle, is nearer to being a "key" to Yeats's thought
> and imagination than anything else in *A Vision*.[66]

Frye is right to emphasize Yeats's ultimate freedom from his own
structure, but that freedom is apparent in more than Yeats's
references to art, Heracles, or the Thirteenth Cone. Yeats never
projects himself or his persona into the system; he remains always
outside of it, observing and evaluating it. Indeed, Yeats's conception of the perfect phase 15 might well describe what *A Vision*
means to him: "All that the being has experienced as thought is
visible to its eyes as a whole, and in this way it perceives, not as
they are to others, but according to its own perception, all orders
of existence" (V, 136).

J. Hillis Miller, ignoring Yeats's commitment to a philosophical
idealism and his discomfort with the traditional Western concept
of God, concludes that the "being" which perceives all "according
to its own perception" in *A Vision* is not human but God:

> The text is the celestial archetypes, and these must be endlessly re-

peated on the stage of history. . . . The audience for this cosmic play, insatiable for suffering and blood, is God. . . . The play he witnesses is the perpetual reincarnation of the congeries of being which is himself. . . . What is joyous self-expression to God is a whirling and a bitterness here.[67]

Yeats's instructors specify in *A Vision* that "neither between death and birth nor between birth and death can the soul find more than momentary happiness; its object is to pass rapidly round its circle and find freedom from that circle" (V, 236). It is from passages such as this one that Miller draws his conclusion that only God apprehends the full meaning of the structure of life and that the individual human being "must suffer not only the eternal return of the same life but also the eternal return of all possible lives. It seems that he will be racked on the wheel of time forever." Miller does perceive an outlet for this miserable creature, in a "movement around the periphery [of the Wheel] so rapid that one would be at all points of the circle at once and thereby reach spherical completeness."[68]

Yeats's instructors have not, however, specified any such rapid movement as inevitable. The Great Wheel, as an archetypal structure, embodies the common characteristics of several superficially different activities: "This wheel is every completed movement of thought or life, twenty-eight incarnations, a single incarnation, a single judgment or act of thought. Man seeks his opposite or the opposite of his condition, attains his object so far as it is attainable, at Phase 15 and returns to Phase 1 again" (V, 81). Rather than of an endless and painful revolution around the Great Wheel, this is more a description of how an act, a thought, or a life may be structured in order to redeem it from the endless flux of experience. In fact, one trip around the Wheel is a fairly accurate description of how Yeats structures his own life in *The Autobiography:* the young child with his unquestioned primary relationship to the world; the adolescent and adult with his growing antithetical habit of projecting qualities admired but not his own onto other people around him, making them heroes; and a return of the aging man to the primary relationship of unity of culture in Lady Gregory's "coterie" and the court of Sweden. Presumably the "I" of *The Autobiography* will have to relive its life after death in reverse course around the Wheel again, as *A Vision* describes, but that is a movement out of the control of the empirical man and in the control of his daimon. *A Vision* also predicts, "Life is an endeavour, made vain by the four sails of its mill, to come to a double contemplation, that of the chosen Image, that of the fated Image" (V, 94). That is, life may be a matter of "vain endeavour" to achieve unity of being, but art, in which the individual can project a persona, is a true means of structuring experience into an integrated and stable whole.

This unity of being in an artistic persona is suggested again at the close of *A Vision:*

> Day after day I have sat in my chair turning a symbol over in my mind, exploring all its details, defining and again defining its elements, testing my convictions and those of others by its unity, attempting to substitute particulars for an abstraction like that of algebra. I have felt the convictions of a lifetime melt though at an age when the mind should be rigid, and others take their place, and these in turn give way to others. . . . Then I draw myself up into the symbol and it seems as if I should know all if I could but banish such memories and find everything in the symbol.
>
> But nothing comes—though this moment was to reward me for all my toil. Perhaps I am too old. (V, 301)

This passage recalls the conclusion to "Reveries over Childhood and Youth," in which Yeats frets, "all life weighed in the scales of my own life seems to me a preparation for something that never happens" (A, 71). *A Vision*, however, seems finally to provide that "something," at least in retrospect:

> Then I understand. I have already said all that can be said. The particulars are the work of the *thirteenth sphere* or cycle which is in every man and called by every man his freedom. Doubtless, for it can do all things and knows all things, it knows what it will do with its own freedom but it has kept the secret. (V, 302)

The revelation of meaning Yeats has sought in *The Autobiography* is supplied in the application of "particulars," or the accidents of life and fate that characterize each personality, to the archetypal structure of life forms in *A Vision*. Yeats now sees that an individual is both fated to follow a certain pattern of life and free to experience the details within the pattern of his own unique passage through life; "Do not all intelligible truths lie in [the] passage from egg to dust?" (V, 214). The structure of *A Vision* has come to signify in Yeats's mind "stylistic arrangements of experience comparable to the cubes in the drawing of Wyndham Lewis and to the ovoids in the sculpture of Brancusi" which "have helped me to hold in a single thought reality and justice" (V, 25), the empirical and transcendent. Thus, when Yeats announces to Ezra Pound at the beginning of *A Vision* that the book will, "when finished, proclaim a new divinity" (V, 27), he perhaps implies that the process of envisioning the abstract structure of all human life will lead him to a full understanding of himself as a composite and unified being, what he calls in *The Autobiography* the "re-creation of the man through . . . art, the birth of a new species of man" (A, 183).

> I need some mind that, if the cannon sound
> From every quarter of the world, can stay
> Wound in mind's pondering,
> As mummies in the mummy-cloth are wound;
> Because I have a marvellous thing to say, . . .
> Such thought, that in it bound
> I need no other thing,
> Wound in mind's wandering
> As mummies in the mummy-cloth are wound.
>
> (V, 303–5)

Northrop Frye should appreciate Yeats's understanding of the abstract structure of *A Vision* as geometric "arrangements of experience," for Frye sees the genre of romance as comprising a comparatively bare "narrative structure," free of representational or realistic detail, "just as a cubist or primitive painting would present the geometrical forms of its images more directly than straight representation would do." Also, like Yeats's *A Vision*, Frye's conception of romance is of the "imagination, left to itself, [producing] the rigidly conventionalized," with the "formulaic unit" being the "cornerstone of the creative imagination, the simplest form of what I call an archetype." Moreover, within this archetypal structure is the "standard romance pattern of a double identity": "At the bottom of the mythological universe is a death and rebirth process which cares nothing for the individual; at the top is the individual's regained identity."[69] The individual falls from identity and struggles back toward it, thereby remaking his identity in a journey that is typically identified as the "heroic quest." This journey is itself a "spiral form, an open circle where the end is the beginning transformed and renewed by the heroic quest." All this sounds remarkably Yeatsian, with particular reference to *A Vision*, and it illuminates the significance of that work: "The journey toward one's own identity, which literature does so much to help with, has a great deal to do with escaping from the alleged 'reality' of what one is reading or looking at, and recognizing the convention behind it."[70]

Frye's comment is a fair summary of the experiences of the Yeatsian persona in *A Vision*. The "I" progresses in this work from the passive reception of information about life to an imaginative comprehension of a structure symbolic of life's archetypal characteristics. From an even wider perspective, the Yeatsian persona has experienced both the need to structure the chaos of empirical detail in *The Autobiography* and the complementary need to examine such concrete detail within the stark structure of *A Vision*. The final union of life and structure is foreseen in the persona's development in these two works, but the persona does not achieve an absolute unity of "style and attitude" in the prose, since *The Autobiography* and *A Vision* perfect different aspects of the union, even while recognizing the ultimate need for a medium in which they can naturally and un-self-consciously merge. It is poetry that affords Yeats traditional structures which can be realized in personal details; as Yeats says, "prose, unlike verse, had not those simple forms that like a masquer's mask protect us with their anonymity."[71] *The Collected Poems* is the complete structure of Yeats's quest toward this unified identity, in which the development of the persona constitutes the unification itself.

4
"Whither?":
The Quest for a Unified Identity

NEAR the end of his life Yeats wrote "A General Introduction for My Work" to clarify the implications of his lifetime of creative labor, both for himself and for his readers. At the end of the essay, Yeats defends his poetics of self-concern by contrast to the newly emerging generation of "young English poets" who "reject dream and personal emotion" and write to celebrate not the self but the objective world, "that they may be modern":

> Young men teaching school in some picturesque cathedral town, or settled for life in Capri or in Sicily, defend their type of metaphor by saying that it comes naturally to a man who travels to his work by Tube. . . . As they express not what the Upanishads call "that ancient Self" but individual intellect, they have the right to choose the man in the Tube because of his objective importance.[1]

Ironically, these more "modern" poets seem light-years behind Yeats, for he has anticipated their objective art of individuality which causes the "egg" of unity of being "instead of hatching" to "burst,"[2] and all of his work has been a battle against this gratuitous disintegration of identity. Yeats thus presents himself in the peculiar role of responding to his own poetic successors, as if he were their heir:

> I am joined to the "Irishry" and I expect a counter-Renaissance. . . . I make no complaint; I am accustomed to the geometrical arrangement of history in *A Vision*, but I go deeper than "custom" for my convictions. When I stand upon O'Connell Bridge in the half-light and notice that discordant architecture, all those electric signs, where modern

heterogeneity has taken physical form, a vague hatred comes up out of
my own dark and I am certain that wherever in Europe there are minds
strong enough to lead others the same vague hatred rises; in four or five
or in less generations this hatred will have issued in violence and imposed some kind of rule of kindred. I cannot know the nature of that
rule, for its opposite fills the light; all I can do to bring it nearer is to
intensify my hatred.[3]

What Yeats hates in "modern heterogeneity" is the denial of the
possibility of unity of being, the abandonment of the quest for an
integrity of identity. The new English poets, as Yeats portrays
them, are far from pursuing unity of being; they are fundamentally
insincere in choosing to live their lives one way (in beautiful places
reminiscent of integrated cultures of the past) while celebrating the
antithesis of that life-style in their work (the man dominated by an
objective, mechanical environment, symbolized by the "Tube").
Yeats's response to this disunity of being that allows the separation
of internal values from external events is one of hatred, hatred as an
emotion that liberates the self. In hating rather than accepting
disunity, Yeats at least keeps open the possibility of unity of being.

The "counter-Renaissance" that Yeats expects is, again paradoxically, akin to the literary renaissance in Ireland that Yeats did so
much to advance early in his career, in that Yeats expects it to
celebrate the union of the individual, empirical self to ideal archetypes it expresses. Yeats feels that modern poets have forgotten or
denied that archetypal aspect of the self, which he has expressed in
the specific terms of Irish mythology and in the more abstract
terms of *A Vision,* and Yeats sees this lapse on the part of poets as
being most serious, for it is the poet above all men who has the
ability to merge individual and archetypal selves, or style and attitude, in his work. The very rules of structure in art, as Yeats
discusses them in the preceding section of "A General Introduction for My Work," enable the poet to achieve a transcendence of
the personal into universal issues and identities. Thomas Parkinson
puts it well:

> The aim of poetry is paradoxically to individualize and generalize at
> once; the fully rendered particular image must, under the pressure of
> poetic art, become the universally cognizable general symbol; through
> the poet's language the individual person must become the universal
> type; what is essential to the artist must become common to the race.[4]

Parkinson finds that "Yeats trusted the poem, and as he moved from initial shape to final form he learned through that process the meaning of his work and destiny.["]5 An analysis of any of Yeats's revisions of a poem in manuscript, especially of those that develop from conception in prose to final publishable form, shows that Yeats did use the discipline of art to raise empirical feelings to archetypal significance:

> [Yeats] shaped rather than merely voiced the ideas and feelings that came to him in the accidents of experience, but the manuscripts do not reveal a poet performing acts of composition out of the stale habit of being a writer. Instead they display the coöperative action of craftsmanlike knowledge, intense feeling, dramatic imagination, laborious thought, and passionate apprehension of immediate qualitative experience. Yeats thought of such an action as a reconciliation of opposites, a marriage of sun and moon, an approximation to Unity of Being possible only, perhaps, in the "marmorean stillness" of his study. Poetry for him was a transmuting process that liberated a man to the greatest realization of his possibilities.[6]

Yeats's autobiography is also a record of his early realization of, and lifelong commitment to, the concept of art as a realm where "personal utterance" transcends "egotism" through the development of style into attitude. He says in *The Autobiography* of himself, "To oppose the new ill-breeding of Ireland, . . . I can only set up a secondary or interior personality created out of the tradition of myself, . . . (alas, only possible to me in my writings)." His analyses of other poets, both in *The Autobiography* and in other contexts, frequently refer to the poet's life as an "experiment in living" that is embodied in his verse:

> I have no sympathy with the mid-Victorian thought to which Tennyson gave his support, that a poet's life concerns nobody but himself. A poet is by the very nature of things a man who lives with entire sincerity, or rather the better his poetry the more sincere his life; his life is an experiment in living and those that come after have a right to know it. Above all it is necessary that the lyric poet's life should be known that we should understand that his poetry is no rootless flower but the speech of a man. To achieve anything in any art, to stand alone perhaps for many years, to go a path no other man has gone, to accept one's own thought when the thought of others has the authority of the world behind it, that it should seem but a little thing to give one's life as well as one's words which are so much nearer to one's soul, to the criticism of the world.[7]

Richard Ellmann discusses the close alliance of artistic style and personal morality in Yeats in a manner that illuminates Yeats's characteristic assimilation of impersonal form and personal experience in verse:

> Stages of stylistic development were stages of personal development. . . . Every poem embodies a schematization, conscious as well as unconscious, of his way of living and seeing; and all his poems form a larger scheme which we can watch in the process of evolving. The stature of his work, which seems to tower over that of his contemporaries, comes largely from this ultimate adhesion of part to part to form a whole.[8]

Several critics have identified "stages" in Yeats's poetic canon; division of poems into early, middle, and late stages is quite common. However, few critics other than Ellmann have argued for a consistent development or an integrated maturation of the poet in the poetry. Northrop Frye is one who does; he characterizes Yeats's growth as metamorphic:

> His technique, his ideas, his attitude to life, are in a constant state of revolution and metamorphosis. He belongs with Goethe and Beethoven, not with the artists who simply unfold, like Blake and Mozart. This phenomenon of metamorphic growth, which must surely have reached its limit in Picasso, seems to be comparatively new in the arts. . . . Yeats, then, may have been compelled to "grow" by a personal search for symbols.[9]

Fundamentally, both Ellmann and Frye are concerned with Yeats's search for identity through the vehicle of poetry; they differ only in that Ellmann sees the progress as largely intentional and inner-directed on Yeats's part, whereas Frye sees it as accidental and dictated by external circumstances. These two related positions parallel Yeats's theories of self and anti-self or *anima hominis* and *anima mundi;* they are complementary perspectives on the persona in the verse. The important point that Ellmann and Frye seem to hold in common is that it is the continuity and integrity of identity of Yeats's *one* poetic persona (and *not* a succession of masks) that unifies the poetic canon. Yeats's poetic canon is a record of the confrontation and conglomeration of personality and form, or empirical and transcendent selves in one poetic identity; it resembles best what Harold Bloom has called the internalized quest-romance: "The poet takes the patterns of quest-romance and transposes them into his own imaginative life, so that the entire rhythm of the quest is heard again in the movement of the poet himself from poem to poem."[10]

Yeats does not consciously "take" and "transpose" the quest structure into his lyric canon, as he does, for instance, in his epic narrative poem, "The Wanderings of Oisin,"[11] which was written as one artistic unit with a preconceived story line. Rather, Yeats discovers or enacts or embodies the quest structure through the interrelations of the lyrics that comprise *The Collected Poems*—bit by bit, in the process of his search for unity of being through the attempted assimilation in each poem of empirical and transcendent identities. In effect, Yeats's conscious quest for an integrated identity leads him unconsciously through the larger structure of an archetypal quest. The persona never "knows" in any one poem that he is attaining unity of being; he rather "embodies" it through his actions *in toto*. In *The Collected Poems*, as in life itself, the poet cannot see the final form as long as he is in the process of becoming that form. The poet differs from others only in having faith in that larger form and in attempting to live up to it, "with entire sincerity," as Yeats puts it, much as the hero of the traditional literary quest has faith in the existence of the object of his efforts and disciplines his life to attaining it. The empirical poet, Yeats or Tennyson, does not achieve unity of being in his life, but his poetic double does achieve this unity in that the persona of the lyric canon embodies the process of becoming within the whole structure of being, which is the quest archetype.

Yeats's comment on the relation of life and art in regard to Tennyson addresses this union of becoming and being in the persona within the structure of a quest, since he sees the lyric poet's "experiment in living" to be reflected in his achievement "in art." Yeats identifies in that comment four stages in the lyric poet's quest: "to stand alone perhaps for many years, to go a path no other man has gone, to accept one's own thought when the thought of others has the authority of the world behind it, . . . to give one's life as well as one's words . . . to the criticism of the world." In Yeats's scheme, the poet may not realize until the last stage of his quest that his life has actually taken such form, and then he can consciously dedicate personal life as well as artistic work to its implications. Up to that final stage of realization, the quest is a lonely one, consisting primarily of personal sincerity, of being true to internal direction even in the face of all external contradictions and distractions. Yeats's persona moves through these four stages in *The Collected Poems*.

Harold Bloom identifies two general periods in the internalized quest, but these periods partially contradict the movement that Yeats describes from internally to externally directed attention:

> Generally, Prometheus is the poet-as-hero in the first stage of his quest, marked by deep involvement in political, social, and literary revolution, and a direct, even satirical attack on the institutional or-thodoxies of European and English society. . . . The Real Man, the Imagination [of Blake], emerges after terrible crises in the major stage of the Romantic quest, which is typified by a relative disengagement from revolutionary activism, and a standing aside from polemic and satire, so as to bring the search within the self and its ambiguities.[12]

Bloom is concerned with how the Romantic poets have "internalized" the traditional literary quest, which involves a hero and his confrontations with dragons and the like on the road to attaining a sacred object or achieving an ideal act. As he does with the modern connotations of the word *persona*, however, Yeats over-looks the modern connotations of internalizing the quest and focuses on the classical qualities of the quest itself, much as Frye has defined it: "Translated into dream terms, the quest-romance is the search of the libido or desiring self for a fulfillment that will deliver it from the anxieties of reality but will still contain that reality."[13] Thus, the quest may be characterized as an effort to unite real and ideal, whether that union be internal or external. The classical external quest, though, as Frye outlines it, involves more subtle gradations of experience than Bloom's internal quest and more fully resembles the four stages that Yeats identifies in his comments on Tennyson and enacts in his poetic canon through his persona.

Where Bloom locates only two phases, Frye finds six.[14] Phase one, the "myth of the birth of the hero," is irrelevant to Yeats's lyric canon, as Yeats's persona is in the process of discovering a quest and not relating the completed quest of his own life from beginning to end. Phase two, however, resembles Yeats's first stage of standing alone and even more strongly evokes the atmo-sphere of Yeats's early poetry, that of the first three volumes in *The Collected Poems*: "Crossways," "The Rose," and "The Wind Among the Reeds."

> The second phase brings us to the innocent youth of the hero. . . . In literature this phase presents a pastoral and Arcadian world, generally a pleasant wooded landscape, full of glades, shaded valleys, murmuring brooks, the moon, and other images closely linked with the female or maternal aspect of sexual imagery. . . . It is often a world of magic or desirable law, and it tends to center on a youthful hero, still over-shadowed by parents, surrounded by youthful companions. The archetype of erotic innocence is less commonly marriage than the kind of "chaste" love that precedes marriage; the love of brother for sister, or of two boys for each other. Hence, though in later phases it is often recalled as a lost happy time or Golden Age, the sense of being close to a moral taboo is very frequent. . . . [There is a] feeling of malaise and longing to enter a world of action.

This is a period of extreme self-consciousness, as the hero is aware simultaneously of the ideal, inner-directed innocence of youth and the real, outer-directed experience of maturity. Yeats's phrase for this stage, "to stand alone," captures the lonely experience of the first confrontation of transcendent and empirical aspects of identity.

Frye's phase three is the "normal quest theme," which involves the physical confrontation of ideal and real or good and evil, often in terms of hero versus dragon. This phase, like the first, is not fully relevant to Yeats's canon, since it involves a consciousness of intention that Yeats's mode of discovery does not allow. Rather, Yeats's second stage of taking a path different from all others constitutes, in effect, Yeats's confrontation in the persona of idealistic hero and empirical world, in the more general terms of Frye's phase four: "In romance the central theme of this phase is that of the maintaining of the integrity of the innocent world against the assault of experience," where the "integrated body to be defended may be individual or social, or both." With Yeats, it is both individual and social; the social poetry of his early theater years, that of "In the Seven Woods," "From 'The Green Helmet and Other Poems,'" and "Responsibilities," seeks to maintain the personal integrity of innocence found in the early poetry as well as the ideal society that supports that innocence.

In Frye's fifth phase, as in Yeats's third, the hero withdraws from conflict but continues to meditate on the opposing natures of his internal ideals and the social reality, "to accept one's own thought when the thought of others has the authority of the world behind it":

> The fifth phase . . . is a reflective, idyllic view of experience from above, in which the movement of the natural cycle has usually a prominent place. It deals with a world very similar to that of the second phase [Yeats's first stage] except that the mood is a contemplative withdrawal from or sequel to action rather than a youthful preparation for it. It is, like the second phase, an erotic world, but it presents experience as comprehended and not as a mystery.

The poetry of Yeats's philosophic period, in "The Wild Swans at Coole" and "Michael Robartes and the Dancer," does indeed present a reflective, contemplative persona re-creating imaginatively the ideals he has conceived in innocent youth. This period is analogous to the Blakean concept of organized innocence; the real world is accepted but refined into similarity to the ideal.

Finally, following this reorganization, the hero/persona moves into, as it were, his ideal real world, in "The Tower," "The Winding Stair and Other Poems," and "Last Poems," making his "life as well as [his] words" symbolic of his experience and open to the "criticism of the world." Frye calls this final state the *"penseroso* phase" and characterizes it as marking the "end of a movement from active to contemplative adventure": "A central image of this phase, a favorite of Yeats, is that of the old man in the tower, the lonely hermit absorbed in occult or magical studies." Whereas Frye remarks that this phase also borders on the fairy tale, or what he terms "cuddle fiction," Yeats lived in his tower as well as writing of it; it was no escape from reality but a symbolic expression of an alternative reality.[15] Yeats's poetic persona has its empirical roots in the historical poet but its transcendent potential in the archetypal form of art itself; the "I" of *The Collected Poems,* that is, steers a middle course between the "I"s of *The Autobiography* and *A Vision.* Yeats's quest differs from the traditional literary quest in that its object is not preconceived and fully identifiable, such as the Holy Grail, but is itself the process of becoming. The quest for unity of being is completed with the persona's realization, at the end of the poetic canon, of the form his life has taken; that conscious identification of process and product within the persona himself is the fulfillment of the quest and the consummation of unity.

The only extended analysis to date of the quest for unity of being in the persona of *The Collected Poems* is the doctoral dissertation of Bryant Edward Hoffman, entitled "This Sedentary Trade: Aesthetic Unity and the Poet-*Persona* in the Lyric Poetry of William Butler Yeats." Hoffman focuses on any poetic character, the "I" of Yeats himself or the voice of his other speakers, which he believes to represent a poet-figure, a "manifestation of Yeats's secondary, aesthetic personality." Hoffman also sees four stages of development in the canon, in which Yeats "seems to move from a traditional, popular poet-figure to a private, subjective one, and then after his formulation of the systems contained within *Per Amica Silentia Lunae* and *A Vision,* he combines them to create a *speaker* at once intensely personal and totally objective."[16] Since Hoffman allows that any voice speaking for the concerns of the poet may be analyzed within this scheme of development, his findings are not fully applicable to the one continuous voice of the poet, his "I." Any critical implications regarding the persona's development must be subordinate to controls on the figure being examined. In the romantic quest itself, there is only one hero who progresses through all six phases from birth to *"penseroso"* maturity. He confronts other characters, but they are tangential to the internal development of the quester. Likewise, in Yeats's poetic canon, there is only one character that appears from beginning to end, and that is the anonymous "I"— anonymous because it lacks the external or objective identity the other poetic characters have, but ultimately it is the voice of the meditating poet himself, the two being linked by common empirical experience. It is this poetic identity, this "I," that develops through *The Collected Poems* in parallel with the empirical development of W. B. Yeats through his life and functions as subject and object of the quest structure. Yeats's poetic persona is, in essence, the skeleton of the poetic canon, the continuity of identity on which the many other variegated poetic characters depend for the structural context that gives them value and meaning.

Under the quadripartite quest structure, the first period, which is usually designated as that of Yeats's "early poetry," includes the first three sections of *The Collected Poems,* "Crossways," "The Rose," and "The Wind among the Reeds," and differs markedly in tone from the succeeding satirical volumes. This is the period of "innocent youth" and dawning recognition of internal ideals. The "I" of these early poems, however, is often assumed to be also the voice of various objective poetic characters and is frequently criticized for being more abstract essence than concrete identity:

> In Yeats' later work the image of the poet is objectified and can be studied within the context of the poetry itself; but in the early poetry . . . all reference to personality is excluded by the canon of "purity" and the image of the poet must be constructed. That is not to say that the early poetry is any less autobiographical than the later; merely that it is so purely psychological that its processes have been rendered virtually anonymous.[17]

In making this evaluation, Allen Grossman fails to distinguish the subjective poetic "I" from other objective poetic characters. The poetic "I" makes relatively few appearances in these early books, but when he does he is always differentiated from other poetic voices by the absence of name or title. Only two poems in "Cross-ways," for instance, present Yeats's poetic persona rather than a dramatic speaker: "To an Isle in the Water" and "Down by the Salley Gardens." All other poems in the section, such as the first two, "The Song of the Happy Shepherd" and "The Sad Shepherd," are obvious dramatizations of fairly standard poetic characters: shepherds, lovers, kings. The happy shepherd's song is expressive of the characteristics of the poetic persona of this period, as are all the other poems in the early books. This character argues that words and dreams only are good and true, that the eternal reality is internal, and that external reality is temporal. The shepherd thus recognizes that the ideal he knows from a golden past conflicts with empirical reality, but he does not enter the conflict. The recognition and the warning suffice. Such poems spoken by objective poetic characters thus state variations on the themes that are preoccupying the persona in that particular stage of development.

Similarly, the "I" of "To an Isle in the Water" (CP, 20) and "Down by the Salley Gardens" (CP, 20) perceives a difference between what he intuitively expects of life and how it actually turns out, but he acts out this recognition rather than speaking of it didactically. In the first simple lyric, domestic life and dreamy flight exist paradoxically side by side:

> She carries in the dishes,
> And lays them in a row.
> To an isle in the water
> With her I would go.

The difference between this poetic persona and the happy shepherd is one of intention. The shepherd expounds a doctrine to an audience that simultaneously embodies the empirical realm against which he protests and represents a body of potential converts to his idealist philosophy. The "I" of "To an Isle in the Water" is conscious of no audience, not even in the person of the "shy one" he observes; he can hardly even be described as speaking. The poem is more a meditation: a moment of recognition that real and ideal exist separately but as complements, and an act of mind that momentarily unites them.

> Underlying the *Crossways* poems, and indeed all of Yeats's work, is the assumption that there is some transcendent unity which will embrace the seemingly irreconcilable antinomies of the real and the ideal. . . . Although ultimate unity may lie far beyond human attainment, it is deemed no less worthy of the poet's commitment, because the poet's imagination insists upon its reality even if it cannot be seen in the limited world of the senses.[18]

Frank Murphy's analysis of "Crossways" applies to all its poetic speakers, but where the dramatic characters vocalize these concerns, the poetic persona enacts them, through mental discovery or imaginative embodiment. In "Down by the Salley Gardens" (CP, 20), the persona similarly unites a memory of ideal love with an expression of real pain of loss by juxtaposing the two in his poetic lament. The agony of loss is implicit in the glow of love, and it is only because the persona, "being young and foolish," ignores the inevitable impingement of real on ideal that he unwittingly sacrifices what he would keep to what he would banish and ends "full of tears."

Almost as if in response to this loss of ideal love precipitated by ignorance of the real world, the persona of the subsequent collection, "The Rose," speaks in a more aggressive tone and with a conscious resolution to look steadily at the opposing elements of real and ideal experience and to attempt to unite them:

> Yeats announces in the first poem of *The Rose* his confident conviction that there *is* something better: a mystic wisdom which will compensate for all such miseries by revealing them as only a portion of a vast and orderly scheme of creation. . . . He will seek the eternal in the ephemeral, the mystic in the commonplace, and the ideal in the real. Whereas in *Crossways* such antinomies constituted polar opposites, in *The Rose* they have become intermixed to such a degree that one force is contained within its opposite. . . . As Yeats moves from the basically egocentric search of *Crossways* to a more objective and vigorous confrontation with experience, *The Rose* poems show evidence of his

keener consciousness of the physical world and its inhabitants. Obviously such an expanded scope is necessary if one seeks reconciliation through a vision of the entire cosmos and its pattern.[19]

"Down by the Salley Gardens" and "To an Isle in the Water" demonstrate an intermixture of real and ideal even in "Crossways," but Murphy's observations on the greater vigor and objectivity of vision in "The Rose" poems are largely true. In part, this enhancement of poetic power and control is the result of a discovery of the infinite suggestibility in the rose symbol. Yeats need no longer portray the confrontation of real and ideal in terms of the conflicting personal emotions they evoke when he can project them into the paradoxical temporal/transcendent symbol of the rose. Richard Ellmann reveals one such application of the symbol's value, as Yeats knew it from his apprenticeship in the occult tradition:

> The conjunction of rose and cross . . . is the central myth of Rosicrucianism. . . . The conjunction is often referred to as a "mystic marriage," as the transfiguring ecstasy which occurs when the adept, after the long pain and self-sacrifice of the quest in this world, a world in which opposites are forever quarrelling, finds his cross—the symbol of that struggle and opposition—suddenly blossom with the rose of love, harmony, and beauty.[20]

In "To the Rose upon the Rood of Time" (CP, 31), the rose as well as the rood symbolizes the dialectical nature of the quest rather than its fulfillment. In this introductory poem, which Murphy identifies as "perhaps the first time we can confidently assume that we hear the poet's own voice rather than that of a persona [character],"[21] the confrontation of ideal and real is both thematic and structural, anticipating the later poetic dialogues of self and soul.

Yeats's note on the rose symbol, that the "quality symbolized as The Rose differs from the Intellectual Beauty of Shelley and of Spenser in that I have imagined it as suffering with man and not as something pursued and seen from afar" (CP, 447), applies obviously to this first rose poem. The first stanza celebrates the magical, mystical powers of the symbolic rose:

> Red Rose, proud Rose, sad Rose of all my days!
> Come near me, while I sing the ancient ways. . . .
> Come near, that no more blinded by man's fate,

> I find under the boughs of love and hate,
> In all poor foolish things that live a day,
> Eternal beauty wandering on her way.

The rose thus embodies a transcendent power; by contemplating it, the persona seems to rise out of empirical "fate" and into the untainted realm of the "eternal" ideal. Notably, however, Yeats places that ideal world not in some far-off heaven but among other images of the world of fate, "under the boughs of love and hate." As a result, the persona finds in the second stanza that he must temper the power of that ideal aspect of the rose's symbolic nature by insisting on its empirical roots:

> Come near, come near, come near—Ah, leave me still
> A little space for the rose-breath to fill!
> Lest I no more hear common things that crave . . .
> And learn to chaunt a tongue men do not know.

Murphy reads this thematic/structural duality of the rose not in terms of vacillation, as Harold Bloom does, not in Ellmann's terms of the fulfillment of a quest, but as being essentially "*about* the need for balance in the new quest to which the poet is committing himself."[22] Certainly the persona is embarking on a quest in this poem rather than completing one, and the quest is presented in terms of finding a middle road between ideal and real and of embodying that reconciliation in the balancing act of mind which is the poem. And the goal of the quest, unity of a dualistic being, is embodied in, symbolized in, the rose.

"To the Rose upon the Rood of Time" is thus the signal poem of the persona's first stage of development; the poems that follow in "The Rose" and "The Wind among the Reeds" are stronger for being built on the persona's "innocent" and youthful belief in his ability to merge real and ideal. "The Lake Isle of Innisfree" (CP, 39), for instance, is a much more powerful poem than its thematic predecessor, "To an Isle in the Water," because the slightly more self-conscious persona of the later poem describes in detail his idealized real world rather than merely referring to it. Yeats has described "The Lake Isle of Innisfree" as "my first lyric with anything in its rhythm of my own music"[23] and has recorded in several sources his boyhood memories of the island. The autobiographical context for the poetic persona increases steadily from this point through *The Collected Poems*, lending concreteness of detail to the poem's aesthetic structures and liberating the "I" from confusion with the archetypal poetic characters of other poems. Rather than hiding the autobiographical origins of his poems, Yeats obviously wanted his readers to be aware of them; thus he discussed them openly in many sources. The autobiographical element is, however, only one facet of the dialectic the persona embodies, the empirical aspect; the persona moves in the poem between this empirical grounding and an aesthetic ideal:

> I will arise and go now, for always night and day
> I hear lake water lapping with low sounds by the shore;
> While I stand on the roadway, or on the pavements grey,
> I hear it in the deep heart's core.

In this poem, the persona attains internally an idealized mental landscape, whereas in life the poet was impeded from physically visiting the island either by his residence in London or by his fear of the forest ranger.[24] A similar historical irony lies behind the composition of "The White Birds" (CP, 41); A. N. Jeffares reveals that the poem was written in response to an expression of affection for sea gulls by Maud Gonne the day after she refused Yeats's first proposal of marriage.[25] In poetry, if not in life, the real can become the ideal, with some readjustment of symbolic identity:

> I am haunted by numberless islands, and many a Danaan shore,
> Where Time would surely forget us, and Sorrow come near us
>   no more;
> Soon far from the rose and the lily and the fret of the flames
>   would we be,
> Were we only white birds, my beloved, buoyed out on the foam
>   of the sea!

Other than their autobiographical context, another historically distinguishing factor of the persona poems is their relative freedom from Yeats's characteristically thorough textual revisions. Although many of the early character poems undergo extensive rewrites between printings, often to the extent of alterations in meaning for the purpose of purging "passages that are sentimental from lack of thought,"[26] the "I" poems in *The Collected Poems* exist largely unrevised. In the major revisions of "The Dedication to a Book of Stories Selected from the Irish Novelists" (CP, 44–45), for example, the connotations of Ireland and Irish tradition are considerably altered,[27] but the persona's metaphorical action of tearing a branch from the tree of Irish tradition and re-presenting it as a book of Irish stories is unchanged. Obviously, Yeats's historical act of publishing such a book renders the poetic act permanent, but the fact that the actions of the "I" in its other appearances are also hardly retouched argues that Yeats chooses to or is able to speak through the poetic "I" only when he is confident of the sincerity of his expression. In a letter to his father written in 1913, Yeats distinguishes between poems of poetic characters and poems of the poetic persona:

> My dear Father: I thought your letter about "portraiture" being "pain" most beautiful and profound. All our art is but the putting our faith and the evidence of our faith into words or forms and our faith is in ecstasy. Of recent years instead of "vision," meaning by vision the intense realization of a state of ecstatic emotion symbolized in a definite imaginative region, I have tried for more self-portraiture. I have tried to make my work convincing with a speech so natural and dramatic that the hearer would feel the presence of a man thinking and feeling.[28]

This letter explains not only the increasing proportion of "I" poems in the canon but also some of the logic behind Yeats's revisions. When seeking to transmit or attain "vision," Yeats employs poetic characters, each in essence a "definite imaginative region," to embody the vision. Hence, "The Lamentation of the Old Pensioner" (CP, 45–46) employs the archetypal *senex* figure to transmit an emotional insight the young Yeats could never have embodied in his own poetic persona, not only because the insight develops from old age but because it is thus also a limited (albeit intense) meaning: "I spit into the face of Time / That has transfigured me."

Yeats thus felt it necessary to revise his character poems more frequently because one limited vision is harder to create and maintain than the process of experience that the "I" expresses. A later Yeats would be understandably more tempted to perfect an abstract vision or alter it to reflect his more mature concerns than he would be to tamper with the concrete expression in his poetic persona of a stage in his own poetic development.[29] Yeats takes great care to distinguish poems of limited vision and poetic character from poems of present "thinking and feeling"; Yeats identifies character poems as such by naming the characters in the poems' titles, thereby conferring objective existence on them, and/or by structuring the poems as dramatic monologues, dialogues, or dramatic scenes. The unnamed "I" proceeds from the only poetic character that can actually think and feel in the poem—Yeats himself. The development of the poetic persona in the first stage of its quest from and beyond these other poetic characters also suggests that the archetypal identities that Yeats intuited in such traditional figures were being slowly internalized and united to the personal concrete identity, enabling the personal to expand into more universal modes of expression. Those other characters, as Yeats suggests in the final two poems of "The Rose," represent an epical, racial, traditional ground out of which the individual persona emerges, a ground akin to the supernatural world, the "anima mundi," and the "anti-self" of the prose. Yeats suggests as much in these lines from "To Some I Have Talked with by the Fire" (CP, 49):

> While I wrought out these fitful Danaan rhymes,
> My heart would brim with dreams about the times
> When we bent down above the fading coals
> And talked of the dark folk who live in souls
> Of passionate men, like bats in the dead trees . . .;

and in these from "To Ireland in the Coming Times" (CP, 49–50):

> *Know, that I would accounted be*
> *True brother of a company*
> *That sang, to sweeten Ireland's wrong,*
> *Ballad and story, rann and song. . . .*
> *Nor may I less be counted one*
> *With Davis, Mangan, Ferguson,*
> *Because, to him who ponders well,*
> *My rhymes more than their rhyming tell*
> *Of things discovered in the deep,*
> *Where only body's laid asleep. . . .*
> *I cast my heart into my rhymes,*
> *That you, in the dim coming times,*
> *May know how my heart went with them*
> *After the red-rose-bordered hem.*

Following this poetic statement of personal commitment, the absence of the poetic persona from the next volume, "The Wind among the Reeds," is puzzling. Archetypal characters abound, and in only one poem, "The Secret Rose" (CP, 67), does the "I" speak in its own right: "I, too, await / The hour of thy great wind of love and hate." Rather than aiming at self-expression in this poem, however, the persona seeks to be "enfolded" by the mystical rose and made one with the heroic characters of Irish mythology; that is, the "I" awaits identity to be imposed from without rather than generating it from within, through "thinking and feeling." The only voices that achieve anything resembling "self-portraiture" in this volume are curiously labeled in the third person in the poem's titles, as "He" or "The Lover," and the printing history of these poems reveals that they were originally written as the "visions" of objective poetic characters, one vision often being shuffled from one named character to another.[30] In the first printing of "The Wind among the Reeds" (1899), in which the titles still name poetic characters although the number of different names has been reduced from those that occur in the original separate publications of the poems, Yeats explains that "Aedh," "Hanrahan," and "Michael Robartes" are used "more as principles of the mind than as actual personages":

> Hanrahan is the simplicity of an imagination too changeable to gather permanent possessions, or the adoration of the shepherds; and Michael Robartes is the pride of the imagination brooding upon the greatness of its possessions, or the adoration of the Magi; while Aedh is the myrrh and frankincense that the imagination offers continually before all that it loves.[31]

Aedh, Robartes, and Hanrahan thus represent isolated (if esoteric) facets of the poet's own imagination. Perhaps this objectification of these elements, which ordinarily constitute the poetic persona, as external poetic characters indicates a rapid and fitful growth in Yeats's understanding of his persona's potential to embody an artistic unity of being in terms of projections of the transcendent aspect of identity. Allen Grossman, in his study of the volume, suggests as much:

> *The Wind among the Reeds* is a history of the poet's archetypal self-finding the achievement of which, though necessarily incomplete, enables him to emerge after 1900 as if reborn into a new phase of life characterized by portraiture of a self which had not previously existed as a creative possibility. . . . The period of Yeats's development [in *The Wind among the Reeds*] . . . is the moment prior to the irony which the

ironic medium of twentieth-century poetry was to take as its subject matter. Above all, however, it is evidence of a great mind struggling in a complex proto-modern culture toward that archetypal self-identification which is the substance of all poetic knowledge.

Where Grossman concludes, however, that the turn to archetypal identity in "The Wind among the Reeds" involves the "extinction of personality" and the abolition of "personal identity" as an "abstract unity,"[32] Richard Ellmann recognizes that the archetypalism of this volume is essentially a misjudgment on Yeats's part, fine as the poems are in their own right:

> *The Wind Among the Reeds* . . . reflects this intention. . . . Only at those moments when we lose ourselves and become archetypal can poetry be made. Certainly there is only idealization, and no indication of "our own excited faces" in the book. Although the poems use "I" and "we" freely, they are curiously anonymous and devoid of intimacy. . . . This was the distilled self, archetypal and not personal. . . . In his attempt to guard against reproducing what was merely intimate and transitory, Yeats fell into a more remote art than he intended.[33]

The structural development of the persona through *The Collected Poems* would seem to bear out Ellman's contention that the abstract archetypalism of the "I" in "The Wind among the Reeds" is an anomaly, since the subsequent volumes reintroduce a highly autobiographical poetic persona. However, Grossman's observation on the proto-ironic mood of the volume is useful in reading the poems within the volume itself. In his gradual refinement of so many of the poetic characters from named personages to states of mind abstractly referred to as "He," Yeats has apparently attempted to implant the capacity for limited but objective visions into his subjective persona. Yeats was not entirely successful—the "He"s in the titles mix oddly with the "I"s speaking in the poems—but the poems are consequently valuable for the insights they provide into this conflict of external and internal, or objective and subjective, aspects of the poetic identity.

Irony is perhaps unintentional in many of these poems, but it is an inevitable consequence of the disjunction of inner and outer. The title character in "The Lover Tells of the Rose in His Heart" (CP, 54), for example, wishes to honor his beloved by re-creating the empirical world as a golden casket, and the speaker of "He Remembers Forgotten Beauty" (CP, 60–61) confuses internal ideals and empirical reality and abandons the latter to the former:

"When my arms wrap you round I press / My heart upon the loveliness / That has long faded from the world." If, as Ellmann argues, Yeats pursues such abstractions in this volume to escape a reductive subjectivity, he also ultimately sacrifices the foundation of the real world and the very body of his beloved in the process— a compromise with the duality of identity that he previously rejects in defining his quest as one of embodying both real and ideal in "To the Rose upon the Rood of Time." The attempt to objectify subjective vision results, paradoxically, in granting the subjective vision an unwarranted power over its own originator. Whereas in previous volumes the persona envisions the ideal in images from the natural world (rose, bird, island) but internalizes those images in the process of mediating real and ideal, suddenly in this volume, the internal ideal comes to seem external and apocalyptic and annihilates the persona's process of mediation.

A comparison of "To an Isle in the Water" to "He Hears the Cry of the Sedge" (CP, 65), a poem of similar concern in "The Wind among the Reeds," reveals the magnitude of the change:

> I wander by the edge
> Of this desolate lake
> Where wind cries in the sedge:
> *Until the axle break*
> *That keeps the stars in their round,*
> *And hands hurl in the deep*
> *The banners of East and West,*
> *And the girdle of light is unbound,*
> *Your breast will not lie by the breast*
> *Of your beloved in sleep.*

Perhaps this turn-of-the-century apocalyptic mood that pervades the volume is what prevents the speakers of these poems from assimilating vision and life; one seems to preclude the other. This extremely radical idealism, however, is still expressive of the first stage of "innocent youth" in the persona's quest for a unified identity. Magic, chaste love, and the "feeling of malaise and longing to enter a world of action," which Frye identifies as its characteristics, are all in evidence. The desire to achieve unity of being is ever apparent, as well, and only the means of implementation are lacking, itself a proof of innocence, as in "He Wishes for the Cloths of Heaven" (CP, 70):

> Had I the heavens' embroidered cloths,
> Enwrought with golden and silver light,

The blue and the dim and the dark cloths
Of night and light and the half-light,
I would spread the cloths under your feet:
But I, being poor, have only my dreams;
I have spread my dreams under your feet;
Tread softly because you tread on my dreams.

The next three volumes in *The Collected Poems* make up the
second stage in the development of Yeats's poetic "I," and in them
the persona makes an abrupt turn from his previous preoccupation
with the ideal to a confrontation with the real. Specific place
names, concrete physical details, and autobiographical allusions all
serve to anchor this poetry and its persona in the empirical world.
At first this concentration on the real world would seem to contradict Frye's characterization of this phase in the quest archetype
as the "maintaining of the integrity of the innocent world" of the
first phase "against the assault of experience," but on closer inspec-
tion it is clear that the persona addresses the empirical world precisely in order to manipulate it into relation with the ideal despite
itself or else to condemn it. To reword Frye's description, the
persona of this second stage attempts to redirect the "assault of
experience," through poetic irony, to the "maintaining of the integrity of the innocent world." The persona of "In the Seven
Woods," "From 'The Green Helmet and Other Poems,'" and
"Responsibilities" pays full attention to external reality but is in no
way conciliatory in his allegience to the internal ideal. Yeats describes the role of this persona, with apparent reason, as traveling
"a path no other man has gone"; the quest toward embodying the
duality of a unified identity has recommenced, and it is necessarily
a lonely journey. Ellmann describes this phase of Yeats's poetic
development as one of "noble isolation"[34]; Parkinson speaks of it
in starker and less heroic terms:

In the poems from 1903 to 1914 Yeats speaks in address to others or in
soliloquy to himself, presenting in a speech radically composed of
common language and rendering against a simple scenic background
the poet's personality moving toward unity with what he conceives as
God through the whirling and bitterness of life, and without scanting
the confusion, the waste, the indignity. There is no ultimate solution
except death perhaps; all that is possible is an occasional moment of
dramatic unity, of revelation, of meaning.[35]

Parkinson's pessimistic reading of the poems of this second phase, like Ellmann's disappointed response to those of "The Wind among the Reeds," results from too limited a critical scope. From the developmental perspective of a quest structure in *The Collected Poems*, these poems of isolation are a natural expression of a stage in the progression toward unity of being; they do not in themselves achieve unity, but they do lay a groundwork, which is necessary for the achievement of unity at a later stage. Frank Murphy also analyzes the poems of this period in too narrow a context: "Yeats is preoccupied with saying the old things in the new way. . . . Instead of reconciliation and consequent unity, Yeats slips backward in the social issue, into division and disharmony."[36] Murphy fails to appreciate that a conscious recognition of social disunity implies some consideration of resolving it into an orderly ideal structure and that this represents a great step forward; the persona would never have emerged from a rather solipsistic idealism into unity of being without this empirical counterstep. Murphy's perspective nevertheless offers an interesting reading of the first poem of this period, "In the Seven Woods" (CP, 75). He sees an ironic disjunction of symbolism in the poem, a "surface for secular consumption and an underlying level for the initiates." Murphy interprets the common imagery of nature in this poem as a bone thrown to the masses and the mystical connotations of "Quiet" and the "Great Archer" as tidbits offered to the subtle-minded, and he believes that this disunified duality represents Yeats's response to the difficulties of reconciling real and ideal in the public medium of poetry—a capitulation to disunity.[37]

Turning from the objectivity of the symbols and toward the poetic persona, however, it becomes clear that there is a good dose of irony in this poem, but it rests not in the poem's imagery but in the persona's overemphasized protestations of peace: "I have . . . put away / The unavailing outcries and the old bitterness / That empty the heart. I have forgot awhile / Tara uprooted, and new commonness / Upon the throne and crying about the streets. . . . / I am contented." This is not a withdrawal into the Seven Woods or into the symbols of mysticism but a particularly powerful expression of active engagement. In this first poem of a new volume, there is no precedent or antecedent for the evils the persona professes to be able to transcend. "In the Seven Woods" thus simultaneously draws these social inequities to the attention of the reader and announces that the persona possesses a fresh method of countering such reality. The quest is again confirmed in this poem and in a very sophisticated fashion—quite an advance, at least over the comparatively simplistic statement of "To the Rose upon the Rood of Time." Here the persona embodies both aspects of the dialectic in the ironic attitude he assumes; in the former poem he could entertain only one at a time in the bipartite structure of the symbol and of the poem itself. This new ironic attitude, however, entails a certain amount of suffering as well as isolation; unity of being does not yet come readily. The reality of life that surrounds the persona in this volume gives him "not a crumb of comfort, not a grain"; he knows that the "folly of being comforted" (CP, 76) lies in the inability of externals to satisfy the heart. Conversely, the natural world seems no longer able, as the rose and the "boughs of love and hate" once did, to bear the weight of his dreams: *"No boughs have withered because of the wintry wind; / The boughs have withered because I have told them my dreams"* (CP, 77–78).

The poems of this second stage predictably turn toward social issues, as the persona seeks to understand the external world. "Adam's Curse" (CP, 78–79) reflects the casual comforts and ultimate impotence of social intercourse; poetry, beauty, love—all require labor:

> I said: "It's certain there is no fine thing
> Since Adam's fall but needs much labouring.
> There have been lovers who thought love should be
> So much compounded of high courtesy
> That they would sigh and quote with learned looks
> Precedents out of beautiful old books;
> Yet now it seems an idle trade enough."

Maud Gonne has recorded in her memoirs that the events of the poem did occur in much the same sequence,[38] so the poem is autobiographical on an empirical level. It is self-revealing, too, on a symbolic level, for the persona speaks of his labor of writing verse and of the labor of love in the presence of the woman he writes for and loves. She, however, utters no word and makes no move in the poem; the poet's labor is unrequited and now "seems an idle trade enough," and love grows "As weary-hearted as that hollow moon." The persona has need of some external confirmation of his ideals but seems to find no reliable response: "I loved long and long, / And grew to be out of fashion / Like an old song" (CP, 81).

"From 'The Green Helmet and Other Poems'" shows the persona in full consciousness of the conflict between his profession and his love, which by now have become symbolic of internal ideals and external reality. In "A Woman Homer Sung" (CP, 87–88), the persona establishes a history for the conflict: in youth jealousy and pride govern him; in middle age he labors at poetry to capture his love's beauty for eternity; finally, in advanced age he has raised her to the level of Helen, "a woman Homer sung," but the memory of her youth that his verses still provoke paradoxically makes "life and letters seem / But an heroic dream." "Words" (CP, 88–89) tells a similar story. The persona's lack of fulfillment in both word and woman ironically lends itself to effecting their mutual compatibility; verse raises woman to immortality, and the woman's immortal qualities inspire the verse. Whereas the empirical man has suffered, which is verified in Yeats's *Memoirs,* the persona of the poetry thrives, for ideal reconciliations can be achieved in verse as they cannot in life. Richard Ellmann has justly described the symbolic value of Yeats's long and frustrated love for Maud Gonne as having more significance than everyday needs of sexual and emotional security:

> To abandon himself to a hopeless passion and all its attendant suffering has the fruitful result of glorifying the beloved and, by implication, the perfect concord which his imagination conceives but cannot proffer. The lover's failure becomes symbolic of the defect of all life.[39]

It is not only unrequited love that spurs the persona to a realization of defects in life which require poetic repair. In "The Fascination of What's Difficult" (CP, 91–92), it is "Theatre business, management of men" that drives the persona to despair over his lyrical gifts, paralleling Yeats's complaints in *The Autobiography* that political and theatrical concerns are preventing him from writing poetry.[40] This second stage of development in *The Collected Poems* is the closest that Yeats comes to writing autobiography in verse. This is not to say that poems in preceding and succeeding volumes are not drawn from life, but these poems of defending the innocent world against the intrusions of the real depict the Yeatsian persona at his most extended and vulnerable moments. Frank Murphy calls the persona of "The Green Helmet" a "naked 'I'":

> The entire volume reflects this sense of confusion concerning [Yeats's] relationship with the crowd. Not yet equipped with the intricate series of personality types, explainable by moon phase, which were to be

included in *A Vision*, Yeats is like a drowning man in a sea of hostile personalities, from Maud Gonne to the stranger who attends his plays. . . . Only through an objective distillation of his personality can Yeats eventually achieve a harmonious conjunction of opposite personalities. The more fully dramatized "I" of the later poems is both aesthetically and philosophically superior to the undramatized, naked "I" of the *Green Helmet* poems.[41]

Understandably, this precariously exposed persona occasionally despairs of his quest and wishes to opt out of it entirely, as in "All Things Can Tempt Me" (CP, 95–96): "[I] would be now, could I but have my wish, / Colder and dumber and deafer than a fish."

"Responsibilities," however, the next volume, announces in title, epigraph, and poetry a new attitude in the questing persona. Each volume seems to renew the quest with vigor, and "Responsibilities," as Murphy notes, reaffirms it in a "highly personal, deeply committed, emotional, combative, and urgent" manner.[42] Occasional poetry is the strength of this volume, marking a more immediate concern on the part of the Yeatsian persona to patch over the defects of life with poetry, to the extent even of asking "pardon" in the introductory rhyme (CP, 99) of his ancestors for his shortcomings in life by offering instead of children his poems:

> *Pardon that for a barren passion's sake,*
> *Although I have come close on forty-nine,*
> *I have no child, I have nothing but a book,*
> *Nothing but that to prove your blood and mine.*

Again, autobiography plays a key role in this volume. The introductory poem that recalls Yeats's ancestors is followed by "The Grey Rock" (CP, 101–4), which associates fellow poets of Yeats's youth with ancient deities of traditional Irish lore; the "tragic generation" is once again immortalized, as in *The Autobiography*. Events and persons from history are thus paired throughout the volume with visionary acts, traditional and current; by placing the defective real beside or close by the inner-inspired ideal, Yeats hopes to unite the two. Where satire is used to break down the corrupt reality, vision fills in the gaps that are thereby created.

Compare, for example, "Paudeen" (CP, 107), one of a number of attacks in this volume on the Irish mercantile class in response to their rejection of Hugh Lane's offer to donate a collection of art to Dublin if a museum were provided:[43]

> Indignant at the fumbling wits, the obscure spite
> Of our old Paudeen in his shop, I stumbled blind
> Among the stones and thorn-trees, under morning light;
> Until a curlew cried and in the luminous wind
> A curlew answered; and suddenly thereupon I thought
> That on the lonely height where all are in God's eye,
> There cannot be, confusion of our sound forgot,
> A single soul that lacks a sweet crystalline cry;

and "The Cold Heaven" (CP, 122–23), a visionary poem with no known specific historical incident as source:

> Suddenly I saw the cold and rook-delighting heaven
> That seemed as though ice burned and was but the more ice,
> And thereupon imagination and heart were driven
> So wild that every casual thought of that and this
> Vanished, and left but memories, that should be out of season
> With the hot blood of youth, of love crossed long ago;
> And I took all the blame out of all sense and reason,
> Until I cried and trembled and rocked to and fro,
> Riddled with light. Ah! when the ghost begins to quicken,
> Confusion of the death-bed over, is it sent
> Out naked on the roads, as the books say, and stricken
> By the injustice of the skies for punishment?

The echoes between the two poems are numerous and complex, but the experiences of the persona in each are fairly simply opposed. In "Paudeen," the persona begins in blind hatred and then is called into a larger imaginative context by the cries of birds and the expanse of heaven they traverse. This perceptual movement from earthly concerns to symbolic ideals is taken to be the imagination's message, as well—that limited empirical life can be transcended and made to assume ideal form. In "The Cold Heaven," birds and sky forcefully blind the persona to all consciousness of his empirical surroundings and drive his imagination inward, where it surveys old memories and emotions. This poem ends with a question, however, concerning the ideal fate of the soul. The parallelism of images and themes in these two poems implies that a symbolic compensation for an external, defective reality is a much simpler issue than an imaginative exploration of the internal realm, which is also a necessary activity in the quest for unity of being, one that will be more directly addressed in the next stage of development.

"The Magi" (CP, 124) is also related to these poems, as a synthesis to two theses. Harold Bloom has described "The Cold Heaven" and "The Magi" as "lyric cries of the solitary ego," where that ego is not the "voice of a single man, but a communal voice, or primal sound of universal human process."[44] Yet the "I" of "The Magi" is not troubled as the "pale unsatisfied ones" he envisions are. The profound significance of the persona's activity in the first line rather contrasts with the inability of the other characters in the poem to achieve vision because they seek it in objective form, as "The uncontrollable mystery on the bestial floor." The persona's experience is by contrast one of internally accessible vision: "Now as at all times I can see in the mind's eye." This is the true strength of the persona in his confrontation with Paudeen, no matter how unsettling the vision, as in "The Cold Heaven," can be.

The final two poems in the volume proclaim with certainty what the persona has discovered in his second stage of confrontation, and they look forward to the third stage of withdrawal and meditation. In "A Coat" (CP, 125), the persona declares that he no longer needs the archetypal structural supports of "old mythologies" or the garments of society; he has discovered the complementary and compensatory capacity for vision within his own imagination and finds "there's more enterprise / In walking naked." Free of all encumbrances, the persona is not only fit and ready to defend his ideal beliefs against reductive realities, he is himself a symbolic embodiment of that defense. As "naked" implies, however, the persona temporarily lacks objective forms to express his internal ideals, since he has condemned the social world as inadequate. This need is reconsidered in the next stage, where the persona turns again to nature in its capacity of symbolic expression. In the closing rhyme (CP, 126), the persona openly declares that the ideal power of the imagination, *That reed-throated whisperer,* has passed from the external world in "The Wind among the Reeds" and in the first stage to the internal realm in "Responsibilities" and the second stage, with the result that the persona is fortified against and *can forgive* all external indignities. The "integrity of the innocent world" has been well maintained against the "assault of experience"; it is now safely anchored within the persona and is available for sustenance, internal and external, in future stages of development.

Although most critics recognize a fundamental difference between the persona in Yeats's early and middle poetry and the persona in his mature work, critical opinion is much divided on the characteristics of the later persona. Vivienne Koch finds that the "man who suffered and the man who wrote were, in the most creative sense of suffering, *one,*" that the late poems embody Yeats's tragic consciousness of having become a "great poet" but not a "great man."[45] By contrast, Thomas Parkinson feels that the "difference between the early and later career . . . reside[s] particularly in [Yeats's] later capacity for looking on his knowledge and experience as *not* his own" but archetypal:

> The poetry to about 1915 seems to be striving toward accomplishment and recognition, asking us to observe what the poet has done, but from 1917 on there is in the poetry the passionate coldness, the neglect of self, that he ascribed to Shakespeare's heroes and heroines. . . . He acted his role, and social or aesthetic criteria had no relevance.[46]

How can these two opposing interpretations of the same persona be reconciled? Obviously, there must be a duality of identity in this persona, for he is not essentially different from the persona of preceding stages but an embodiment of another stage in a continuous line of development. Curtis Bradford catches the essence of the persona's continuity from early to late manifestations and indicates also how it can appear alternately subjective and objective to different critics:

> Perhaps the greatest paradox in Yeats's development as a poet was that he became a truly public poet only after he had become a private one; eventually he came to express whatever was nearest to hand, say a statuette carved in lapis lazuli standing on the mantle in his study, in the mode of public speech.[47]

The persona in the third stage of the quest structure is still the paradoxical embodiment of private and public, empirical and universal, but the balance of the combination has shifted again. In the two volumes of poetry that comprise this period, "The Wild Swans at Coole" and "Michael Robartes and the Dancer," Yeats's persona has gained a capacity for projecting his ideal vision on the real world. This ability is won at the cost of retreating, in terms of subject matter, from the frays of empirical life; idyllic estates and symbolic towers begin to replace the shops, city streets, and theater work of the second period. The persona, however, takes a great stride forward in the quest to achieve unity of being by learning to identify and utilize those aspects of the real that correspond to his internal ideals and to reshape others in his imagination. It is at this time in his life that Yeats looks back to the ideals of his youth within the context of his more mature concept of the duality inherent in unity of being:

> One day when I was twenty-three or twenty-four this sentence seemed to form in my head, without my willing it, much as sentences form when we are half-asleep: "Hammer your thoughts into unity." For days I could think of nothing else, and for years I tested all I did by that sentence. I had three interests: interest in a form of literature, in a form of philosophy, and a belief in nationality. None of these seemed to have anything to do with the other. . . . Now all three are, I think, one, or rather all three are a discrete expression of a single conviction. I think that each has behind it my whole character and has gained thereby a certain newness—for is not every man's character peculiar to himself?—and that I have become a cultivated man.[48]

The title poem, which opens "The Wild Swans at Coole," demonstrates this new confidence of unity, or in Frye's phrase, of a "reflective, idyllic view of experience from above," a "contemplative withdrawal from or sequel to action." Whereas in the first stage of development, the persona assumes that the internal ideal can be realized and that there is no inherent separation of it from external reality, the persona of phase three has been through the agonizing divisive experience of phase two and survives by realizing that the ideal is projected on nature by the mind and has no place in nature apart from the individual perceiving mind. This realization, which reflects Yeats's own growing interests in philosophical idealism (his correspondence on Berkeley and Gentile with T. Sturge Moore takes place a few years later), is both tragic and hopeful; the persona has abandoned belief in an external unity of being, but an internal union seems to be viable. The first two stanzas of the poem "The Wild Swans at Coole" (CP, 129–30) establish the division of nature and mind, the first being an objective depiction of a static autumn landscape with swans and the second a subjective emotional response to that view. Common to these two descriptions, however, is the imagery of autumn, and the persona turns in the third stanza to the theme of aging, which autumn suggests, and finds that time leaves the external world largely unchanged (one autumn in nature is like another) but not the heart and body of man:

> Among what rushes will they build,
> By what lake's edge or pool
> Delight men's eyes when I awake some day
> To find they have flown away?

The poem's question actually draws attention away from the future activities of the swans, although this is its literal import, and toward the persona's state of mind. Expectations of awakening "some day" imply a duality in existence: the life being experienced now versus the life that will be experienced then. Whether or not this awakening is a reference to death, it is presented in terms of a change in perceptual contexts, and it is directly linked to the swans. The persona's current state of mind, which has persisted for at least nineteen years, is symbolized in the natural, unaging swans; his anticipated awakening is presented in terms of the swans' flight from his view. Graham Martin interprets this shift in perspective as indicating the bowing of the subjective viewpoint to the objective:

> In following their imaginary flight into a future which excludes him the speaker thus begins to transcend his own nostalgia and despair. The action of the poem embodies his discovery that far from commanding the swans he is commanded by them and must resign himself to the situation they represent (for him): physical-emotional life as an order of transcendence.[49]

The persona does not, however, imaginatively follow the swans' flight; he leaves their destination a question, literally and purposefully. The persona rather uses his imagination to banish the too-persistent swans, which "drift on the still water, / Mysterious, beautiful" and draw his attention to the surface unity of the natural world. The final focus of the poem is on the persona himself and on his power to attend to or dismiss objects in the natural world at will. In the mood of an aging man, he has used the swans as symbols of the attractive but static natural world against which he can realize the full import of his own loneliness and mutability; with new hopes for an internal unity, another aspect of mutability, the swans are no longer an appropriate emblem.

Free of the tyranny of nature, the persona anticipates awakening to his own command of the natural world, and he does so awaken in "The Collar-Bone of a Hare" (CP, 134–35). Here nature is reduced to a dead bone through which the "I" sees the world of society in all its inconsequence:

> I would find by the edge of that water
> The collar-bone of a hare
> Worn thin by the lapping of water,
> And pierce it through with a gimlet, and stare
> At the old bitter world where they marry in churches
> And laugh over the untroubled water
> At all who marry in churches,
> Through the white thin bone of a hare.

The poem begins, "Would I could", but the activity of the "I" in this poem proves that the poet can. Whereas the imagined flight to Innisfree in the first stage is dependent on the actual existence of that lake island, the persona of this stage has the capacity to flee into an ideal world within his own imagination. All is possible in a world flexible to the imagination and to the poet who strives to "accept one's own thought when the thought of others has the authority of the world behind it."

The poignance of this dual revelation—the loss of identification with the physical world and the gain in visionary freedom—is the dominant theme of the volume. The "I" is isolated and self-consciously so; age is given as the causative factor, but it is age in the sense of the discovery of some limitations and other potentials, which are signs of emotional maturity more than physical decline. In "The Living Beauty" (CP, 137), the persona invokes artistic beauty, despite its limitations, as a compensation for "The living beauty [that] is for younger men." In "Lines Written in Dejection" (CP, 143–44), the persona feels that the mythological mysteries he once found in the natural world have been lost to him along with that world and that he is left with only an empty, unresponsive reality:

> The holy centaurs of the hills are vanished;
> I have nothing but the embittered sun;
> Banished heroic mother moon and vanished,
> And now that I have come to fifty years
> I must endure the timid sun.

This is a picture of static isolation, indeed, and certainly an occasion for dejection. However, the very next poem, "The Dawn" (CP, 144), presents a revival of the correlative, visionary faculty. If the persona has "nothing but the embittered sun," then that sun becomes the foundation of a new unified, mythological perspective on the world. The persona arbitrarily endows his old symbol of stark reality, the sun, with a new value of isolation and universal perspective:

> I would be ignorant as the dawn
> That has looked down
> On that old queen measuring a town
> With the pin of a brooch,
> Or on the withered men that saw
> From their pedantic Babylon
> The careless planets in their courses,
> The stars fade out where the moon comes,
> And took their tablets and did sums;
> I would be ignorant as the dawn
> That merely stood, rocking the glittering coach
> Above the cloudy shoulders of the horses;
> I would be—for no knowledge is worth a straw—
> Ignorant and wanton as the dawn.

Here is the refrain of the conditional again: "I would . . . I would . . . I would." Its incantatory tones carry the persona beyond positing possibilities and into a realization of the possible. In this poem particularly, the refrain specifies what state of mind the persona is invoking—the state of being as opposed to knowing. The sun cannot participate in human affairs, but from the perspective of the sun's continuous, self-sufficient existence, or being, human affairs appear trite and "pedantic." The persona "would *be*," like the dawn, an elemental presence, a passive but eternal mode of perception that illuminates all without being subject to the limitations of life. He is reaching inside for his archetypal identity, from which he can view the changing world as from a stable plateau. If achieved, this archetypal identity would certainly represent an awakening into universal perceptions that would render insignificant those swans which seem so firmly entrenched in the unity of nature from the perspective of the individual in the mutability of his life cycle.

In this volume there are two related consequences of the persona's will to universal being, one personal and one impersonal. Impersonal poems based on Yeats's concurrent philosophical concerns from "Per Amica Silentia Lunae" and the inception of *A Vision* begin to appear toward the end of "The Wild Swans at Coole": "Ego Dominus Tuus," "The Phases of the Moon," "The Double Vision of Michael Robartes," to name the most dogmatic. These are pronouncements from an objective system, an archetypal structure that the poet is using as a means of viewing all the details in the world in their proper positions, much as the sun impassively chronicles the rise and fall of all things by virtue of its own constancy. There is no poetic persona in these doctrinal poems, however, since the presence of a perceiving and evaluating mind would disrupt the static and abstract nature of the structure. In other poems, the persona continues to play its central role in a manner that achieves a coordination of the ideal visionary faculty and the real limits of animate life. These poems achieve what might be called a mythological autobiography; they cast real experience in the transcendent frame of an archetypal ideal. In "A Prayer on Going into My House" (CP, 160) what is real is defended as long as it can be "simple enough / For shepherd lads in Galilee" or "what the great and passionate have used / Throughout so many varying centuries." What has been common to generations of men has achieved a permanence of being, against which an individual man may measure his personal aspirations. Moreover, what is archetypal or ideal persists despite human ignorance and error, as in "A Deep-Sworn Vow" (CP, 152):

> Others because you did not keep
> That deep-sworn vow have been friends of mine;
> Yet always when I look death in the face,
> When I clamber to the heights of sleep,
> Or when I grow excited with wine,
> Suddenly I meet your face.

Other than memory, imagination is the means of re-creating the real in ideal form. "The Fisherman" (CP, 145–46) tells of an act of vision that has been achieved in despite of reality, the creation of an ideal subject / audience in the traditional form of a fisherman. The persona has "looked in the face / What I had hoped 'twould be / To write for my own race / And the reality"—the idealistic hopes of the first stage of the quest. The reality of the second stage, however, has resulted in despair over the possibility of a fit audience, and the persona now reaches his third stage of "imagining a man," "In scorn of this audience":

> A man who does not exist,
> A man who is but a dream;
> And cried, "Before I am old
> I shall have written him one
> Poem maybe as cold
> And passionate as the dawn."

The persona's act of reaching inside for an archetypal image and projecting it in poetry as both his theme and his audience is an act of personal as well as poetic transcendence. The primitive, archetypal figure that once spoke for the persona in his first stage of development is now under the poetic control of that persona—as his audience, as his subjective imaginative creation rather than his objective peer. In these poems of the third stage, the dual aspects the persona perceives in himself and the world are most conspicuously interrelated, as if Yeats were experimenting with the possibility of uniting the two by considering them in rapid alternation. Much as in the opening poem, the persona in "Broken Dreams" (CP, 151–52) moves through two parallel courses. One is apparent in the opening line, "There is grey in your hair"; this is the well-worn poetic path of praising the ideal beauty in a real woman. The other course becomes apparent in the final stanza, which anticipates the conclusion of the second edition of *A Vision:*

> The last stroke of midnight dies.
> All day in the one chair
> From dream to dream and rhyme to rhyme I have ranged
> In rambling talk with an image of air:
> Vague memories, nothing but memories.

The poem is, in this dual frame, both an object constructed in praise of a woman and an act of participation in that ideal construct, though the persona remains still more sharply conscious of the loss of the original world of ideal innocence than of his compensatory power to re-create that world from its remembered remains in the present.

The consummate expression of the concerns of this volume is, however, its second poem, "In Memory of Major Robert Gregory" (CP, 130-33). The specific genre of this poem, elegy for a friend, supplies the context of an imperfect reality and the challenge of redeeming some ideal meaning from an aborted life. Yeats rises to the occasion magnificently, not just by writing an elegiac poem but by inculcating that symbolic activity into the structure of

his own life, as persona in the poem. That is, the persona's homage
to his friend achieves the ritual qualities of the extraordinary
rooted in the ordinary. The first verse establishes the empirical
context:

> Now that we're almost settled in our house
> I'll name the friends that cannot sup with us
> Beside a fire of turf in th'ancient tower,
> And having talked to some late hour
> Climb up the narrow winding stairs to bed:
> Discoverers of forgotten truth
> Or mere companions of my youth,
> All, all are in my thoughts to-night being dead.

This poem begins where "Broken Dreams" ends, with an act of
memory; the act is deliberate and symbolic and a far cry from the
semiconscious dismissal of the natural world in the preceding
poem, "The Wild Swans at Coole." The persona is in the comfort
of his tower home and is consciously arranging this physical context to facilitate his imaginative task, no longer discomfited by the
independent and static symbolism of nature. He welcomes old
friends one by one to his new home, as if he were carrying out the
custom of a housewarming, but because these friends are dead, he
invokes them through memory. What an emblem this is of the
heroic re-creation of an ideal world from what is left of the real!
The re-creation is by necessity internal, for the characters now live
only in the persona's memory and imagination, and the carefully
arranged context of empirical existence is also internalized, if only
momentarily:

> They were my close companions many a year,
> A portion of my mind and life, as it were,
> And now their breathless faces seem to look
> Out of some old picture-book.

The friends that are re-created in the memory are then thrust
back into the world again, but only after the persona has reshaped
their lives into archetypal forms. The form the persona imaginatively gives to the life of each friend resembles the present form of
his own act of ritualistic remembering: each friend "comes" with
his own version of the eternal duality of real world and personal
ideals. Lionel Johnson "loved his learning better than mankind";
John Synge "dying chose the living world for text"; and George

Pollexfen from "muscular youth" turned to the "opposition, square and trine" of mysticism. And yet each man attains in the persona's act of memory, if not unity, a taste of it: Johnson in his studies, Synge among the peasants, and Pollexfen in contemplation. Perhaps because of these partial successes, the persona can accept their deaths.

> I am accustomed to their lack of breath,
> But not that my dear friend's dear son,
> Our Sidney and our perfect man,
> Could share in that discourtesy of death.

Most critics have noted that the Johnson, Synge, and Pollexfen portraits anticipate qualities that are subsequently praised in Robert Gregory—scholarship, artistry, sportsmanship. Few have recognized that the persona's presentation of the Gregory portrait differs qualitatively from that of the first three. Where the lives of Johnson, Synge, and Pollexfen are described as completed structures because they are dead, the persona imaginatively resurrects Gregory as if to replay his life, the better to understand its unique form, but also as if the persona himself were reliving Gregory's life for the consolation and compensation that imaginative activity affords him.

Marjorie Perloff interprets the persona-Gregory relationship as one of opposition: "The speaker or persona of the poem is consistently presented as one who has heroically survived the turmoil and temptations of the fledgling artist to achieve the Unity of Being denied to Robert Gregory in his lifetime."[50] Certainly the aging, contemplative poet settling into home and marriage contrasts with the young, active Renaissance man he calls to mind. But in Yeats's poetry and in the presentation of his persona, opposition always implies complementarity. Notably, whereas the first three visitors are identified by name, the persona is not, as usual, but neither is Robert Gregory, except in the poem's title. He is named as an archetype rather than as an individual: "Our Sidney and our perfect man." This exaggeration of the subject's significance is not out of place in an elegy, though even in *Lycidas* Milton provides a mythological name and identity for his subject. In Yeats's poem, Gregory's archetypal qualities suggest both that the persona casts Gregory as the artist of his own completed life, much as Yeats portrays the departed Synge in *The Autobiography*, and that the persona projects his own efforts and aspirations into the finished form of Gregory's life. Poetic details confirm the persona's identification with the idealized Gregory:

> For all things the delighted eye now sees
> Were loved by him; . . .
> We dreamed that a great painter had been born
> To cold Clare rock and Galway rock and thorn,
> To that stern colour and that delicate line
> That are our secret discipline.

The present perceptions and thoughts of the persona participate in those that define the sensibility of the "perfect man." Other phrases suggest that the persona is completing what Gregory could only begin. Stanza X recalls Gregory's artistic "counsel" on the restoration of the tower that now serves as the setting of the poem and the persona's home. Stanza VII views the tower in its natural setting of vegetation and animal life and concludes, "He might have been your heartiest welcomer." Like the persona, "he" was an artist who "had the intensity / To have published all to be a world's delight"; in fact he is presented as having had a security of public reception that even Yeats's persona feels he lacks and must create.

The ideal structures that Gregory once envisioned are presently inhabited by the persona; the comparisons and contrasts are thus startling:

> Some burn damp faggots, others may consume
> The entire combustible world in one small room
> As though dried straw, and if we turn about
> The bare chimney is gone black out
> Because the work had finished in that flare.
> Soldier, scholar, horseman, he,
> As 'twere all life's epitome.
> What made us dream that he could comb grey hair?

Gregory is now, like Synge in *The Autobiography*, a finished, "perfect" work, because the life structure is visible in the remembered actions—at least from the persona's perspective of his own ongoing struggle to assimilate life and art, process and product. The quick blaze of straw leaves a much sharper image in the mind than the slowly smoldering fire.[51] The two poems that follow this elegy provide an ironic chorus to the persona's experience of this dual identity by projecting each aspect separately and in an extreme form. The dramatic speaker of "An Irish Airman Foresees His Death" (CP, 133–34) relinquishes life for a blaze of glory; the speaker of "Men Improve with the Years" (CP, 134) stands inanimate as a statue amid the stream of life. Ironically in these poems death becomes heroic and life becomes static. The persistent "damp faggots" of the persona's life flare a bit in the elegy, however, as he imagines his still-smoldering life in conjunction with Gregory's quick combustion. The persona has momentarily transcended his own life and attained an imaginative apprehension of unity of identity that finally silences speech when self-consciousness returns:

> I had thought, seeing how bitter is that wind
> That shakes the shutter, to have brought to mind
> All those that manhood tried, or childhood loved
> Or boyish intellect approved,
> With some appropriate commentary on each;
> Until imagination brought
> A fitter welcome; but a thought
> Of that late death took all my heart for speech.

What the persona achieves internally in "In Memory of Major Robert Gregory" is expanded into societal significance in "Easter 1916" (CP, 177–80), a poem written two years before the Gregory elegy but withheld from inclusion in a collected volume until "Michael Robartes and the Dancer" (1921) for political reasons. It is obviously a poem of the same stage of quest, however, that of "contemplative withdrawal" and consolidation of internal ideals, despite being an occasional poem celebrating a specific public event. As Marjorie Perloff describes it, "the political event that is the occasion for this poem is not viewed from the outside . . . the center is rather the 'I' who must come to terms with the public event,"[52] the public event being the Irish nationalist rebellion against England in 1916, which succeeded momentarily in the "occupation" of Dublin but resulted eventually in the execution of the most prominent rebels. Many of these rebels were friends or acquaintances of Yeats and are remembered as such by his persona:

> I have met them at close of day
> Coming with vivid faces
> From counter or desk among grey
> Eighteenth-century houses.

The empirical context is so common, even so trite, that the persona professes "Being certain that they and I / But lived where motley is worn." The characters are described as passing through lives of conflicting intentions, some worse than others, but in the act of rebellion each "has resigned his part / In the casual comedy; / He, too, has been changed in his turn, / Transformed utterly: / A terrible beauty is born."

Each has transformed himself in an act of willful unification, by an empirical, physical enactment of ideal nationalist hopes. But each is also transformed in the perceptions of the persona; one is even remembered as being a "drunken, vainglorious lout," in the persona's response to their unforeseen valour: "I number him in my song."

> We know their dream; enough
> To know they dreamed and are dead;
> And what if excess of love
> Bewildered them till they died?
> I write it out in verse—
> MacDonagh and MacBride
> And Connolly and Pearse
> Now and in time to be,
> Wherever green is worn,
> Are changed, changed utterly:
> A terrible beauty is born.

The poet's act of registering the result of the rebels' efforts is inseparable from the results themselves. It is more than a personal response that the persona records; it is a universal one, expressed most clearly in the imagery of nature in the third stanza. The stone suggests both the absolute, unthinking quality of the rebels' commitment to their cause and the inevitable reminder it becomes to others in the society of the limits of death on life and of reality on ideal hopes: "The stone's in the midst of all." Life does not stop because of the rebellion or the martyrdom, as a stream is only "troubled" and not dammed by a stone in its midst, but the act provokes a slight transcendence of communal consciousness. Consciousness is conflict, say the instructors in *A Vision*,[53] and conflict produces consciousness in this poem of the tragic necessity of conflict itself as the means to unity of being or unity of culture.

The natural images that occur in "In Memory of Major Robert Gregory" ("damp faggots" and "dried straw") and "Easter 1916" ("stone" and "stream") as dramatic symbols of the poems' thought processes suggest that the persona has not quite banished the external world, as he seems to do in "The Wild Swans at Coole." Rather, the persona has come to recognize his internal control of empirical nature through the power of poetic symbolizing, to understand that a symbolic relationship of mind and nature in a poem is, in effect, their unification. The later poems develop this technical power of achieving a poetic union in their characteristic development of a climactic symbol from an image from nature. "A Prayer for My Daughter" (CP, 185–87) anticipates in this third stage the technical success of the fourth stage. It is constructed on a complex framework of natural imagery that serves as both the physical setting for the poem and a symbolic expression of the values the persona hopes will exist in the future maturity of his child, much as the images of burning in the Gregory elegy play the dual role of hearth and life-style. In "A Prayer for My Daughter," the natural world threatens to overcome the new-found symbolic balance of the persona's imagination; a storm threatens "haystack" and "roof," man's physical barriers against the chaos of the natural world. The persona, "because of the great gloom that is in my mind," walks and prays:

> Imagining in excited reverie
> That the future years had come,
> Dancing to a frenzied drum,
> Out of the murderous innocence of the sea.

Gradually, the persona transforms in his imagination the threatening objectivity, or "murderous innocence," of the natural world to human characteristics of pride and hatred, which, in turn, he counters with their social checks, custom and ceremony. These qualities, in turn, recall such traditional, humanized natural symbols as the horn of plenty and the laurel tree. The physically threatening wind becomes "intellectual hatred," which the self-possessed imagination can transcend:

> Considering that, all hatred driven hence,
> The soul recovers radical innocence
> And learns at last that it is self-delighting,
> Self-appeasing, self-affrighting,
> And that its own sweet will is Heaven's will;
> She can, though every face should scowl
> And every windy quarter howl
> Or every bellows burst, be happy still.

The persona thus wills his newborn daughter his art of meditative union of internal ideal and external real, which in this poem is the imaginative power to transform windblown haystack and linnet tree to the "rich horn" of ceremony and the "laurel tree" of custom. He can only do so, however, even in imagination, by projecting himself or a surrogate, his daughter's bridegroom, into her future, for it is only the process of the individual imagination that can effect the transformation of unpleasant realities to "custom and . . . ceremony / . . . innocence and beauty." The power lies in the imaginative symbol produced in the mind and not in the external forms of nature or society. John Holloway, who reads "A Prayer for My Daughter" as anticipating the triumphant "self-possession and power" of language in "The Tower" volume, finds that in this poem "Yeats has in effect created for himself a private language." It is a language that, though addressing public events, remains only internally viable: "All the important words of his sentence take their meanings from a progressive charging which they receive from the developing poem."[54]

That "A Prayer for My Daughter" is more an act of idealizing nature than a celebration of lasting social values, more process than product, is suggested by the poem which precedes it, "The Second Coming" (CP, 184–85), in which the persona invokes a vision of the future state of society that is far from custom and ceremony. In this poem, an external image becomes a symbol that directs the movement of the persona's mind: circling falcon, anarchy, "The blood-dimmed tide is loosed, and everywhere / The ceremony of innocence is drowned." The persona looks for some "revelation" in this quick succession of symbolic values that possess his mind. "Surely . . . surely," he invokes it, and a vision appears of an animate sphinx, suggesting what has existed previous to the present social structure and what will likely succeed it. "A Prayer for My Daughter," in following this semivoluntary revelation, suggests that it is the mind's role to counter external truth with internal values and that the confrontation is an ongoing, personal process. The poem that precedes "The Second Coming" anticipates, though in fairly abstract terms, the experiential findings of both the following poems. "Demon and Beast" (CP, 183–84) celebrates a rare moment of unity of being as it is perceived in the external world rather than in the mind:

> For certain minutes at the least
> That crafty demon and that loud beast

> That plague me day and night
> Ran out of my sight;
> Though I had long perned in the gyre,
> Between my hatred and desire,
> I saw my freedom won
> And all laugh in the sun.

Most critics follow the lead of Peter Ure in interpreting "demon" as "hatred" and "beast" as "desire," both images of a "state of intense self-absorption and subjectivity."[55] This interpretation seems rather unnecessarily forced, however; the context of the poem and the dual character of the persona throughout the poetic canon allow "demon" and "beast" to be interpreted almost literally. Freedom from the beast allows the persona to participate in the ideal values embodied in certain portraits: "For all men's thoughts grew clear / Being dear as mine are dear." That is, transcendence of the empirical restrictions of the body liberates the mind to mingle in "sweet company" with other minds. On the other hand, when free from his demon the persona can find "aimless joy" in the movements of a "stupid happy creature." His "whole nature" is roused in sympathy with the play of birds without the necessity of mentally realizing their symbolic value or interpreting the "gyring . . . perning" movements in the context of a system of universal import. Beast is quite simply the empirical nature, and demon is the spiritual or transcendent nature[56]; they have warred incessantly in Yeats's persona, alternately gaining control of, and occasionally being reconciled in, the persona's mind.

Suddenly they are eliminated as opposing elements in this poem by being united in a flash of recognition: body becomes mind in art, mind takes body as form in life. It is "mere growing old, that brings / Chilled blood, this sweetness brought," muses the persona. The process of aging does bring images of death and life together; the mature persona, who has been so beleaguered by the dual elements of his being, is finally in a position to embody their union, to project himself as a symbol of unity of being, to "give [his] life as well as [his] words . . . to the criticism of the world," as Yeats defines the final stage of the quest in his comment on Tennyson. "Demon and Beast" does not celebrate the consummate union of mind and world. The persona remains convinced that "every natural victory / Belongs to beast or demon, / That never yet had freeman / Right mastery of natural things"; and the final stanza of the poem is a reminder of the fate of those who willfully seek such mastery by imposing an internally conceived ideal on the real. The verse that concludes the volume, however, and the evidence of a growing mental control of natural symbols throughout "The Wild Swans at Coole" and "Michael Robartes and the Dancer," identify the individual mind of the poetic persona as the specific locus of the union of ideal and real that confers value on all existence. Thus, in the final verse, the persona assumes his most concrete identity ever, an identity of man and work "To Be Carved on a Stone at Thoor Ballylee" (CP, 188):

> I, the poet William Yeats,
> With old mill boards and sea-green slates,
> And smithy work from the Gort forge,
> Restored this tower for my wife George;
> And may these characters remain
> When all is ruin once again.

Northrop Frye labels the final stage of the romantic quest the "*penseroso* phase" and illustrates it with the image, a "favorite image of Yeats . . . that of the old man in the tower, the lonely hermit absorbed in occult or magical studies." This may be a "favorite" image for Yeats, but it is more characteristic of the persona of the third rather than fourth stage of development, in "In Memory of Major Robert Gregory" and "A Prayer for My Daughter," or of the objective characters of the systematic poems, such as the poet of "The Phases of the Moon." The persona of "The Tower," "The Winding Stair," and "Last Poems" is indeed at the "end of a movement from active to contemplative adventure," but his contemplation takes place conspicuously amid the ongoing activity of the world and not entirely within an isolated tower, although the world seems all the more chaotic in the light of the persona's meditative wholeness. This late persona is, as Yeats was himself at this time, quite conscious of being a symbolic figure to the world, and many of the late poems are presented as the dramatic utterances of the persona as an archetypal being. The persona is no longer in the process of becoming; the late "I," though still dynamic, is an achievement of unity of being. Whereas in previous stages the persona visibly, but not wholly consciously, wavers between a wholehearted ideal belief and a thorough disillusionment with the real world, this persona has internalized that vacillation and maintains it in a dynamic state of being which is not bliss but a labor that produces unity.

John Holloway's impressive study of style and language in the later poems finds that a change in style "contributes something to the *persona* of the author":

> The *forming ritual* of these poems, one may say, is the solemnised calling-up of objects by the poet to people the world of his imagination. . . . But these ritual phrases reveal the *ontology* of what constitutes Yeats's world: the kind of reality, the status of reality, which is possessed by the objects in it. It is part of the nature of these poems that they do not offer to depict and describe things which the reader is invited to envisage as having prior, independent existence. On the contrary, the reader is invited to see them as called into being by the *fiat* of the poet, peopling a world *ab initio* as part of the creative act.[57]

In these poems of maturity, the poet/persona can and does legitimately reflect that he has become "mythical even to myself."[58] With such mental power to integrate ideal and real, there would seem to be a temptation to retire from external conflict and indulge only in personal thoughts: "My temptation is quiet," says the persona in "An Acre of Grass" (CP, 299). But perfection of the work is not accompanied by perfection of life; the body ages as the imagination grows supple, and the conflict of duality continues unabated within the one identity.[59] The mind may command, as in "Sailing to Byzantium" (CP, 191–92), "Soul clap its hands and sing, and louder sing / For every tatter in its mortal dress," and in that effort sail off to the "holy city of Byzantium," away from the world of generation and into the "artifice of eternity." But even in Byzantium the imagination sings "of what is past, or passing, or to come"; it is irretrievably tied to the physical world of "whatever is begotten, born, and dies" and cannot escape the body's influence.

In "The Tower" (CP, 192–97), one of the several great long lyrics of personal meditation in this final stage, the persona accepts his inherent duality as the necessary condition of a poetic unity:

> What shall I do with this absurdity—
> O heart, O troubled heart—this caricature,
> Decrepit age that has been tied to me
> As to a dog's tail?
> > Never had I more
> Excited, passionate, fantastical

> Imagination, nor an ear and eye
> That more expected the impossible.

With acute consciousness of embodying this duality of decrepit body and "fantastical imagination," the persona of "The Tower" surveys the environment atop his tower, "send[s] imagination forth," and finds not a hostile or intransigent reality but one peopled with figures he has, during his career, either imaginatively resurrected from history and legend or created himself. The persona discovers beyond duality an ideal reality—not a misperceived idealistic reality, that of the persona's first stage—but a real landscape peopled with imaginative figures and invested with internal values.

"The Circus Animals' Desertion" (CP, 335–36) tells the same story, though from the perspective of dead memories rather than living ones. The persona, the aging poet, recalls how his past works have expressed his emotional needs: "What can I but enumerate old themes?" Oisin, the persona recalls, was "set . . . to ride" by the persona's own need to realize the ideal, "starved" as he was "for the bosom of his faery bride."

> And then a counter-truth filled out its play,
> *The Countess Cathleen* was the name I gave it. . . .
> I thought my dear must her own soul destroy,
> So did some fanaticism and hate enslave it,
> And this brought forth a dream and soon enough
> This dream itself had all my thought and love.

Finally, in the saga of Cuchulain, "It was the dream itself enchanted me":

> Character isolated by a deed
> To engross the present and dominate memory.
> Players and painted stage took all my love,
> And not those things that they were emblems of.

The persona of "The Tower" finds some comfort in the living presence of his creations and even calls Hanrahan back from the dead to question him as an authority on love, but the "I" of "The Circus Animals' Desertion" feels out of touch with those characters, which he finds to be emblems and not companions. Nonetheless, in perceiving them as emblems of the dreams of his own heart, the persona inductively discovers the progression of his own development, as he has outlined it in his remarks on Tennyson: from the "innocent world" of Oisin, through a bitter "maintaining of the innocent world against the assault of experience" in Cathleen, to the "contemplative withdrawal" and defense of "one's own thought" that characterize Cuchulain's last acts. The final stage, that of giving "one's life as well as one's words . . . to the criticism of the world," involves an understanding that life has always been the foundation of literature:

> Those masterful images because complete
> Grew in pure mind, but out of what began? . . .
> I must lie down where all the ladders start,
> In the foul rag-and-bone shop of the heart.

The persona's immediate purpose in this poem is to revive the source of art, which he ultimately finds to be internal, but he has along the way achieved a return to his beginnings. The ideal world he has projected in the story of Oisin, once only internal, is now still available amid the empirical trappings of subsequent experience. It embodies, in fact, the ideal structure the persona has attempted to impose on reality during his development.

In the poem "The Tower," the somewhat more philosophically inclined persona writes his will as an act of communicating his understanding of reality as internally conceived:

> And I declare my faith:
> I mock Plotinus' thought
> And cry in Plato's teeth,
> Death and life were not
> Till man made up the whole,
> Made lock, stock and barrel
> Out of his bitter soul,
> Aye, sun and moon and star, all
> And further add to that
> That, being dead, we rise,
> Dream and so create
> Translunar Paradise.[60]

In the meantime, this faith will support the aging persona in his continual activity of reconciling body and mind, world and imagination:

> Now shall I make my soul,
> Compelling it to study

> In a learned school
> Till the wreck of body . . .
> Seem but the clouds of the sky
> When the horizon fades,
> Or a bird's sleepy cry
> Among the deepening shades.

Death is an important theme in these poems of stage four. Death and old age are significant themes throughout the poetic canon and occasionally something of a joke among Yeats's critics,[61] who find it indecorous for the young poet of the early poems to anticipate death so keenly. In this final stage, however, death is not only a necessary and appropriate consideration, it is constructive. Death has always served as a reminder of the finitude of life in Yeats's poetry, but when death becomes an immediate prospect, as it is for the late persona, it provokes an appreciation of life as structure as well as process. The persona not only perceives the philosophical value of death, as in such poems as "An Acre of Grass" and "A Prayer for Old Age" (CP, 281), he also uses the presence of death to instill a sharper sense of his own life as form in his poetry. "Meditations in Time of Civil War" (CP, 198–204) captures, in both title and text, the "Befitting emblems of adversity" that inform life in the face of death. The structure and details of the poem are openly autobiographical, and the persona performs the mental acts of mediation and meditation necessary to maintain the unity of opposites, of life and death:

> I turn away and shut the door, and on the stair
> Wonder how many times I could have proved my worth
> In something that all others understand or share;
> But O! ambitious heart, had such a proof drawn forth
> A company of friends, a conscience set at ease,
> It had but made us pine the more. The abstract joy,
> The half-read wisdom of daemonic images,
> Suffice the ageing man as once the growing boy.

The persona of this fourth stage, reviewing his life and work in expectation of death, grows progressively more archetypal in bearing and in interests. The "I" becomes an externally stable embodiment of an internally dynamic duality, and the outside world grows comparatively more chaotic. In part, Yeats's apocalyptic expectations of a new cycle or a "Second Coming" affect his pre-

sentation of social flux, but aesthetically, the persona's growing
stability and integrity inevitably cast a proportionately increasing
appearance of chaos into the world around him. As becomes clear
in "At Algeciras—A Meditation upon Death" (CP, 241), the persona is an embodied unity but not The Unity, which is God:

> Greater glory in the sun,
> An evening chill upon the air,
> Bid imagination run
> Much on that Great Questioner;
> What He can question, what if questioned I
> Can with a fitting confidence reply.

What the persona can no longer assimilate into his life's structure
and symbols, that which belongs to a future age, is left for others
to tackle and thus, from the persona's viewpoint, becomes a growing chaos.

One response that Yeats makes to this exclusive unity of his late
persona is to create other poetic characters that still participate in
the flux: Crazy Jane, Old Tom, Ribh, "A Man Young and Old,"
"A Woman Young and Old." Each of these archetypal characters
sees the world from a different perspective and thus creates an
ordered context of mediated realities around the persona, much as
the very young persona is himself surrounded by such traditional
figures as shepherds, fishermen, an "old pensioner," and Fergus.
There is a return also to ballad forms in the late poetry as well,
which supplements the texture of a traditional reality that is still in
existence about the persona. The later poetic characters, however,
are more fully individual, products of a rich, experienced poetic
mind; indeed, they often undergo minor developments of their
own, which are analogous to the progress of the persona through
the canon, though on a greatly reduced scale. They relate to the
poetic "I" in much the manner the objective characters of "The
Secret Rose" and "Stories of Red Hanrahan" relate to the "I" of
"The Celtic Twilight" in *Mythologies*. J. R. Mulryne describes
them as "Yeats's 'personal archetypes' by imaginative knowledge
of whom the poet becomes endowed with 'joy.' "[62] The persona,
secure in his own identity, is free to appreciate other characters in
their traditional forms and even finds the activity self-affirming, as
in "Lapis Lazuli" (CP, 291–93), where the persona's response to
"hysterical women" who "are sick of the palette and fiddle-bow, /

Of poets that are always gay," is to imagine a positive act of transcendence and gaiety by contemplating the rewards for others of the quest for identity, as carved in an art form:

> Two Chinamen, behind them a third,
> Are carved in lapis lazuli. . . .
> Every discoloration of the stone,
> Every accidental crack or dent,
> Seems a water-course or an avalanche,
> Or lofty slope where it still snows
> Though doubtless plum or cherry-branch
> Sweetens the little half-way house
> Those Chinamen climb towards, and I
> Delight to imagine them seated there;
> There, on the mountain and the sky,
> On all the tragic scene they stare.
> One asks for mournful melodies;
> Accomplished fingers begin to play.
> Their eyes mid many wrinkles, their eyes,
> Their ancient, glittering eyes, are gay.

Other poems project the dual aspects of the completed identity in the abstract terms of an internal dialogue rather than in separate objective characters. "A Dialogue of Self and Soul" (CP, 230–32) is perhaps the most affirmative of all Yeats's dialogue poems, because it achieves a communion of the two opposite entities, which cannot occur intrapoetically when the characters are separate identities. The mind of Yeats or the poem as a whole can unite Hic and Ille or Robartes and Aherne, but the characters themselves cannot be cognizant of such unity. "Self" and "Soul" in this poem are versions of the empirical and transcendent identities. Soul urges transcendence of physical life, "I summon to the winding ancient stair," as a means to spiritual deliverance:

> Think of ancestral night that can,
> If but imagination scorn the earth
> And intellect its wandering
> To this and that and t'other thing,
> Deliver from the crime of death and birth.

In contemplating such deliverance, however, Soul is struck dumb, for a pure transcendence from life would negate all vehicles of knowledge and expression: "For intellect no longer knows / *Is* from the *Ought*, or *Knower* from the *Known*." Soul concludes,

"Only the dead can be forgiven." Interspersed with Soul's presentation of its concerns is Self's verbal preoccupation with Sato's sword, emblem of "A charter to commit the crime once more," to remain in the cycle of life, though ironically the sword itself shows little sign of use: "Still razor-keen, still like a looking-glass / Unspotted by the centuries." In part II, Self responds to Soul's objections to empirical life by affecting a nonchalance: "What matter if the ditches are impure? / What matter if I live it all once more?" The terms that Self uses to describe life, however, betray that nonchalance: "toil," "ignominy," "distress," "clumsiness." The emotion turns to bravado,

> I am content to live it all again
> And yet again, if it be life to pitch
> Into the frog-spawn of a blind man's ditch,
> A blind man battering blind men . . . ,

and finally to pride in the meaning inherent in the process of life, a meaning which redeems life from ignominy:

> I am content to follow to its source
> Every event in action or in thought;
> Measure the lot; forgive myself the lot!
> When such as I cast out remorse
> So great a sweetness flows into the breast
> We must laugh and we must sing,
> We are blest by everything,
> Everything we look upon is blest.

Critics have traditionally read this final stanza as a victory in the debate for Self. Ellmann concludes, "Self and soul are not reconciled, but their opposition has generated in the victorious self a new knowledge and a new strength." Bloom worries, "We are moved by the reciprocal blessings . . . yet we might be a touch uneasy also, for the self happily is blessing the self."[63] Is the Self's triumphant finale mere solipsism? Yeats himself described the poem, while he was writing it, as involving the "choice of rebirth rather than deliverance from birth,"[64] which suggests not an obstinate but an enlightened empiricism. Within the poem itself, Self's discovery, through emphatic concentration on the characteristics of physical life, of a transcendent quality within itself resembles Soul's perception of unity in transcendence that is so perfect that it inhibits all expression or knowledge. Self alone, the "frog-spawn of a blind man's ditch," could not have achieved the final state of blessedness, which is dual: the passive receiving of blessings and the active bestowing of them. To the extent that blessing involves the attention and care of Heaven, the Soul's abilities and concerns are immediately involved.

Holloway finds in his study of the poem's imagery that the "transition from ditch to source is no transition from an event merely back to its cause, but one from the whole life of the sensual world, back to its origin in the world of the soul. The supramundane meaning of the poem is written into the very grain of its imagery."[65] This complementarity of Self and Soul accepted, the meaning of the final verse is clear. Self is responsible for accounting for life (measuring "the lot") and for realizing and accepting its limited potential (forgiving oneself "the lot"). The humility gained from assuming this partially transcendent perspective (casting "out remorse") inevitably involves Soul, which is after all partner to Self in life and fellow inhabitant of the tower in this poem. Self and Soul together, two "I"s as "we," celebrate the wonder of a spiritual liberation that remains grounded in the perceived world. There is no acceptable antecedent for "we" in the poem other than the complementary relationship of Self and Soul that is suggested by the poem's title and in its structure. And there is no compelling reason for blessings and joy at the end other than the union of these two complementary aspects of identity. Self's final expression of the dual achievement of the whole being and the structure of the poem itself both embody the essential fate and freedom of every man.

"A Dialogue of Self and Soul" provides an interior view of that phenomenon of freedom that is presented externally in "Demon and Beast," an internal view inherent in the self-consciously symbolic persona of the final stage but not available to the isolated "I" of stage three. "Stream and Sun at Glendalough" (CP, 250) reemphasizes the persona's position of being representative of the concerns of "common man" but more open to the potential for rebirth in a transcendent state than those who perceive themselves as living static lives. In "Byzantium" (CP, 243–44), too, the persona "hail[s] the superhuman; / I call it death-in-life and life-in-death," where spirits straddle the "dolphin's mire and blood." "Vacillation" (CP, 245–47), however, is probably the supreme dialogue poem of this last stage, because of its success in inculcating the abstract oppositions of death and life, body and soul, with the remembered empirical experiences of the whole man. It is not a dialogue of abstract qualities but an accounting for the whole of existence in one individual. The opening verse sets the theme:

> Between extremities
> Man runs his course;
> A brand, or flaming breath,
> Comes to destroy
> All those antinomies
> Of night and day;
> The body calls it death,
> The heart remorse.
> But if these be right
> What is joy?

Part II of the poem recalls the early imagery of trees of good and evil in "The Two Trees" (CP, 47–48), but here they are made one tree, "half all glittering flame and half all green" and a source of the duality that leads to unity: "he that Attis' image hangs between / That staring fury and the blind lush leaf / May know not what he knows, but knows not grief." That old symbol of mask is used here as the instrument of uniting two opposites, but it is clearly the action of hanging the mask between the two parts of the tree that unites them. The persona continues to embody that unifying action in this last stage of his development. Blessedness overcomes the persona in part IV, responsibility and remorse overcome him in part V. Soul and Heart debate in part VII, and in part VIII the persona realizes,

> I—though heart might find relief
> Did I become a Christian man and choose for my belief
> What seems most welcome in the tomb—play a predestined
>   part.
> Homer is my example and his unchristened heart.

Again, soul and self (or heart) must comply, but together a secular holiness is achieved, built on the symbolic value of the archetypal life, the "predestined part" that Homer has done so much to establish and that the persona himself has just re-created by memory of his dualistic life experiences.

"Vacillation" is very much a poem of the final stage of development in its presentation of historical detail within an archetypal structure. The more specifically autobiographical poems of this stage also achieve the transcendence of unity but by an alternate

174 A New Species of Man

route. They present details of empirical experience and discover the structural values within them, similar to the basic perceptual structure of *The Autobiography*. "Coole Park, 1929" (CP, 238) and "Coole Park and Ballylee, 1931" (CP, 239) return to the subject matter of "The Wild Swans at Coole," but all the natural detail noticed in the earlier poem has in the later poems become self-conscious, even defiant, symbolism. "What's water but the generated soul?" Yeats asks in "Coole Park and Ballylee, 1931":

> At sudden thunder of the mounting swan
> I turned about and looked where branches break
> The glittering reaches of the flooded lake.

> Another emblem there! . . .
> So arrogantly pure, a child might think
> It can be murdered with a spot of ink.

"The Municipal Gallery Revisited" (CP, 316–18) recalls "In Memory of Major Robert Gregory." The persona confronts pictures of past friends, though this time physical portraits rather than images re-created from memory. These portraits, like the nationalistic paintings surrounding them, are not copies of the empirical subjects but their ideal images, what " 'the poets have imagined, terrible and gay.' " And yet the portraits can only approximate the ideal images of the persona's memory, which have been forged from repeated past contacts with those friends amid all the chaos of their empirical lives:

> Heart-smitten with emotion I sink down,
> My heart recovering with covered eyes;
> Wherever I had looked I had looked upon
> My permanent or impermanent images: . . .

> And I am in despair that time may bring
> Approved patterns of women or of men
> But not that selfsame excellence again.

Having outlived his friends, Yeats is in the paradoxical position of carrying out their ideals in his act of remembering them:

> John Synge, I and Augusta Gregory, thought
> All that we did, all that we said or sang
> Must come from contact with the soil, from that
> Contact everything Antaeus-like grew strong.

Thus, the persona renews his own strength and revives his own imagination, "Antaeus-like," in remembering the living acts of his peers and how they have assumed their places in the still-evolving ideal structure of his own life. The final couplet is not the cliché some critics have found it to be, for it is not a eulogy of his friends in their isolated acts but a recognition of how the parts contribute to the unity of a life: "Think where man's glory most begins and ends, / And say my glory was I had such friends."

"Among School Children" (CP, 212–14) addresses a similar experience of memory and unity of being, but its resolution, being objectively portrayed in terms of the impersonal images of dancer and tree, seems somehow more affirmative and more universal than the concluding remarks of the persona in "The Municipal Gallery Revisited." Again the persona finds himself confronting the paradoxes of life and death; here he is self-consciously a "sixty-year-old smiling public man," a "comfortable kind of old scarecrow" in the eyes of the scarcely self-conscious children. As Cleanth Brooks sees it, this is a confrontation of the children's as yet unthreatened innocence, which constitutes a premature unity of being, with the persona's established attitude of experience: "The world of becoming must always suffer when measured against the world of pure being." The persona reacts by recalling his youth and the unity of self and loved one that seems, in retrospect, to have informed it: "It seemed that our two natures blent / Into a sphere from youthful sympathy." But, as Brooks also acknowledges, and as the persona discovers in the course of this meditative experience, the individual in a state of experience or becoming has the advantage of being able to imagine unity of being, whereas a child in the state of primary being cannot, by definition, know himself: "One cannot know the world of being through the world of becoming (though one must remember that the world of becoming is a meaningless flux apart from the world of being which it implies)."[66] The persona can thus conceive the justification for the labor of childbirth, of study, of worship—the empirical pain of each is more than compensated for by the transcendent image of being the laborer works to realize in his own life or mind. Similarly, the persona delivers himself of his two images of unity of being: the chestnut tree that simultaneously embodies age in the life-supporting structure of trunk or bole, maturity in the leaf, and youth in its blossoms; and the dancer, whose empirical identity becomes assimilated with transcendent expression in the process of dance.

The poem is both a discovery of these images of unity and an embodiment of their viability in the human imagination. The poet has labored to make this poem as well, but his labor is a "blossoming or dancing" in that it is indistinguishable from the internal experience of imagination which redeems the empirical identity by association with the transcendent. The imagination attains the transcendent state, which gives the empirical identity it perceives a context of values:

> Yeats's "world" in the major later poems comprises not simply the objects which he promulgates, but also and along with them the acts of thought by which these are promulgated and manipulated. This is what follows from—or creates, depending on how one looks at it—the passionate subjectivity of the poem: an ever-present continuity in them of their vehemently feeling, thinking, willing creator.[67]

The working drafts of "Among School Children" reveal that Yeats originally planned a poem on the betrayal of the soul by the aging body; apparently the experience of contemplating youth and age together precipitated their union and the final ecstatic verse.[68] In "Among School Children," the acts of "feeling, thinking, willing" can hardly be separated from the objects they produce, and the fact that these objects are empirically realistic as well as subjectively ideal finally ratifies this poem as the persona's ultimate attainment of unity of being, of Giovanni Gentile's "mind as pure act."[69] The laboring artist of "Adam's Curse" has finally found his reward, in the realization that his own art and thought, and not a woman's response, complete his identity.

Yeats thought of "The Tower," the volume that contains "Among School Children," and of its sequel, "The Winding Stair," as "evidence . . . that my poetry has gained in self-possession and power" since the "incredible experience" of archetypal structuring that is recorded in *A Vision*.[70] Denis Donoghue takes this comment to indicate that "in those books his doctrine of the Mask has been realised, certified," with the "Mask" implying the poet's facility "to cast himself in 'interesting' roles; the randy old man, the Blueshirt singer, the Fascist Celt."[71] Surely in the light of these later poems, the "self-possession and power" of the mask must be interpreted from the more integrated perspective of the continuous poetic persona, which has indeed developed radically over the course of *The Collected Poems.*

J. R. Mulryne offers an alternative reading of the later poetry, specifically that of the volume "Last Poems," which accounts for this continuous integrity and developing unity on the part of the persona. He sees the later poems as realizing the theory of persona that Yeats presents in the first part of "A General Introduction for My Work":

> The hypnotic logic of this passage offers the poetic act as a true re-demption of the Self; to write poetry is to be re-born, and to be so re-born, as to conquer "accident," "incoherence," "tragedy." The syntax brooks no argument: with this version of the "personal archetypes," artistic remaking of the poet and his beloved, as type, passion, *dramatis personae,* can render nature no longer hostile, but enabling, "part of our creative power." The passage is interesting as theory; more immediately important, its language and its assumptions richly anticipate those of *Last Poems.* The *dramatis personae* of the prose reappear in the verse. . . . The assumptions about actual and imagined reality, and about the poet's access to "creative power," serve as an arena within which are drawn up the encountering dispositions and commitments of *Last Poems.*[72]

Mulryne's thesis has two implications. On the one hand, the persona of "Last Poems" makes archetypal *dramatis personae* of the people, objects, and events of his life by casting them in art, particularly in the medium of sculpture: Maud Gonne in "A Bronze Head," the portraits of "The Municipal Gallery Revisited," the carved "Lapis Lazuli" itself, and the statue of Cuchulain suggested in "The Statues." More significant than the ability to cast these images in sculpted poetry, however, is the persona's persistent act of communicating with them, reinvesting them with empirical flesh from memory and borrowing from them in turn their structured forms with which to shape his own life. Far different from the ironic statue in "Men Improve with the Years," the sculpture in "Last Poems" is a part of life itself: "boys and girls, pale from the imagined love / Of solitary beds, . . . / pressed at midnight in some public place / Live lips upon a plummet-measured face" ("The Statues," CP, 322-23). Mulryne concludes:

> The originality of "The Statues" . . . is that the fixity of the marble becomes, not the antagonist of the living, but the potential locus of life-

enhancing knowledge. The release of this knowledge is accomplished by the exertion of imaginative energy, by the imaginative possession of the archetype as discovered in the statue.[73]

"The Man and the Echo" (CP, 337–39) captures something of the dynamic quality of this interaction of life and death, process and product in the form of a dialogue between the empirical "I" of "Man" and his archetypal identity, the oracular "Echo." Man ponders aloud some questions arising from his own life that plague him for answers, as anticipation of death provokes the need to form a whole identity from the loose ends of life. Echo responds, presumably rendering oracular advice but actually merely repeating the end words of Man. The effect is that Man debates the meaning of his life with himself, and much as in "A Dialogue of Self and Soul," the empirical aspect consults an imagined ideal aspect, which reflects only those qualities of thought that are of lasting value. Man measures his identity against eternity and produces some semblance of unity of being. It may be an internal dialogue, but it is not solipsistic, since it involves two aspects within the self and becomes a union of "mind as pure act."

The final poem of the lyric canon, "Under Ben Bulben" (CP, 341–44), carries this interchange of man and archetype to its natural conclusion. David Lynch objects that Yeats did not intend this poem to conclude *The Collected Poems* and that its power is therefore deceptive:

> The power of Yeats's artifice in "Under Ben Bulben" is reflected by our willingness to read it as if it really were his last poem. It was not, nor was it his intention that it seem to be. His own ordering of *Last Poems and Two Plays* that are now the second half of his "last poems" was quite different from the one adopted by his posthumous editors in the *Collected Poems*. It begins rather than ends with the testament of "Under Ben Bulben"; it concludes (as it were, posthumously) with the "foul rag-and-bone shop of the heart" in "The Circus Animals' Desertion" and the "wild old wicked man" of "Politics." The last three lines of "Under Ben Bulben" have been cut above the poet's grave in Drumcliff churchyard; the table of contents of the *Last Poems and Two Plays* suggests that Yeats might have preferred
>
>> But O that I were young again
>> And held her in my arms![74]

Although Lynch's admonition must be considered in any argument for an intentional aesthetic structure in "Last Poems,"[75] it does not apply to an analysis of the total structure of development of the poetic persona, which proceeds in stages rather than from poem to poem. "Under Ben Bulben" is the final word of this persona, and for a rather paradoxical reason—the poem is not spoken by the "I" but speaks itself, largely in the imperative mood, from the completed identity of the persona as it has evolved through the poetic canon.[76]

The voice that enjoins the reader, "Swear . . . Swear," like the ghost of Hamlet senior; the voice that pronounces on human fate, "Many times man lives and dies / Between his two eternities, / That of race and that of soul / And ancient Ireland knew it all"; the voice that coaxes, "Irish poets, learn your trade, / Sing whatever is well made, . . . / That we in coming days may be / Still the indomitable Irishry"—each issues from the persona who has confronted his own oracle, who has lived the archetypal life of his race, who has sought "perfection" of life in art, and who is anticipated by the author of "A General Introduction for My Work," who proclaims: "I am joined to the 'Irishry' and I expect a counter-Renaissance." The persona does not venture to dictate the details of this Renaissance to his successors, either in poem or in prose, and he cannot. He does not "know," he "embodies" truth. The truest depiction of the individual's hope for unity of being is the empirical persona in his grave, a completed symbol, the essence of his transcendent labor written above for all to see:

> Cast a cold eye
> On life, on death.
> Horseman, pass by!

Yeats originally conceived the epitaph as a quatrain, beginning with the line, "Draw rein, draw breath."[77] He perhaps deleted the first line, because its message is redundant: epitaphs, by the very fact that they exist "as something visibly set up," "arrest the passer-by and compel him to read."[78] The persona's identity has become monolithic, archetypal; it arrests the passer-by but only to admonish him to pass on, after having coldly considered both life and death as impartial archetypal structures. The road to individual unity of being must be traveled with few stops either on the side of life or on that of death; it is the tension between empirical experience and transcendent structure and the struggle to assimilate one with the other, the ongoing "act of mind," that determines the individual's success in arriving at the transcendent "whither" of a unified identity. The epitaph of "Under Ben Bulben" is thus the persona's final symbolic act in the quest for unity of being, but the paradoxical character of that quest—a continuous process of experience within an established archetypal structure—is perhaps more accurately and ironically portrayed in the self-explanatory but unresolved depiction of the persona's development in another late poem, "What Then?" (CP, 299–300):

> His chosen comrades thought at school
> He must grow a famous man;
> He thought the same and lived by rule,
> All his twenties crammed with toil;
> *"What then?" sang Plato's ghost. "What then?"*
>
> Everything he wrote was read,
> After certain years he won
> Sufficient money for his need,
> Friends that have been friends indeed;
> *"What then?" sang Plato's ghost. "What then?"*
>
> All his happier dreams came true—
> A small old house, wife, daughter, son,
> Grounds where plum and cabbage grew,
> Poets and Wits about him drew;
> *"What then?" sang Plato's ghost. "What then?"*
>
> "The work is done," grown old he thought,
> "According to my boyish plan;
> Let the fools rage, I swerved in naught,
> Something to perfection brought";
> *But louder sang that ghost, "What then?"*

Conclusion

THAT chestnut tree of "Among School Children," which is such an ecstatic image of unity of being in its simultaneous embodiment of age, maturity, and new life in bole, leaf, and blossom, has its roots in an essay Yeats wrote in 1893 entitled "Nationality and Literature." The tree of this early article is not an expression of simultaneous being, as is the tree of "Among School Children," but of progressive becoming. Yeats's purpose in this early essay is to illustrate the "general course of literary development and set it apart from mere historical accident and circumstance" by analogy to the natural growth of a tree:

> It grows from a simple seed, and having sent up a little green sprout of no great complexity, though much more complex than its seed, it develops a complex trunk at last and all innumerable and intricate leaves, and flowers, and fruits. Its growth is from unity to multiplicity, from simplicity to complexity, . . . it takes place through a constant sub-division of the constituent cells. I hope to show you that a literature develops in an analogous way, and that this development takes place by a constant sub-division of moods and emotions, corresponding to the sub-division of the cells in the tree. In its youth it is simple, and in its mid-period it grows in complexity, as does the tree when it puts forth many branches, and in its mature age it is covered by an innumerable variety of fruits and flowers and leaves of thought and experience.[1]

The three stages of literature that correspond to the growth of a tree are: "First, the period of narrative poetry, the epic or ballad period; next the dramatic period; and after that the period of lyric poetry." The epic phase is marked by "great racial or national movements and events," a literature that is fundamentally related to its social context, like a tree trunk to the soil. The dramatic phase sees a subdivision of these massive movements "into the

181

characters who lived and wrought in them"; it is a period of the individual expression of archetypes, like branches that divide from but remain attached to the trunk of a tree. The final phase is that of lyric poetry, in which "not only have the racial events disappeared but the great personages themselves, for literature has begun to centre itself about this or that emotion or mood." Like flowers on a tree, lyric poems are most tenuously related to the structure that supports them, while being also that structure's consummate expression of being and its promise of regeneration.[2]

As his organic analogy dictates, Yeats is not interested in isolating and excising any one part of the tree of literature for separate attention; that would only injure the organism. His very position as a lyric poet in a nation he sees as still undergoing its epic-ballad period of development establishes Yeats as witness to the fact that the parts do not exist in isolation from the whole, which is, indeed, his message: literature "must go through these periods no matter how greatly we long for finality," and "our desire should be to make each [period] perfect after its kind." Finally, as nature and literature develop, so do society, mankind, and even the universe:

> Granted fit time and fit occasion, I could apply the same law of division and sub-division and of ever increasing complexity to human society itself—to human life itself—and show you how in the old civilizations an endless šub-division of society to trades and professions, and of human life to habits and rules, is making men every day more subtle and complex, less forcible and adaptable. . . . If time and fit occasion offered, I could take you upon that path, beaten by the feet of the seers, and show you behind human society and human life the causal universe itself, "falling," in the words of my master, William Blake, "into division," and foretell with him "its resurrection into unity."[3]

The flower of lyric poetry will eventually drop to earth, refertilizing the soil of all existence and regenerating new trees, reenacting thereby the universal law. By implication, the poet who would participate in this universal process and embody it in his poetry must be wary of falling into a static concentration on only one phase in the process. The lyric poet, above all, must be aware of the epic and dramatic origins of his verse, which constitute also that verse's destiny, as well as providing the context for the structure of his own life.

This is the basis of Yeats's dislike, in section IV of "A General Introduction for My Work," of poets who celebrate "modern heterogeneity" and of his hatred for its physical manifestations. He anticipates a return to "some kind of rule of kindred," the regeneration of the epic trunk of the tree by the flower of lyricism, but those modern poets who ratify the chaos of the present blind themselves to its future implications. They put their faith in a linear tradition rather than in a cyclic process and so demean the present by isolating it and intensifying its characteristic proliferation of blossoms into a chaos of perceptual experiences: "I feel as neither Eliot nor Ezra do the need of old forms, old situations that, as when I re-create some early poem of my own, I may escape from scepticism. . . . The 'modern man' is a term invented by modern poetry to dignify our scepticism."[4] Yeats's "I" turns inward, to the "tradition of myself," and finds a cyclic integrity that saves him from self-dispersion, which is death in poetry. Unlike those modern poets Yeats refers to in "A General Introduction for My Work" who live in Capri and write of the man who rides the Tube, Yeats, through his poetic persona, speaks primarily of himself and of the world that supplies the meaning and value of the self: "The one reason for putting our actual situation into art is that the struggle for complete affirmation may be, often must be, that art's chief poignancy. I must, though [the] world shriek at me, admit no act beyond my power, nor thing beyond my knowledge, yet because my divinity is far off I blanch and tremble."[5] Where Yeats tempts the derision of the world in defending his self-integrity, other modern poets deter the same derision by openly rejecting the possibility of self-integrity in their art; Yeats sees this weakness particularly in two of his poetic heirs, T. S. Eliot and Ezra Pound.

Yeats readily admits Eliot's "revolutionary" impact on poetry but qualifies it as "stylistic alone": "No romantic word or sound, nothing reminiscent. . . . Poetry must resemble prose, and both must accept the vocabulary of their time; nor must there be any special subject-matter. . . . We older writers disliked this new poetry, but were forced to admit its satiric intensity."[6] For a poet who believes the "struggle for complete affirmation" to be "art's chief poignancy," being forced to admit Eliot's satirical power is not much of a submission; indeed, in his "Introduction" to *The Oxford Book of Modern Verse*, Yeats states plainly, "I think of him as satirist rather than poet."[7] Eliot writes satire because he projects poetic characters as "puppets" rather than as individuals struggling in the archetypal quest for unity of being: "Eliot has produced his great effect upon his generation because he has described men and women that get out of bed or into it from mere habit." Prufrock,

Sweeney, and Gerontion are all poetic characters of limited integrity; they reflect how the world has shaped them rather than how the human mind can shape the world. "In describing this life that has lost heart his own art seems grey, cold, dry"; even when Eliot's "I" seems to speak as a poetic persona, reflecting Eliot's own identity, it is curiously detached from, rather than engaged with, reality: "Eliot's genius is human, mundane, impeccable, it seems to say 'this man will never disappoint, never be out of character. He moves among objects for which he accepts no responsibility, among the mapped and measured.' "[8] Yeats's euphonic paralleling of "heart" and "art" reveals the grounds of his judgment of Eliot—the poet who does not invest his heart in his work does not produce art. Eliot has created some memorable poetic characters but not Yeats's art of "affirmative capability," to use Richard Ellmann's term:

> It begins with the poet's difficulties but emphasizes his resolutions of them. . . . [It consists of] positive statements which were the active expression of a man, distinguished from beliefs or ideas which were outside structures to which the man submitted himself. . . . Yeats requires an art based on affirmations, then, by representing it as the expression of the fundamental urge of living beings, to transcend themselves.[9]

Where Yeats finds Eliot to err in the direction of poetic characterization, projecting satiric portraits of partial beings, he conceives of Ezra Pound as losing control, at the other end of the poetic equation, of poetic structure: "Ezra Pound has made flux his theme."[10] In his introductory material to *A Vision*, Yeats discusses the structure of Pound's massive work, *The Cantos:*

> I have often found there brightly printed kings, queens, knaves, but have never discovered why all the suits could not be dealt out in some quite different order. Now at last [Pound] explains that it will, when the hundredth canto is finished, display a structure like that of a Bach Fugue. There will be no plot, no chronicle of events, no logic of discourse, but two themes, the Descent into Hades from Homer, a Metamorphosis from Ovid, and, mixed with these, mediaeval or modern historical characters. He has tried . . . to achieve a work as characteristic of the art of our time as the paintings of Cézanne . . . as *Ulysses* and its dream association of words and images, a poem in which there is nothing that can be taken out and reasoned over, nothing that is not part of the poem itself.[11]

It is telling that Yeats devotes extensive attention to Pound's *Cantos* in *A Vision*. The two poets have demonstrated similar urges toward creating a large abstract structure that would encompass all reality and then filling that structure with details from their own experiences in particular and from human history in general. Where Yeats erects that structure in the prose of *A Vision*, however, and only assimilates it into his poetry primarily in terms of the persona's consciousness of his own developmental cycle, Pound attempts to conceive the structure in the poetry itself. Yeats has misgivings about the resultant mixture of noble style with "its direct opposite, nervous obsession, nightmare, stammering confusion": "Has the author been carried beyond reason by a theoretical conception? . . . This loss of self-control . . . is rare . . . among men of Ezra Pound's culture and erudition. Style and its opposite can alternate, but form must be full, sphere-like, single."[12]

If either structure or persona becomes detached from the writer's poetic identity, the poetry will reflect "modern heterogeneity" and not the quest toward unity of being. In Yeats's poetic canon, the structure reflects the development of the persona, as the persona unites both Yeats's empirical identity and his transcendent yearnings made concrete in the archetypal forms of art. Poetic persona and poetic structure cannot be separated in Yeats's art and cannot be fully divorced from Yeats himself. As editor of *The Oxford Book of Modern Verse*, Yeats has been severely criticized for favoring friends and fellow countrymen and for neglecting his truly great poetic peers. In his "Introduction" to the volume, however, Yeats justifies his selection in terms of the relationship of poetic persona and poetic structure and concludes with a self-portrait that embodies his preference for process over product in art and for experience over evaluation:

> I have said nothing of my own work, not from modesty, but because writing through fifty years I have been now of the same school with John Synge and James Stephens, now in that of Sturge Moore and the younger "Michael Field": and though the concentration of philosophy and social passion of the school of Day Lewis and in MacNeice lay beyond my desire, I would, but for a failure of talent have been in that of Turner and Dorothy Wellesley.[13]

This self-denigration is a false modesty, for Yeats has not only lived through these periods and more, he has written some of the best poetry of each. The important point, however, is that his

lyrics still cling to the boughs and trunk of his artistic identity; his
persona has developed in stages, but the development in its totality
is an integrated whole.

In his being at once the voice of a lyric mood and the representative of a stage in a developmental structure, Yeats's poetic persona
achieves that unity of being which the "great-rooted blossomer" of
"Among School Children" embodies, and he participates as well in
the confluence of epic, dramatic, and lyrical art which Yeats illustrates with a tree in "Nationality and Literature." In his prefatory
notes to that essay, John Frayne argues that Yeats achieved in
himself the dramatic stage of literary development in founding the
Irish national theater, and that his achievement of the lyric phase
was self-evident, but that he "abandoned" the epic phase following
"The Wanderings of Oisin."[14] If Yeats's achievements are assessed
in terms of his poetic persona, however, it is obvious that the
development of that persona through the poetic canon constitutes
an archetypal image of the human situation that is epic in scale.
The blossoming lyric expressions grow from the boughs of dramatic interaction between empirical and transcendent aspects of
identity, which, in turn, branch off from the governing structure
of a quest for identity. The unity of being that Yeats achieves in the
process of his persona's development within the product of the
structured poetic canon is the universal movement of "resurrection
into unity":

A little lyric evokes an emotion, and this emotion gathers others about
it and melts into their being in the making of some great epic; and at
last, needing an always less delicate body, or symbol, as it grows more
powerful, it flows out, with all it has gathered, among the blind instincts of daily life, where it moves a power within power, as one sees
ring within ring in the stem of an old tree.[15]

Notes

INTRODUCTION

1. W. B. Yeats, *The Letters*, ed. Allan Wade (London: Rupert Hart-Davis, 1954), p. 548.

2. W. B. Yeats, "Friends of My Youth": Lecture Transcript and Notes, *Yeats and the Theatre*, ed. Robert O'Driscoll and Lorna Reynolds (London: Macmillan & Co., 1975), pp. 38–39.

3. Ibid., p. 32.

4. W. B. Yeats, *The Autobiography* (New York: Macmillan, 1965), pp. 185–234.

5. Yeats, "Friends of My Youth," p. 76.

6. Ibid., pp. 77–78; italics added.

7. Horace Gregory, "W. B. Yeats and the Mask of Jonathan Swift," *The Southern Review* 7 (1941–1942): 493.

8. Richard Ellmann, *Yeats: The Man and the Masks* (New York: Macmillan, 1948), pp. 171–76.

9. Richard Ellmann, *The Identity of Yeats*, 2d ed. (New York: Oxford University Press, 1954), pp. 5–6.

10. Thomas Parkinson, *W. B. Yeats: The Later Poetry* (Berkeley: University of California Press, 1964), pp. 42–57.

11. Ellmann, *The Identity of Yeats*, pp. 5–6.

12. Giovanni Gentile, *Theory of Mind as Pure Act*, trans. H. Wildon Carr (London: Macmillan & Co., 1922), pp. 5–6.

13. Harold Bloom, *Yeats* (New York: Oxford University Press, 1970), p. 184.

14. W. B. Yeats, *The Collected Poems* (New York: Macmillan, 1956); except where otherwise noted, all quotations from Yeats's poetry refer to this edition and are cited throughout the text of this study following the designation "CP."

15. Helen Regueiro, *The Limits of Imagination: Wordsworth, Yeats, and Stevens* (Ithaca, N.Y.: Cornell University Press, 1976), pp. 122–23.

16. See Adolf Trendelenburg, "A Contribution to the History of the Word Person," *The Monist* 20 (1910): 336–59.

17. Yeats, "Friends of My Youth," p. 78.

18. Gentile, *Theory of Mind as Pure Act*, p. 6.

19. Yeats, *The Autobiography*, p. 128.

20. Hugh Kenner, "The Sacred Book of the Arts," in Hugh Kenner, *Gnomon* (New York: Ivan Obolensky, 1958), pp. 14, 22.

21. Yeats, "Friends of My Youth," p. 80.

22. W. B. Yeats, "A General Introduction for My Work," in W. B. Yeats, *Essays and Introductions* (New York: Macmillan, 1961), pp. 509–26.

CHAPTER 1

1. W. B. Yeats, "A General Introduction for My Work," in W. B. Yeats, *Essays and Introductions* (New York: Macmillan, 1961), p. 509.

2. W. B. Yeats, *The Variorum Edition of the Poems*, ed. Peter Allt and Russell K. Alspach (New York: Macmillan, 1957), p. 778. This poem was originally published as the epigram to volume 2 of the Stratford-on-Avon edition of Yeats's *Collected Works in Verse and Prose* (1908).

3. *The Ten Principal Upanishads*, trans. Shree Purohit Swami and W. B. Yeats (New York: Macmillan, 1937). See "Eesha-Upanishad," for instance: "The Self is one. Unmoving, it moves faster than the mind. The senses lag, but Self runs ahead. Unmoving, it outruns pursuit. Out of Self comes the breath that is the life of all things" (p. 15).

4. W. B. Yeats, "Dramatis Personae, 1896–1902," in *The Autobiography* (New York: Macmillan, 1965); on Browning, see W. B. Yeats, *Letters to the New Island*, ed. Horace Reynolds (Cambridge, Mass.: Harvard University Press, 1934), p. 98; W. B. Yeats, "J. M. Synge and the Ireland of His Time," in Yeats, *Essays and Introductions*, p. 330; W. B. Yeats, "Swedenborg, Mediums and the Desolate Places," in W. B. Yeats, *Explorations* (New York: Macmillan, 1962), p. 56; see also W. B. Yeats, *A Vision: A Reissue with the Author's Final Revisions* (New York: Macmillan, 1956), pp. 23, 227.

5. *Webster's Third New International Dictionary of the English Language Unabridged* (Springfield, Mass.: G. & C. Merriam, 1961); *The Concise Oxford Dictionary of Current English*, 6th ed. (Oxford: Clarendon Press, 1976).

6. This is the finding of Robert O. Payne; see "Chaucer's Realization of Himself as Rhetor," in *Medieval Eloquence: Studies in the Theory and Practice of Medieval Rhetoric*, ed. James J. Murphy (Berkeley: University of California Press, 1978), p. 278.

7. Plato, *The Dialogues*, 4th ed., trans. B. Jowett (Oxford: Clarendon Press, 1953), pp. 241, 480, 479.

8. George T. Wright, *The Poet in the Poem: The Personae of Eliot, Yeats, and Pound* (Berkeley: University of California Press, 1960), p. 9.

9. Adolf Trendelenburg, "A Contribution to the History of the Word Person," *The Monist* 20 (1910): 345.

10. Yeats, *A Vision*, p. 272; W. B. Yeats, "Per Amica Silentia Lunae," in *Mythologies* (New York: Macmillan, 1959), pp. 319–69. Yeats's understanding, or lack of understanding, of the Stoic doctrine is unclear. Perhaps his condemnation of the Stoics reflects primarily his enthusiasm for Nietzsche, who harangues Stoic philosophy in *Beyond Good and Evil:* "You desire to *live* 'according to Nature'? Oh, you noble Stoics, what fraud of words! . . . While you pretend to read with rapture the canon of your law in Nature, you want something quite the contrary, you extraordinary stage-players and self-deluders! In your pride you wish to dictate your morals and ideals to Nature." From Friedrich Nietzsche,

Beyond Good and Evil: Prelude to a Philosophy of the Future, trans. Helen Zimmern (Edinburgh: T. N. Foulis, 1909), p. 13.

11. Robert Langbaum, *The Mysteries of Identity: A Theme in Modern Literature* (New York: Oxford University Press, 1977), p. 160.

12. *A Dictionary of Modern Critical Terms*, ed. Roger Fowler (Boston: Routledge & Kegan Paul, 1973).

13. Wayne C. Booth, *The Rhetoric of Fiction* (Chicago: University of Chicago Press, 1961), pp. 70–71, 73.

14. For representative opposing positions in the debate, see: E. Talbot Donaldson, "Chaucer the Pilgrim," *Publications of the Modern Language Association of America* 69 (1954): 928–36; Donald Howard, "Chaucer the Man," *Publications of the Modern Language Association of America* 80 (1965): 337–43; and, more recently, Thomas J. Garbáty, "The Degradation of Chaucer's 'Geffrey'," *Publications of the Modern Language Association of America* 89 (1974): 97–104.

15. Leo Spitzer, "Note on the Poetic and the Empirical 'I' in Medieval Authors," *Traditio* 4 (1946): 415–16, 417.

16. Yeats, "Per Amica Silentia Lunae," p. 329.

17. Yeats, *The Autobiography*, p. 101.

18. Walter J. Ong, S. J., "Voice as Summons for Belief," in *Literature and Belief: English Institute Essays, 1957*, ed. M. H. Abrams (New York: Columbia University Press, 1958), pp. 86–87.

19. Virginia Moore, *The Unicorn: William Butler Yeats's Search for Reality* (New York: Macmillan, 1954), pp. 187–88; Moore's source in this passage is Israel Regardie, *The Golden Dawn: An Account of the Teachings, Rites and Ceremonies of the Order of the Golden Dawn*, 4 vols. (Chicago: Aries Press, 1937–40). A. Norman Jeffares also gives an account of the biographical development of "Yeats's Mask," in *English Studies* (1949), reprinted in *The Circus Animals: Essays on W. B. Yeats* (New York: Macmillan, 1970), pp. 3–14.

20. Edward Dowden, *Studies in Literature, 1789–1877*, 5th ed. (London: Kegan Paul, Trench, 1889), p. 240.

21. Yeats, *The Autobiography*, p. 58.

22. W. B. Yeats, "The Poetry of Sir Samuel Ferguson, II," in *Dublin University Review* (Nov. 1886), as reprinted in W. B. Yeats, *Uncollected Prose*, vol. 1, ed. John P. Frayne (New York: Columbia University Press, 1970), p. 89.

23. W. B. Yeats, "Friends of My Youth": Lecture Transcript and Notes, *Yeats and the Theatre*, ed. Robert O'Driscoll and Lorna Reynolds (London: Macmillan & Co., 1975), p. 74.

24. Yeats, *The Autobiography*, pp. 89–90. Yeats gives the year as 1887 or 1888; Richard Ellmann fixes it at 1888, in *Eminent Domain: Yeats among Wilde, Joyce, Pound, Eliot, and Auden* (New York: Oxford University Press, 1967), p. 13.

25. Oscar Wilde, "The Decay of Lying," in *The Artist as Critic: Critical Writings of Oscar Wilde*, ed. Richard Ellmann (New York: Random House, 1968), pp. 297, 307, 320.

26. Yeats, *The Autobiography*, pp. 92–93.

27. Ellmann, *Eminent Domain*, p. 16.

28. Wright, *The Poet in the Poem*, p. 99.

29. In *The Autobiography*, Yeats records that his father introduced him to Blake at age fifteen or sixteen (p. 76), and that he began his study of Blake with Ellis in 1889 (p. 108).

30. Edwin John Ellis and William Butler Yeats, *The Works of William Blake: Poetic, Symbolic, and Critical,* vol. 1 (London: Bernard Quaritch, 1893), p. 89.

31. Ibid., vol. 1, pp. 242–43. Yeats wrote in the margin of his personal copy of *The Works of William Blake,* "The greater part of the 'symbolic system' is my writing"; see Hazard Adams, *Blake and Yeats: The Contrary Vision* (Ithaca, N.Y.: Cornell University Press, 1955), pp. 46–48.

32. Ellis and Yeats, *The Works of William Blake,* vol. 2, p. 244.

33. Northrop Frye, in *Fearful Symmetry: A Study of William Blake* (Princeton, N.J.: Princeton University Press, 1947), is the premier authority on Blake and his system; accordingly, I consult him throughout for the accuracy of the interpretations of Yeats and Ellis.

34. See Northrop Frye, "Yeats and the Language of Symbolism," *University of Toronto Quarterly* 17 (1947); as reprinted in *Fables of Identity: Studies in Poetic Mythology* (New York: Harcourt, Brace & World, 1963), p. 234; and Harold Bloom, *Yeats* (New York: Oxford University Press, 1970), p. 73.

35. W. B. Yeats, "William Blake and His Illustrations to the *Divine Comedy,*" in *Essays and Introductions,* p. 119.

36. Yeats, "Nationality and Literature," *United Ireland* (27 May 1893); as reprinted in *Uncollected Prose,* vol. 1, p. 273.

37. Adams, *Blake and Yeats,* pp. 7, 17–18.

38. Ellis and Yeats, *The Works of William Blake,* vol. 2, pp. 17, 76, 275.

39. Ibid., vol. 2, p. 276.

40. Bloom, *Yeats,* pp. 76–79.

41. Ellis and Yeats, *The Works of William Blake,* vol. 2, pp. 288, 294.

42. Ibid., vol. 2, pp. 290, 288.

43. Robert Snukal, *High Talk: The Philosophical Poetry of W. B. Yeats* (Cambridge: Cambridge University Press, 1973), p. 2.

44. See, for instance, Denis Donoghue, *William Butler Yeats* (New York: Viking, 1971), pp. 52–60; Richard Ellmann, *The Identity of Yeats* (New York: Oxford University Press, 1964), pp. 92–98; and Thomas R. Whitaker, *Swan and Shadow: Yeats's Dialogue with History* (Chapel Hill: University of North Carolina Press, 1964), passim. Yeats declares that "Nietzsche completes Blake and has the same roots," in W. B. Yeats, *The Letters,* ed. Allan Wade (London: Rupert Hart-Davis, 1954), p. 379.

45. *W. B. Yeats and T. Sturge Moore: Their Correspondence, 1901–1937,* ed. Ursula Bridge (London: Routledge & Kegan Paul, 1953).

46. Donald T. Torchiana, *W. B. Yeats and Georgian Ireland* (Evanston, Ill.: Northwestern University Press, 1966), p. 226.

47. See W. B. Yeats, "Pages from a Diary Written in Nineteen Hundred and Thirty," in *Explorations,* p. 323.

48. Yeats, "Bishop Berkeley," in *Essays and Introductions,* p. 398.

49. Ibid., p. 400.

50. Ibid., pp. 405, 408n.

51. *W. B. Yeats and T. Sturge Moore,* pp. 79–80.

52. Yeats, "Bishop Berkeley," pp. 404–5.

53. Ibid., p. 408.

54. Ibid., p. 409.

55. Torchiana, *W. B. Yeats and Georgian Ireland,* p. 252; and Moore, *The Unicorn,* pp. 322–26. See also, Donald T. Torchiana, " 'Among School Children' and the Education of the Irish Spirit," in *In Excited Reverie: A Centenary Tribute*

to William Butler Yeats, 1865–1939, ed. A. Norman Jeffares and K. G. W. Cross (New York: St. Martin's, 1965), pp. 123–50.

56. W. B. Yeats, "The Child and the State," in W. B. Yeats, *The Senate Speeches,* ed. Donald R. Pearce (Bloomington: Indiana University Press, 1960), p. 173.

57. Giovanni Gentile, *The Reform of Education,* trans. Dino Bigongiari (New York: Harcourt, Brace, 1922), p. 231.

58. *W. B. Yeats and T. Sturge Moore,* p. 89; Yeats, *The Letters,* p. 782.

59. Yeats, *A Vision,* p. 70; see also p. 81n.

60. Giovanni Gentile, *Theory of Mind as Pure Act,* trans. H. Wildon Carr (London: Macmillan & Co., 1922), p. 147. For Gentile's term *transcendental* I substitute *transcendent* in this work, in order to avoid any unwarranted associations with other specific schools of philosophy which use the former term as well.

61. Ibid., pp. 31–32; Blake, *The Poetry and Prose,* pp. 481, 36.

62. Gentile, *Theory of Mind as Pure Act,* p. 251.

63. Ibid., p. 101.

64. Ellis and Yeats, *The Works of William Blake,* vol. 2, pp. 403–5.

65. Gentile, *Theory of Mind as Pure Act,* p. 152.

66. Ibid., pp. 224, 207, 220.

67. Yeats, "Friends of My Youth": Lecture Notes, in *Yeats and the Theatre,* p. 74.

68. Gentile, *Theory of Mind as Pure Act,* p. xxvii; the tree metaphor nicely complements Torchiana's reading of "Among School Children" in *In Excited Reverie.*

69. Wright, *The Poet in the Poem,* p. 123.

70. Langbaum, *The Mysteries of Identity,* pp. 159, 173–74.

CHAPTER 2

1. W. B. Yeats, "A General Introduction for My Work," in W. B. Yeats, *Essays and Introductions* (New York: Macmillan, 1961), pp. 519, 520.

2. Ibid., pp. 519, 510–11.

3. Ibid., p. 518.

4. Richard J. Finneran, "Yeats's Revisions in *The Celtic Twilight,* 1912–1925," *Tulane Studies in English* 20 (1972): 99; Professor Warwick Gould, of the University of London, confirms by private correspondence that "Per Amica Silentia Lunae" was not included in the early unpublished "Mythologies."

5. Richard J. Finneran, ed., *John Sherman & Dhoya* (Detroit: Wayne State University Press, 1969), p. 128, n. 26.

6. W. B. Yeats, *The Letters,* ed. Allan Wade (London: Rupert Hart-Davis, 1954), p. 22.

7. Richard Ellmann, *Yeats: The Man and the Masks* (New York: Maemillan, 1948), pp. 78–80.

8. Richard J. Finneran, *The Prose Fiction of W. B. Yeats: The Search for "Those Simple Forms"* (Dublin: Dolmen, 1973), pp. 27, 30. Finneran has paid some attention to the prose but not at great length.

9. In a letter to Katharine Tynan about the novel Yeats emphasizes Sherman's

Irishness, spells out its virtues, and claims to emulate his own character; see Yeats, *The Letters*, pp. 187–88.

10. Allan Wade, *A Bibliography of the Writings of W. B. Yeats*, 3d ed., ed. Russell K. Alspach (London: Rupert Hart-Davis, 1968), p. 28.

11. W. B. Yeats, *The Celtic Twilight: Men and Women, Dhouls and Faeries* (London: Lawrence & Bullen, 1893), pp. ix–x.

12. Finneran, "Yeats's Revisions in *The Celtic Twilight*," p. 103. Finneran finds among the results of these revisions a "development of a more skeptical attitude by the narrator towards the objective validity of 'Fairyland'" (p. 99).

13. W. B. Yeats, *Mythologies* (New York: Macmillan, 1959); all references to this volume will be given in the text following the designation "M."

14. Yeats, *The Letters*, p. 922.

15. W. B. Yeats, "Pages from a Diary Written in Nineteen Hundred and Thirty," in W. B. Yeats, *Explorations* (New York: Macmillan, 1962), p. 333.

16. Yeats has adapted this phrase from a letter by William Blake; see William Blake, *The Poetry and Prose*, ed. David V. Erdman (New York: Doubleday, 1965), p. 707. For the significance of this letter to Yeats, see W. B. Yeats, *Letters to the New Island*, ed. Horace Reynolds (Cambridge, Mass.: Harvard University Press, 1934), p. 94.

17. Philip L. Marcus, *Yeats and the Beginning of the Irish Renaissance* (Ithaca, N.Y.: Cornell University Press, 1970), pp. 49–50.

18. W. B. Yeats, *The Secret Rose* (London: Lawrence & Bullen, 1897), p. vii.

19. Finneran, *The Prose Fiction of W. B. Yeats*, p. 17.

20. Yeats, *The Letters*, p. 286.

21. Richard J. Finneran, "'Old lecher with a love on every wind': A Study of Yeats's *Stories of Red Hanrahan*," *Texas Studies in Literature and Language* 14 (1972): 354. See also, F. A. C. Wilson, *Yeats's Iconography* (New York: Macmillan, 1960), pp. 46–52; Wilson defines five stages of quest in *Stories of Red Hanrahan* and characterizes them as an "inhibited grail adventure" (p. 52).

22. Michael J. Sidnell, "Versions of the Stories of Red Hanrahan," in *Yeats Studies*, vol. 1. *Yeats and the 1890s* (Shannon: Irish University Press, 1971), p. 119. See also David Lynch, *Yeats: The Poetics of the Self* (Chicago: University of Chicago Press, 1979), pp. 17–28, for an analysis of Hanrahan as surrogate poet-figure in Yeats's explorations of his own poetic fate.

23. Robert O'Driscoll, "*The Tables of the Law*: A Critical Text," in *Yeats Studies*, vol. 1, p. 93.

24. Frank Lentricchia, *The Gaiety of Language: An Essay on the Radical Poetics of W. B. Yeats and Wallace Stevens* (Berkeley: University of California Press, 1968), p. 85: "As a Yeatsian persona, Hanrahan symbolizes the poet caught between two worlds, neither of which will have him."

25. Ellmann, *Yeats: The Man and the Masks*, p. 83; Finneran, *The Prose Fiction of W. B. Yeats*, p. 20; John A. Lester, Jr., "Joyce, Yeats, and the Short Story," *English Literature in Transition* 15 (1972): 310.

26. Hugh Kenner has argued for the latter definition of other personae of modern literature: Prufrock of T. S. Eliot's "The Love Song of J. Alfred Prufrock," and Stephen Dedalus of James Joyce's *A Portrait of the Artist as a Young Man*. See *The Invisible Poet: T. S. Eliot* (New York: Ivan Obolensky, 1959); and *Dublin's Joyce* (Bloomington: Indiana University Press, 1956).

27. Horatio Sheafe Krans, *William Butler Yeats and the Irish Literary Revival* (London: William Heinemann, 1905), pp. 157–58.

28. O'Driscoll, *"The Tables of the Law,"* p. 88.

29. Lentricchia, *The Gaiety of Language*, pp. 86–87.

30. Robert Langbaum, *The Mysteries of Identity: A Theme in Modern Literature* (New York: Oxford University Press, 1977), pp. 179, 181.

31. W. B. Yeats, "Bishop Berkeley," in *Essays and Introductions*, p. 404.

32. The original version of "Rosa Alchemica," which appeared in *The Savoy* in 1896, specifies the death of Michael Robartes; Robartes, of course, is resurrected in the first edition of *A Vision*.

33. Blake, *The Poetry and Prose*, p. 37.

34. O'Driscoll, *"The Tables of the Law,"* p. 93.

35. Ibid., pp. 96–97.

36. Ellmann, *Yeats: The Man and the Masks*, p. 83.

37. W. B. Yeats, "Preface" to *The Wild Swans at Coole* (London: Macmillan, 1919), as reprinted in W. B. Yeats, *The Variorum Edition of the Poems*, ed. Peter Allt and Russell K. Alspach (New York: Macmillan, 1957), p. 852.

38. W. B. Yeats, *Memoirs: Autobiography—First Draft, Journal*, ed. Denis Donoghue (London: Macmillan & Co., 1972), p. 138.

39. Richard Ellmann, *The Identity of Yeats* (New York: Oxford University Press, 1964), pp. 305–6.

40. Harold Bloom, *Yeats* (New York: Oxford University Press, 1970), pp. 198–99.

41. See Langbaum, *The Mysteries of Identity*, p. 163, for an excellent discussion of this poem and its title.

42. Ibid., pp. 163–64; Richard Ellmann records that Ezra Pound identified the two voices as "Hic and Willie," in *Eminent Domain: Yeats among Wilde, Joyce, Pound, Eliot, and Auden* (New York: Oxford University Press, 1967), p. 71.

43. W. B. Yeats, "The Trembling of the Veil," in W. B. Yeats, *The Autobiography* (New York: Macmillan, 1965), p. 208.

44. Peter Ure, *Yeats and Anglo-Irish Literature: Critical Essays*, ed. C. J. Rawson (Liverpool: Liverpool University Press, 1974), p. 96.

45. Bloom, *Yeats*, p. 184.

46. This diary is now published as "Estrangement: Extracts from a Diary Kept in 1909," in Yeats, *The Autobiography*; see pp. 317–18 for the original copy.

47. Blake, *The Poetry and Prose*, p. 151.

48. Langbaum, *The Mysteries of Identity*, pp. 166–67; Langbaum's discussion of mask draws heavily on Yeats's poem, "The Mask" (CP, 286).

49. Giovanni Gentile, *Theory of Mind as Pure Act*, trans. H. Wildon Carr (London: Macmillan & Co., 1922), p. 251.

50. Adolf Trendelenburg, "A Contribution to the History of the Word Person," *The Monist* 20 (1910): 345.

51. Langbaum, *The Mysteries of Identity*, p. 159.

52. Edwin John Ellis and W. B. Yeats, *The Works of William Blake: Poetic, Symbolic, and Critical*, vol. 2 (London: Bernard Quaritch, 1893), p. 405.

53. Yeats, *The Autobiography*, pp. 170, 176; see also, pp. 180–81.

54. Ibid., pp. 170, 181, 176, 182–83.

55. Lentricchia, *The Gaiety of Language*, pp. 75, 64–65; Finneran, in *The Prose Fiction of W. B. Yeats*, argues that Yeats failed to find an anonymous mask in the fictional prose but that this "failure" leads to "triumph" in another genre, that of "direct autobiography" (p. 31).

56. Finneran, Ibid.; Curtis B. Bradford, *Yeats at Work* (Carbondale: Southern Illinois University Press, 1965), pp. 348–49.

57. Ure, *Yeats and Anglo-Irish Literature*, pp. 47–48.

CHAPTER 3

1. W. B. Yeats, "A General Introduction for My Work," in *Essays and Introductions* (New York: Macmillan, 1961), p. 521.

2. Ibid., p. 522.

3. Ibid., p. 524.

4. W. B. Yeats, *The Autobiography* (New York: Macmillan, 1965), pp. 349, 311; for style as a discipline in youth, see pp. 48, 135. All references to *The Autobiography* will apply to this edition and will henceforth appear in the text, following the designation "A."

5. W. B. Yeats, *A Vision: A Reissue with the Author's Final Revisions* (New York: Macmillan, 1956), p. 7; all future references to this, the second, edition of *A Vision* will appear in the text following the designation "V."

6. See, for example, Maud Gonne MacBride, "Yeats and Ireland," in *Scattering Branches: Tributes to the Memory of W. B. Yeats*, ed. Stephen Gwynn (New York: Macmillan, 1940), p. 21.

7. David Lynch, *Yeats: The Poetics of the Self* (Chicago: University of Chicago Press, 1979), p. 5.

8. Marjorie Perloff, " 'The Tradition of Myself': The Autobiographical Mode of Yeats," *Journal of Modern Literature* 4 (1975): 550, 551.

9. Richard Ellmann, *Yeats: The Man and the Masks* (New York: Oxford University Press, 1948), pp. 3, 2.

10. W. B. Yeats, *Memoirs: Autobiography—First Draft, Journal*, ed. Denis Donoghue (London: Macmillan & Co., 1972).

11. See "Memoirs" in William Flint Thrall and Addison Hibbard, *A Handbook to Literature*, rev. ed., ed. C. Hugh Holman (New York: Odyssey, 1960).

12. Yeats, *Memoirs*, p. 19n.

13. Ibid., pp. 40, 42.

14. Denis Donoghue, "Introduction" to Yeats, *Memoirs*, pp. 11–12.

15. Francis R. Hart, "Notes for an Anatomy of Modern Autobiography," *New Literary History* 1 (1969–1970): 486, 492–93.

16. W. B. Yeats, *The Letters*, ed. Allan Wade (London: Rupert Hart-Davis, 1954), p. 589.

17. Roy Pascal, *Design and Truth in Autobiography* (London: Routledge & Kegan Paul, 1960), p. 9.

18. Dillon Johnston, "The Perpetual Self in Yeats's *Autobiographies*," *Éire-Ireland* 9 (1974): 69, 77, 85.

19. Joseph Ronsley, *Yeats's Autobiography: Life as Symbolic Pattern* (Cambridge, Mass.: Harvard University Press, 1968), pp. 3, 11.

20. The "Journal" is now reprinted in Yeats, *Memoirs*.

21. Curtis B. Bradford, *Yeats at Work* (Carbondale: Southern Illinois University Press, 1965), pp. 340–41.

22. Yeats, *The Letters*, p. 627.

23. Ian Fletcher, "Rhythm and Pattern in 'Autobiographies,'" in *An Honoured Guest: New Essays on W. B. Yeats*, ed. Denis Donoghue and J. R. Mulryne (London: Edward Arnold, 1965), p. 166.

24. Pascal, *Design and Truth in Autobiography*, pp. 10–11.

25. This poem and its structure are explored in chapter 4.

26. Pascal, *Design and Truth in Autobiography*, p. 45.

27. Johnston, "The Perpetual Self in Yeats's *Autobiographies*," pp. 71n, 71.

28. Pascal, *Design and Truth in Autobiography*, p. 194.

29. Richard Ellmann, in *The Artist as Critic: Critical Writings of Oscar Wilde* (New York: Random House, 1968), discusses the influence of Pater on Wilde; see pp. xiiff.

30. Morton Dauwen Zabel, "The Thinking of the Body: Yeats in the Autobiographies," *The Southern Review* 7 (1941–1942): 579, 585.

31. "Alastor" is usually taken to refer to the "spirit of solitude" in Shelley's poem that leads the unnamed Poet to his death; Yeats has apparently taken "Alastor" to be the Poet's name.

32. Percy Bysshe Shelley, *Poetical Works*, new ed., ed. Thomas Hutchinson, (New York: Oxford University Press, 1970), p. 159.

33. Ibid., p. 471.

34. Yeats, *The Letters*, p. 922.

35. George Bornstein, *Yeats and Shelley* (Chicago: University of Chicago Press, 1970), p. 55.

36. Johnston, "The Perpetual Self in Yeats's *Autobiographies*," p. 81.

37. Harold Bloom, *Yeats* (New York: Oxford University Press, 1970), p. 57.

38. W. B. Yeats, "The Philosophy of Shelley's Poetry," in *Essays and Introductions*, p. 80; for Yeats's source, see Shelley, *Poetical Works*, p. 34.

39. Yeats, "The Philosophy of Shelley's Poetry," p. 95.

40. W. B. Yeats, "Prometheus Unbound," in Yeats, *Essays and Introductions*, pp. 423–24.

41. Ibid., pp. 424–25.

42. W. B. Yeats, *Letters to the New Island*, ed. Horace Reynolds (Cambridge, Mass.: Harvard University Press, 1934), p. 146.

43. Ronsley, *Yeats's Autobiography*, p. 104.

44. See Ibid., for an account of the Yeats-Moore conflict.

45. Ibid., p. 128.

46. Zabel, "The Thinking of the Body," p. 586.

47. Friedrich Nietzsche, *Beyond Good and Evil: Prelude to a Philosophy of the Future*, trans. Helen Zimmern (Edinburgh: T. N. Foulis, 1909), p. 10; W. B. Yeats, "Introduction to 'The Resurrection,'" in *Explorations* (New York: Macmillan, 1962), p. 397.

48. W. B. Yeats, *A Vision: An Explanation of Life Founded upon the Writings of Giraldus and upon Certain Doctrines Attributed to Kusta Ben Luka* (London: T. Werner Laurie, 1925), pp. ix, xi–xii.

49. Ellmann, *Yeats*, pp. 235–36.

50. Yeats, *A Vision* (ed. 1), pp. xxiii.

51. Ibid., p. xii.

52. Lynch, *Yeats*, p. 84.

53. Cleanth Brooks, "Yeats: The Poet as Myth-Maker," *The Southern Review*

4 (1938), as reprinted in Cleanth Brooks, *Modern Poetry and the Tradition* (Chapel Hill: University of North Carolina Press, 1939), pp. 175, 200.

54. Helen Hennessy Vendler, *Yeats's VISION and the Later Plays* (Cambridge, Mass.: Harvard University Press, 1963), pp. 30, 74–75.

55. Bloom, *Yeats*, p. 216.

56. Richard Ellmann, *The Identity of Yeats* (New York: Oxford University Press, 1964), p. 323.

57. See the research of James Lovic Allen, "Yeats's Phase in the System of *A Vision*," *Éire-Ireland* 8 (1973): 95–96; Allen's contention that Yeats may well have projected himself in phase 13 is provocative but overargued. See also, Stuart Hirschberg, "Why Yeats Saw Himself as a '*Daimonic* Man' of Phase 17: A Complementary View," *English Language Notes* 11 (1974): 202–6, for another ingenious analysis of Yeats in *A Vision*, this one employing astrological mathematics.

58. Contrast pp. 42 and 115 of *The Autobiography* for the transition in self-perception from lonely, introspective youth to "gregarious" adult; both passages are linked with Shelley and together suggest that in assimilating these antithetical selves in the structure of *A Vision* Yeats has superseded Shelley's systemless technique of embodying personae in sequence. Recall also Yeats's statement, "When I was immature I was a different person and can stand apart and judge" (Yeats, *The Letters*, p. 589).

59. Bloom, *Yeats*, p. 243.

60. Yeats, *The Letters*, p. 675.

61. Yeats, *A Vision* (ed. 1), pp. 251–52.

62. Northrop Frye, "The Top of the Tower: A Study of the Imagery of Yeats," *The Southern Review* 5 (1969), as reprinted in Northrop Frye, *The Stubborn Structure: Essays on Criticism and Society* (Ithaca, N.Y.: Cornell University Press, 1970), p. 272. Also, Northrop Frye, *The Secular Scripture: A Study of the Structure of Romance* (Cambridge, Mass.: Harvard University Press, 1976), p. 92.

63. Northrop Frye, "Yeats and the Language of Symbolism," *University of Toronto Quarterly* 17 (1947), as reprinted in Northrop Frye, *Fables of Identity: Studies in Poetic Mythology* (New York: Harcourt, Brace & World, 1963), pp. 230–31.

64. William Blake, *The Poetry and Prose*, ed. David V. Erdman (New York: Doubleday, 1962), pp. 523–24; that Yeats was familiar with Blake's reading of Chaucer is apparent from the reference in E. J. Ellis and W. B. Yeats, *The Works of William Blake: Poetic, Symbolic and Critical*, vol. 2 (London: Bernard Quaritch, 1893), p. 310.

65. See, for instance, Thomas J. Garbáty, "The Degradation of Chaucer's 'Geffrey,'" *Publications of the Modern Language Association of America* 89 (1974): 97–104.

66. Northrop Frye, "The Rising of the Moon: A Study of *A Vision*," in *An Honoured Guest*, pp. 31, 32–33.

67. J. Hillis Miller, *Poets of Reality: Six Twentieth-Century Writers* (Cambridge, Mass.: Belknap/Harvard University Press, 1965), p. 103.

68. Ibid., pp. 105–6.

69. Frye, *The Secular Scripture*, pp. 41, 36, 108, 183.

70. Ibid., pp. 174, 166.

71. Yeats, "Introduction" to *Letters to the New Island*, p. xiii.

CHAPTER 4

1. W. B. Yeats, "A General Introduction for My Work," in *Essays and Introductions* (New York: Macmillan, 1961), p. 525.

2. W. B. Yeats, "The Holy Mountain," in *Essays and Introductions*, p. 468.

3. Yeats, "A General Introduction for My Work," p. 526.

4. Thomas Parkinson, *W. B. Yeats, Self-Critic: A Study of His Early Verse* (Berkeley: University of California Press, 1951), p. 5.

5. Thomas Parkinson, *W. B. Yeats, Self-Critic* and *W. B. Yeats, The Later Poetry: Two Volumes in One* (Berkeley: University of California Press, 1971), p. vi.

6. Thomas Parkinson, *W. B. Yeats: The Later Poetry* (Berkeley: University of California Press, 1964), pp. 81–82.

7. W. B. Yeats, *The Autobiography* (New York: Macmillan, 1965), p. 312; W. B. Yeats, "Friends of My Youth": Lecture Transcript and Notes, in *Yeats and the Theatre*, ed. Robert O'Driscoll and Lorna Reynolds (London: Macmillan & Co., 1975), pp. 74–75.

8. Richard Ellmann, *The Identity of Yeats*, 2d ed. (New York: Oxford University Press, 1964), p. 2.

9. Northrop Frye, "Yeats and the Language of Symbolism," *University of Toronto Quarterly* 17 (1947); as reprinted in Northrop Frye, *Fables of Identity: Studies in Poetic Mythology* (New York: Harcourt, Brace & World, 1963), p. 222.

10. Harold Bloom, "The Internalization of Quest Romance," *The Yale Review* 58 (1969); as reprinted in *Romanticism and Consciousness: Essays in Criticism*, ed. Harold Bloom (New York: W. W. Norton, 1970), p. 5.

11. See, for instance, Harold Bloom, *Yeats* (New York: Oxford University Press, 1970), chap. 6.

12. Bloom, "The Internalization of Quest Romance," p. 11.

13. Northrop Frye, *Anatomy of Criticism: Four Essays* (Princeton, N.J.: Princeton University Press, 1957), p. 193.

14. The following descriptions are from Frye, *Anatomy of Criticism*, pp. 198–202.

15. Several critics have posited stages in a similar developmental sequence for Yeats, the historical individual. See, for instance: Dillon Johnston, "The Perpetual Self of Yeats's *Autobiographies*," *Éire-Ireland* 9 (1974): 69–85; and T. R. Henn, *The Lonely Tower: Studies in the Poetry of W. B. Yeats*, 2d ed. (London: Methuen, 1965), chap. 2. Stages in the life are of course arbitrary, since an individual evolves through a continuous line of development; stages of the persona's development in art reflect the structuring influence of art on the process of life.

16. Bryant Edward Hoffman, *This Sedentary Trade: Aesthetic Unity and the Poet-Persona in the Lyric Poetry of William Butler Yeats* (Ph.D. diss., Rutgers University, 1975), pp. 4, 11.

17. Allen R. Grossman, *Poetic Knowledge in the Early Yeats: A Study of "The Wind among the Reeds"* (Charlottesville: The University Press of Virginia, 1969), p. 47.

18. Frank Hughes Murphy, *Yeats's Early Poetry: The Quest for Reconciliation* (Baton Rouge: Louisiana State University Press, 1975), p. 8.

19. Ibid., pp. 31–32.

20. Ellmann, *The Identity of Yeats*, p. 64.

21. Murphy, *Yeats's Early Poetry*, p. 36.

22. Ibid., p. 39; Bloom, *Yeats*, p. 111.

23. Yeats, *The Autobiography*, p. 103.

24. Ibid., p. 47.

25. A. Norman Jeffares, *W. B. Yeats: Man and Poet*, 2d ed. (New York: Barnes & Noble, 1962), p. 68; see also, W. B. Yeats, *Memoirs: Autobiography— First Draft, Journal*, ed. Denis Donoghue (London: Macmillan & Co., 1972), p. 46: "At the day's end I found I had spent ten shillings, which seemed to me a great sum."

26. W. B. Yeats, *The Variorum Edition of the Poems*, ed. Peter Allt and Russell K. Alspach (New York: Macmillan, 1957), p. 854.

27. Parkinson, *W. B. Yeats, Self-Critic*, pp. 158–165.

28. W. B. Yeats, *The Letters*, ed. Allan Wade (London: Rupert Hart-Davis, 1954), p. 583.

29. Curtis Bradford discusses this type of revision in *Yeats at Work* (Carbondale: Southern Illinois University Press, 1965), p. 15.

30. See Yeats, *The Variorum Edition of the Poems*.

31. Ibid., p. 803.

32. Grossman, *Poetic Knowledge in the Early Yeats*, pp. xiv–xv, 73.

33. Ellmann, *The Identity of Yeats*, pp. 123–24.

34. Ibid., p. 115.

35. Parkinson, *W. B. Yeats, Self-Critic*, p. 110.

36. Murphy, *Yeats's Early Poetry*, p. 89.

37. Ibid., pp. 90–93.

38. Maud Gonne MacBride, *A Servant of the Queen* (London: Victor Gollancz, 1938), pp. 328–30.

39. Ellmann, *The Identity of Yeats*, p. 5.

40. Yeats, *The Autobiography*, pp. 328–29, 333.

41. Murphy, *Yeats's Early Poetry*, p. 109.

42. Ibid., p. 115.

43. For the historical background of these poems, see A. Norman Jeffares, *W. B. Yeats*, pp. 168–73.

44. Bloom, *Yeats*, p. 173.

45. Vivienne Koch, *W. B. Yeats, The Tragic Phase: A Study of the Last Poems* (London: Routledge & Kegan Paul, 1951), pp. 26, 14.

46. Parkinson, *W. B. Yeats: The Later Poetry*, pp. 59, 67.

47. Bradford, *Yeats at Work*, p. 17.

48. W. B. Yeats, "If I Were Four-and-Twenty," in W. B. Yeats, *Explorations* (New York: Macmillan, 1962), p. 263. This 1919 essay has much to say on Yeats's concept of unity of being at mid-life.

49. Graham Martin, " 'The Wild Swans at Coole,' " *An Honoured Guest: New Essays on W. B. Yeats*, ed. Denis Donoghue and J. R. Mulryne (London: Edward Arnold, 1965), p. 62. As Martin notes, in the first publication of the poem in *The Little Review* (June 1917), what is the fifth and last stanza in *The Collected Poems* was then the third and middle stanza; the change in sequence certainly transfers power from the swans to the persona. Thomas Parkinson, in *W. B. Yeats: The Later Poetry*, discusses the swans as symbols of an external unity of being not available to the persona; see pp. 128–29.

50. Marjorie Perloff, "The Consolation Theme in Yeats's 'In Memory of Major Robert Gregory,'" *Modern Language Quarterly* 27 (1966): 307–8. For perhaps the most influential modern reading of the poem, see Frank Kermode, *Romantic Image* (London: Routledge & Kegan Paul, 1961), p. 38.

51. In *The Autobiography*, Yeats clarifies the intentional meaning of these images, in discussing members of the "tragic generation" who burned themselves out so quickly: "They had taught me that violent energy, which is like a fire of straw, consumes in a few minutes the nervous vitality, and is useless in the arts. Our fire must burn slowly" (p. 212).

52. Marjorie Perloff, "Yeats and the Occasional Poem: 'Easter 1916'," *Papers on Language and Literature* 4 (1968): 321. For dates of composition and publication of this poem, see the chronology in Ellmann, *The Identity of Yeats*, pp. 289–90.

53. W. B. Yeats, *A Vision: A Reissue with the Author's Final Revisions* (New York: Macmillan, 1956), p. 214.

54. John Holloway, "Style and World in 'The Tower,'" *An Honoured Guest*, p. 95.

55. Peter Ure, "Yeats's 'Demon and Beast,'" *Irish Writing* 31 (1955); as reprinted in Peter Ure, *Yeats and Anglo-Irish Literature: Critical Essays*, ed. C. J. Rawson (Liverpool: Liverpool University Press, 1974), p. 109.

56. See Virginia Moore on "demon" in *The Unicorn: William Butler Yeats's Search for Reality* (New York: Macmillan, 1954), pp. 287–89; she points to Yeats's title in the Order of the Golden Dawn, "Demon est Deus Inversus," and to a passage in the first edition of *A Vision* in which daimon and demon are used interchangeably.

57. Holloway, "Style and World in 'The Tower,'" pp. 91, 97.

58. Ian Fletcher quotes Yeats as confessing this but gives no source; see "Rhythm and Pattern in 'Autobiographies,'" *An Honoured Guest*, p. 166.

59. Yeats makes a similar comment in *The Autobiography*, p. 365; the concept probably derives from Blake's "Mental Traveller."

60. Yeats has made a curious note on this passage: "When I wrote the lines about Plato and Plotinus I forgot that it is something in our own eyes that makes us see them as all transcendence"; apparently Yeats refers to them as symbols of the reality-as-essence philosophy. See Yeats, *The Variorum Edition of the Poems*, p. 826.

61. See, for instance, David Lynch, *Yeats: The Poetics of the Self* (Chicago: University of Chicago Press, 1979), pp. 10–11.

62. J. R. Mulryne, "The 'Last Poems,'" *An Honoured Guest*, p. 128.

63. Ellmann, *The Identity of Yeats*, p. 9; Bloom, *Yeats*, p. 373.

64. Yeats, *The Letters*, p. 729.

65. Holloway, "Style and World in 'The Tower,'" p. 94; see also Stanley Sultan, *Yeats at His Last* (Dublin: Dolmen, 1975), p. 26: "The integrated 'self,' spirit and body pertually wedded, speaks the whole second part of the poem."

66. Cleanth Brooks, *The Well-Wrought Urn: Studies in the Structure of Poetry* (New York: Harcourt, Brace & World, 1947), pp. 186, 187.

67. Holloway, "Style and World in 'The Tower,'" p. 100.

68. Parkinson, *W. B. Yeats: The Later Poetry*, pp. 93–113.

69. Donald Torchiana explores the influence of Giovanni Gentile in the poem, in "'Among School Children' and the Education of the Irish Spirit," *In Excited Reverie: A Centenary Tribute to William Butler Yeats, 1865–1939*, ed. A. Norman Jeffares and K. G. W. Cross (New York: St. Martin's, 1965), pp. 123–50.

70. Yeats, *A Vision*, p. 8.

71. Denis Donoghue, "On 'The Winding Stair,'" *An Honoured Guest*, pp. 120–21.

72. Mulryne, "The 'Last Poems,'" pp. 124–25.

73. Ibid., p. 130.

74. Lynch, *Yeats*, pp. 82–83.

75. See Sultan, *Yeats at His Last*, who argues that *The Collected Poems* ignores Yeats's own ordering of many of the final poems, in particular his placing "Under Ben Bulben" first, which implies that the other poems are written from the tomb.

76. Jon Stallworthy tells the interesting story of the manuscript revisions of "Under Ben Bulben," in *Vision and Revision in Yeats's "Last Poems"* (Oxford: Clarendon Press, 1969), pp. 148–74. The poem's title originally was "Creed," then "His Convictions." In the first two versions, the poetic persona played a major role, proclaiming "creed" and "convictions" in the first person throughout.

77. Ibid., p. 149.

78. Frye, *Anatomy of Criticism*, p. 296.

CONCLUSION

1. W. B. Yeats, "Nationality and Literature," *United Ireland* (27 May 1893); as reprinted in W. B. Yeats, *Uncollected Prose*, vol. 1, *First Reviews and Articles, 1886–1896*, ed. John P. Frayne (New York: Columbia University Press, 1970), pp. 268–69.

2. Ibid., p. 269.

3. Ibid., pp. 269, 272–73.

4. W. B. Yeats, "Unp. journal," as printed in Richard Ellmann, *The Identity of Yeats*, 2d ed. (New York: Oxford University Press, 1964), p. 240.

5. Ibid.

6. W. B. Yeats, "Modern Poetry: A Broadcast," in W. B. Yeats, *Essays and Introductions* (New York: Macmillan, 1961), p. 499.

7. W. B. Yeats, "Introduction" to W. B. Yeats, ed., *The Oxford Book of Modern Verse, 1892–1935* (Oxford: Clarendon Press, 1936), p. xxii.

8. Yeats, "Modern Poetry," p. 505; Yeats, "Introduction" to *The Oxford Book of Modern Verse*, pp. xxi, xxviii.

9. Ellmann, *The Identity of Yeats*, pp. 238, 241, 242.

10. Yeats, "Introduction" to *The Oxford Book of Modern Verse*, p. xxiii.

11. W. B. Yeats, *A Vision: A Reissue with the Author's Final Revisions* (New York: Macmillan, 1956), p. 4.

12. Yeats, "Introduction" to *The Oxford Book of Modern Verse*, p. xxv.

13. Ibid., pp. xli–xlii.

14. John P. Frayne, prefatory comments to Yeats, "Nationality and Literature," *Uncollected Prose*, vol. 1, p. 267.

15. W. B. Yeats, "The Symbolism of Poetry," in *Essays and Introductions*, pp. 157–58.

Bibliography

Adams, Hazard. *Blake and Yeats: The Contrary Vision.* Ithaca, N.Y.: Cornell University Press, 1955.

―――. "Some Yeatsian Versions of Comedy." *In Excited Reverie: A Centenary Tribute to William Butler Yeats, 1865–1939.* Edited by A. Norman Jeffares and K. G. W. Cross. New York: St. Martin's, 1965, pp. 153–70.

Allen, James Lovic. "Yeats's Phase in the System of *A Vision.*" *Éire-Ireland* 8 (1973): 91–117.

Berwind, Sandra M. Personal manuscript on W. B. Yeats. Bryn Mawr, Pa.: Bryn Mawr College.

Blake, William. *The Poetry and Prose.* Edited by David V. Erdman. New York: Doubleday, 1965.

Bloom, Harold. "The Internalization of Quest-Romance." *Romanticism and Consciousness: Essays in Criticism.* Edited by Harold Bloom. New York: W. W. Norton, 1970, pp. 3–24.

―――. *Yeats.* New York: Oxford University Press, 1970.

Booth, Wayne C. *The Rhetoric of Fiction.* Chicago: University of Chicago Press, 1961.

Bornstein, George. *Yeats and Shelley.* Chicago: University of Chicago Press, 1970.

Bradford, Curtis B. *Yeats at Work.* Carbondale: Southern Illinois University Press, 1965.

Brooks, Cleanth. "Yeats: The Poet as Myth-Maker." *Modern Poetry and the Tradition.* Chapel Hill: University of North Carolina Press, 1939.

―――. "Yeats's Great Rooted Blossomer." *The Well-Wrought Urn: Studies in the Structure of Poetry.* New York: Harcourt, Brace & World, 1947.

Chaucer, Geoffrey. *The Works.* 2d ed. Edited by F. N. Robinson. Boston: Houghton Mifflin, 1957.

Concise Oxford Dictionary of Current English. 6th ed. Oxford: Clarendon Press, 1976.

Davie, Donald. "Yeats, Berkeley, and Romanticism." *English Literature and British Philosophy.* Edited by S. P. Rosenbaum. Chicago: University of Chicago Press, 1971.

Dictionary of Modern Critical Terms. Edited by Roger Fowler. Boston: Routledge & Kegan Paul, 1973.

Donaldson, E. Talbot. "Chaucer the Pilgrim." *Publications of the Modern Language Association of America* 69 (1954): 928–36.

Donoghue, Denis. "On 'The Winding Stair.' " *An Honoured Guest: New Essays on W. B. Yeats.* Edited by Denis Donoghue and J. R. Mulryne. London: Edward Arnold, 1965, pp. 106–23.

———. *William Butler Yeats.* New York: Viking, 1971.

Dowden, Edward. *Studies in Literature, 1789–1877.* 5th ed. London: Kegan Paul, Trench, 1889.

Ellis, Edwin John, and Yeats, William Butler. *The Works of William Blake: Poetic, Symbolic, and Critical.* 3 vols. London: Bernard Quaritch, 1893.

Ellmann, Richard. *Eminent Domain: Yeats among Wilde, Joyce, Pound, Eliot, and Auden.* New York: Oxford University Press, 1967.

———. *The Identity of Yeats.* 2d ed. New York: Oxford University Press, 1964.

———. *Yeats: The Man and the Masks.* New York: Macmillan, 1948.

Engelberg, Edward. *The Vast Design: Patterns in W. B. Yeats's Aesthetic.* Toronto: University of Toronto Press, 1964.

Finneran, Richard J. " 'Old lecher with a love on every wind': A Study of Yeats's *Stories of Red Hanrahan.*" *Texas Studies in Literature and Language* 14 (1972).

———. *The Prose Fiction of W. B. Yeats: The Search for "Those Simple Forms."* Dublin: Dolmen, 1973.

———. "Yeats's Revisions in *The Celtic Twilight,* 1912–1925." *Tulane Studies in English* 20 (1972): 97–105.

Finneran, Richard J., ed. *Anglo-Irish Literature: A Review of Research.* New York: The Modern Language Association of America, 1976.

Fletcher, Ian. "Rhythm and Pattern in *Autobiographies.*" *An Honoured Guest: New Essays on W. B. Yeats.* Edited by Denis Donoghue and J. R. Mulryne. London: Edward Arnold, 1965.

Frye, Northrop. *Anatomy of Criticism: Four Essays.* Princeton, N.J.: Princeton University Press, 1957.

———. *Fearful Symmetry: A Study of William Blake.* Princeton, N.J.: Princeton University Press, 1947.

———. "The Rising of the Moon: A Study of *A Vision.*" *An Honoured*

Guest: New Essays on W. B. Yeats. Edited by Denis Donoghue and J. R. Mulryne. London: Edward Arnold, 1965, pp. 8–33.

———. *The Secular Scripture: A Study of the Structure of Romance.* Cambridge, Mass.: Harvard University Press, 1976.

———. "The Top of the Tower: A Study of the Imagery of Yeats." *The Stubborn Structure: Essays on Criticism and Society.* Ithaca, N.Y.: Cornell University Press, 1970, pp. 257–77.

———. "Yeats and the Language of Symbolism." *Fables of Identity: Studies in Poetic Mythology.* New York: Harcourt, Brace & World, 1963, pp. 218–37.

Garbáty, Thomas J. "The Degradation of Chaucer's 'Geffrey.'" *Publications of the Modern Language Association of America* 89 (1974): 97–104.

Gentile, Giovanni. *The Reform of Education.* Translated by Dino Bigongiari. New York: Harcourt, Brace, 1922.

———. *Theory of Mind as Pure Act.* Translated by H. Wildon Carr. London: Macmillan & Co., 1922.

Gregory, Horace. "W. B. Yeats and the Mask of Jonathan Swift." *The Southern Review* 7 (1941–1942): 492–509.

Grossman, Allen R. *Poetic Knowledge in the Early Yeats: A Study of "The Wind among the Reeds."* Charlottesville: The University Press of Virginia, 1969.

Harris, Daniel A. *Yeats: Coole Park & Ballylee.* Baltimore: Johns Hopkins University Press, 1974.

Hart, Francis R. "Notes for an Anatomy of Modern Autobiography." *New Literary History* 1 (1969–1970): 485–511.

Henn, T. R. *The Lonely Tower: Studies in the Poetry of W. B. Yeats.* 2d ed. London: Methuen, 1965.

Hirschberg, Stuart. "Why Yeats Saw Himself as a '*Daimonic* Man' of Phase 17: A Complementary View." *English Language Notes* 11 (1974): 202–6.

Hoffman, Bryant Edward. *This Sedentary Trade: Aesthetic Unity and the Poet-Persona in the Lyric Poetry of William Butler Yeats.* Ann Arbor, Mich.: University Microfilms International. [Ph.D. diss. Rutgers University, 1975]

Holloway, John. "Style and World in 'The Tower.'" *An Honoured Guest: New Essays on W. B. Yeats.* Edited by Denis Donoghue and J. R. Mulryne. London: Edward Arnold, 1965, pp. 88–105.

Hone, Joseph. *W. B. Yeats, 1865–1939.* 2d ed. London: Macmillan & Co., 1962.

Howard, Donald. "Chaucer the Man." *Publications of the Modern Language Association of America* 80 (1965): 337–43.

Jeffares, A. Norman. *The Circus Animals: Essays on W. B. Yeats.* New York: Macmillan, 1970.

————. *A Commentary on the Collected Poems of W. B. Yeats.* Stanford, Cal.: Stanford University Press, 1968.

————. *W. B. Yeats: Man and Poet.* 2d ed. New York: Barnes & Noble, 1962.

Jochum, K. P. S., ed. *W. B. Yeats: A Classified Bibliography of Criticism.* Urbana: University of Illinois Press, 1978.

Johnston, Dillon. "The Perpetual Self of Yeats's *Autobiographies.*" *Éire-Ireland* 9 (1974): 69–85.

Kenner, Hugh. *Dublin's Joyce.* Bloomington: Indiana University Press, 1956.

————. *The Invisible Poet: T. S. Eliot.* New York: Ivan Obolensky, 1959.

————. "The Sacred Book of the Arts." *Gnomon.* New York: Ivan Obolensky, 1958, pp. 9–29.

Kermode, Frank. *Romantic Image.* London: Routledge & Kegan Paul, 1961.

Koch, Vivienne. *W. B. Yeats, The Tragic Phase: A Study of the Last Poems.* London: Routledge & Kegan Paul, 1951.

Krans, Horatio Sheafe. *William Butler Yeats and the Irish Literary Revival.* London: William Heinemann, 1905.

Langbaum, Robert. *The Mysteries of Identity: A Theme in Modern Literature.* New York: Oxford University Press, 1977.

Leavis, F. R. *New Bearings in English Poetry: A Study of the Contemporary Situation.* London: Chatto & Windus, 1938.

Lentricchia, Frank. *The Gaiety of Language: An Essay on the Radical Poetics of W. B. Yeats and Wallace Stevens.* Berkeley: University of California Press, 1968.

Lester, John A., Jr. "Joyce, Yeats, and the Short Story." *English Literature in Transition* 15 (1972): 305–314.

Levin, Gerald. "The Yeats of the Autobiographies: A Man of Phase 17." *Texas Studies in Literature and Language* 6 (1964–1965): 398–405.

Levine, Bernard. *The Dissolving Image: The Spiritual-Esthetic Development of W. B. Yeats.* Detroit: Wayne State University Press, 1970.

Luce, A. A. *Berkeley's Immaterialism: A Commentary on His "A Treatise Concerning the Principles of Human Knowledge."* New York: Thomas Nelson, 1945.

Lynch, David. *Yeats: The Poetics of the Self.* Chicago: University of Chicago Press, 1979.

MacBride, Maud Gonne. *A Servant of the Queen*. London: Victor Gollancz, 1938.

———. "Yeats and Ireland." *Scattering Branches: Tributes to the Memory of W. B. Yeats*. Edited by Stephen Gwynn. New York: Macmillan, 1940.

Marcus, Phillip L. *Yeats and the Beginning of the Irish Renaissance*. Ithaca, N.Y.: Cornell University Press, 1970.

Martin, Graham. " 'The Wild Swans at Coole.' " *An Honoured Guest: New Essays on W. B. Yeats*. Edited by Denis Donoghue and J. R. Mulryne. London: Edward Arnold, 1965.

Miller, J. Hillis. *Poets of Reality: Six Twentieth-Century Writers*. Cambridge, Mass.: Belknap / Harvard University Press, 1965.

Miyoshi, Masao. *The Divided Self: A Perspective on the Literature of the Victorians*. New York: New York University Press, 1969.

Moore, Virginia. *The Unicorn: William Butler Yeats's Search for Reality*. New York: Macmillan, 1954.

Mulryne, J. R. "The 'Last Poems.' " *An Honoured Guest: New Essays on W. B. Yeats*. Edited by Denis Donoghue and J. R. Mulryne. London: Edward Arnold, 1965, pp. 124–42.

Murphy, Frank Hughes. *Yeats's Early Poetry: The Quest for Reconciliation*. Baton Rouge: Louisiana State University Press, 1975.

Murphy, William M. *Prodigal Father: The Life of John Butler Yeats (1839–1922)*. Ithaca, N.Y.: Cornell University Press, 1978.

Nietzsche, Friedrich. *Beyond Good and Evil: Prelude to a Philosophy of the Future*. Translated by Helen Zimmern. Edinburgh: T. N. Foulis, 1909.

———. *The Birth of Tragedy, or Hellenism and Pessimism*. Translated by William A. Haussmann. New York: Macmillan, 1924.

O'Driscoll, Robert. *Symbolism and Some Implications of the Symbolic Approach: W. B. Yeats during the Eighteen-Nineties*. Dublin: Dolmen, 1975.

———. "*The Tables of the Law:* A Critical Text." *Yeats Studies, 1: Yeats and the 1890s*. Shannon: Irish University Press, 1971, pp. 87–118.

Olney, James. *Metaphors of Self: The Meaning of Autobiography*. Princeton, N.J.: Princeton University Press, 1972.

Ong, Walter J., S.J. "Voice as Summons for Belief." *Literature and Belief: English Institute Essays, 1957*. Edited by M. H. Abrams. New York: Columbia University Press, 1958.

Parkinson, Thomas. "*W. B. Yeats, Self-Critic: A Study of His Early Verse*" *and* "*W. B. Yeats: The Later Poetry*": *Two Volumes in One*. Berkeley: University of California Press, 1971.

Pascal, Roy. *Design and Truth in Autobiography.* London: Routledge & Kegan Paul, 1960.

Payne, Robert O. "Chaucer's Realization of Himself as Rhetor." *Medieval Eloquence: Studies in the Theory and Practice of Medieval Rhetoric.* Edited by James J. Murphy. Berkeley: University of California Press, 1978.

————. *The Key of Remembrance: A Study of Chaucer's Poetics.* New Haven, Conn.: Yale University Press, 1963.

Perloff, Marjorie. "The Consolation Theme in Yeats's 'In Memory of Major Robert Gregory.'" *Modern Language Quarterly* 27 (1966): 306–322.

————. "'The Tradition of Myself': The Autobiographical Mode of Yeats." *Journal of Modern Literature* 4 (1975): 529–73.

————. "Yeats and the Occasional Poem: 'Easter 1916.'" *Papers on Language and Literature* 4 (1968): 308–328.

Plato. *The Dialogues.* 4th ed. Translated by B. Jowett. Oxford: Clarendon Press, 1953.

Regueiro, Helen. *The Limits of Imagination: Wordsworth, Yeats, and Stevens.* Ithaca, N.Y.: Cornell University Press, 1976.

Ronsley, Joseph. *Yeats's Autobiography: Life as Symbolic Pattern.* Cambridge, Mass.: Harvard University Press, 1968.

Rudd, Margaret. *Divided Image: A Study of William Blake and W. B. Yeats.* London: Routledge & Kegan Paul, 1953.

Saul, George Brandon. *Prolegomena to the Study of Yeats's Poems.* Philadelphia: University of Pennsylvania Press, 1957.

Shelley, Percy Bysshe. *Poetical Works.* New ed. Edited by Thomas Hutchinson. New York: Oxford University Press, 1970.

Sidnell, Michael J. "Versions of the Stories of Red Hanrahan." *Yeats Studies, 1: Yeats and the 1890s.* Shannon: Irish University Press, 1971, pp. 119–74.

Snukal, Robert. *High Talk: The Philosophical Poetry of W. B. Yeats.* Cambridge: Cambridge University Press, 1973.

Spitzer, Leo. "Note on the Poetic and Empirical 'I' in Medieval Authors." *Traditio* 4 (1946): 414–22.

Stallworthy, Jon. *Between the Lines: Yeats's Poetry in the Making.* Oxford: Clarendon Press, 1963.

————. *Vision and Revision in Yeats's "Last Poems."* Oxford: Clarendon Press, 1969.

Strong, L. A. G. "William Butler Yeats." *Scattering Branches: Tributes to the Memory of W. B. Yeats.* Edited by Stephen Gwynn. New York: Macmillan, 1940.

Sultan, Stanley. *Yeats at His Last*. Dublin: Dolmen, 1975.

Swami, Shree Purohit, and Yeats, William Butler, trans. *The Ten Principal Upanishads*. New York: Macmillan, 1937.

Thrall, William Flint, and Hibbard, Addison. *A Handbook to Literature*. rev. ed. Edited by C. Hugh Holman. New York: Odyssey, 1960.

Torchiana, Donald T. " 'Among School Children' and the Education of the Irish Spirit." *In Excited Reverie: A Centenary Tribute to William Butler Yeats, 1865–1939*. Edited by A. Norman Jeffares and K. G. W. Cross. New York: St. Martin's, 1965.

————. *W. B. Yeats and Georgian Ireland*. Evanston, Ill.: Northwestern University Press, 1966.

Trendelenburg, Adolf. "A Contribution to the History of the Word Person." *The Monist* 20 (1910): 336–59.

Ure, Peter. *Yeats and Anglo-Irish Literature: Critical Essays*. Edited by C. J. Rawson. Liverpool: Liverpool University Press, 1974.

Vendler, Helen Hennessy. *Yeats's VISION and the Later Plays*. Cambridge, Mass.: Harvard University Press, 1963.

W. B. Yeats and T. Sturge Moore: Their Correspondence, 1901–1937. Edited by Ursula Bridge. London: Routledge & Kegan Paul, 1953.

Wade, Allan. *A Bibliography of the Writings of W. B. Yeats*. 3d ed. Edited by Russell K. Alspach. London: Rupert Hart-Davis, 1968.

Webster's Third New International Dictionary of the English Language. Unabridged. Springfield, Mass.: G. & C. Merriam, 1961.

Whitaker, Thomas R. *Swan and Shadow: Yeats's Dialogue with History*. Chapel Hill: University of North Carolina Press, 1964.

Wilde, Oscar. *The Artist as Critic: Critical Writings of Oscar Wilde*. Edited by Richard Ellmann. New York: Random House, 1968.

Wilson, F. A. C. *Yeats's Iconography*. New York: Macmillan, 1960.

Witt, Marion. "The Making of an Elegy: Yeats's 'In Memory of Major Robert Gregory.' " *Modern Philology* 48 (1950): 112–21.

Wright, George T. *The Poet in the Poem: The Personae of Eliot, Yeats, and Pound*. Berkeley: University of California Press, 1960.

Yeats, William Butler. *The Autobiography*. New York: Macmillan, 1965.

————. *The Celtic Twilight: Men and Women, Dhouls and Faeries*. London: Lawrence & Bullen, 1893.

————. *The Collected Poems*. New York: Macmillan, 1956.

————. *Essays and Introductions*. New York: Macmillan, 1961.

————. *Explorations*. New York: Macmillan, 1962.

————. "Friends of My Youth": Lecture Transcript and Notes. *Yeats and the Theatre.* Edited by Robert O'Driscoll and Lorna Reynolds. London: Macmillan & Co., 1975, pp. 26–41, 63–81.

———. *John Sherman & Dhoya.* Edited by Richard J. Finneran. Detroit: Wayne State University Press, 1969.

———. *The Letters.* Edited by Allan Wade. London: Rupert Hart-Davis, 1954.

———. *Letters to the New Island.* Edited by Horace Reynolds. Cambridge, Mass.: Harvard University Press, 1934.

———. *Memoirs: Autobiography—First Draft, Journal.* Edited by Denis Donoghue. London: Macmillan & Co., 1972.

———. *Mythologies.* New York: Macmillan, 1959.

———. *The Secret Rose.* London: Lawrence & Bullen, 1897.

———. *The Senate Speeches.* Edited by Donald R. Pearce. Bloomington: Indiana University Press, 1960.

———. *Uncollected Prose.* vol. 1, *First Reviews and Articles, 1886–1896.* Edited by John P. Frayne. New York: Columbia University Press, 1970.

———. *Uncollected Prose.* vol. 2, *Reviews, Articles and Other Miscellaneous Prose, 1897–1939.* Edited by John P. Frayne and Colton Johnson. New York: Columbia University Press, 1976.

———. *The Variorum Edition of the Poems.* Edited by Peter Allt and Russell K. Alspach. New York: Macmillan, 1957.

———. *A Vision: A Reissue with the Author's Final Revisions.* New York: Macmillan, 1956.

———. *A Vision: An Explanation of Life Founded upon the Writings of Giraldus and upon Certain Doctrines Attributed to Kusta Ben Luka.* London: T. Werner Laurie, 1925.

———. *The Wind among the Reeds.* London: Elkin Mathews, 1899.

Yeats, William Butler, ed. *The Oxford Book of Modern Verse, 1892–1935.* Oxford: Clarendon Press, 1936.

Zabel, Morton Dauwen. "The Thinking of the Body: Yeats in the Autobiographies." *The Southern Review* 7 (1941–1942): 562–90.

Zwerdling, Alex. *Yeats and the Heroic Ideal.* New York: New York University Press, 1965.

Index

Index of Yeats's Works